5-6 Gini Index
6 Palma Index - US 4 4th
white - Black Diff

2 US Senate Rules & Rich
15 The Issue : how wealth translated into political
influence + outcomes

17 Oligarphic Democracy ?

BILLIONAIRES

19 Polarization + income inequality

35 Watergate

BILLIONAIRES

REFLECTIONS
ON THE
UPPER CRUST

DARRELL M. WEST

BROOKINGS INSTITUTION PRESS
Washington, D.C.

The Brookings Institution is a private nonprofit organization devoted to research,
education, and publication on important issues of domestic and foreign policy. Its
principal purpose is to bring the highest quality independent research and analysis
to bear on current and emerging policy problems. Interpretations or conclusions in
Brookings publications should be understood to be solely those of the authors.

Library of Congress Cataloging-in-Publication data
West, Darrell M., 1954–
Billionaires: reflections on the upper crust / Darrell M. West.
pages   cm
Includes bibliographical references and index.
ISBN 978-0-8157-2582-4 (hardcover : alk. paper) —
ISBN 978-0-8157-2596-1 (pbk. : alk. paper)
1. Wealth. 2. Wealth–Political aspects. 3. Rich people–Political activity.
4. Billionaires. 5. Equality. I. Title.
HC79.W4W465 2014
305.5'234--dc23   2014000450

10 9 8 7 6 5 4 3 2 1

Printed on acid-free paper

Typeset in Sabon

Composition by Oakland Street Publishing

To Karin

who has brought a different kind of wealth into my life

Contents

BILLIONAIRES

1 *The Controversy over Billionaires*

AT THE TIME of his reelection campaign, several conservative billionaires were unhappy with the job performance of President Barack Obama. The economy was not doing well. There was uncertainty in foreign policy. Many of them believed that Obama was a poor leader. Irate about how things were going, they decided to devote several hundred million dollars to defeating the president. Individuals such as Sheldon Adelson, David and Charles Koch, and the late Harold Simmons and a group of wealthy donors assembled by Republican strategist Karl Rove felt that they needed to speak out to ensure that the country had stronger leadership and moved in what they considered a better direction.

But they were not the only super-wealthy people who were politically active. In recent elections, there has been an explosion of activism by the rich. Billionaires such as Michael Bloomberg, George Soros, and Tom Steyer have poured extensive resources into supporting their favored candidates and causes. In addition, wealthy individuals have bankrolled advocacy campaigns at the state level—for example, in support of same-sex marriage and marijuana legalization or in opposition to Obama's health care reform and higher taxes on the wealthy. Aided by friendly Supreme Court rulings and the rising cost of election campaigns, affluent people have discovered that they are in a strong position to affect a variety of different issues.

In researching this subject, I discovered that it is not just an American development but something that is happening globally. Billionaires have run for office in Austria, Australia, France, Georgia, India, Italy, Lebanon, the Philippines, Russia, Thailand, Ukraine, and the United Kingdom as well as the United States. Most of them have won. Oligarchs in Russia, so-called "princelings" in China, and tycoons in many other countries are becoming politically active and affecting public policy. Their political involvement raises important questions about excessive influence, especially in places where there is weak rule of law, overt corruption, and limited opportunities for social or economic advancement. The activism of the super rich is taking place against a backdrop of poor transparency, weak news coverage, accountability problems, and performance challenges on many different fronts in political systems around the world. With the "wealthification" of politics, those in the upper echelon, who as a group hold policy views that differ significantly from those of the general population, have access to many ways to influence the political process.

Wealth—its uses and its abuses—is a subject that has intrigued me since my youth in the rural Midwest. I was born on a dairy farm and grew up poor. When asked what our house was like when my parents moved to Ohio in 1947, my mother said, "There was no running water in it or hot water of any kind. No bathroom." Water was carried in from the barn. It was not until 1952, two years before I was born, that the house got cold running water. Indeed, because of the cows, the barn had running water before our house did. To do the laundry, Mom heated water on a gas stove, washed the clothes in a manual washer, ran them through a hand-cranked wringer, and then hung them on a line outside to dry. She didn't have an automatic dryer until much later in her life. Hot running water and an indoor bathroom were added in 1960, when I was six years old; the bathroom replaced the outhouse that the family had used before. In 1965, we got a furnace to replace the coal stoves in the kitchen and living room.

The contrast between the poverty of my youth and the privilege of my adulthood makes me very attuned to the role that wealthy people play in the United States and around the world. Not only has it made me curious about the lives of the rich, it has led me to ask questions regarding their political impact. The world's billionaires have had a major influence on other people. They have created new businesses, launched new products, and altered how people live, work, play, and communicate.

Yet much of the current debate regarding the political role of billionaires suffers from ideological short-sightedness. Progressives fear political activism when it is undertaken by conservative billionaires yet applaud it when liberal billionaires swing into action. Conservatives get worried when left-leaning billionaires dump a lot of money into elections but appreciate the advocacy efforts of their own billionaires and pro-business special interest groups. What each side misses are the challenges raised by billionaire activism for the system as a whole. Billionaires' extensive resources and advocacy efforts provoke questions about political influence, transparency, and accountability. At a time of high income concentration and dysfunctional political institutions, it is important to understand the impact that the ultra rich have on national life and the need for policies that promote better disclosure, governance, and opportunity.

Here, too, I have a personal perspective. From my perches in both the Ivy League, at Brown University, and the Brookings Institution, I have seen Americans of great wealth do positive things with their money and improve the lives of other people. Most of those that I know personally display admirable traits—vision, innovativeness, and entrepreneurship. Moreover, having received research grants from leading foundations as well as people of great wealth over a number of years, I have benefited professionally from their philanthropy. Some of those discussed in this book are or have been benefactors of Brown and others of Brookings, and they are identified as such. Their careers and practices illustrate different themes and observations, but what they have in common is a respect for institutional independence, academic freedom, and public transparency regarding sources of funding.

It is possible to admire individual billionaires but also fear their overall influence on elections, governance, and public policy. According to *Forbes* magazine, there are 1,645 known billionaires around the world, 492 of whom live in the United States. In this book, I study their political efforts in the United States and other countries and describe how they have pioneered more activist forms of politics and philanthropy. I argue that such activism presents major challenges in the areas of political influence, accountability, transparency, and system performance. Countries everywhere need policies that promote better disclosure and governance and preserve opportunities for a broader range of people.

Income Concentration

The assets of the U.S. super wealthy—as reported on the *Forbes* list of billionaires—have more than doubled over the past decade. Ten years ago, these individuals controlled around $1 trillion; now their wealth has risen to more than $2 trillion.[1] Economists Marco Cagetti and Mariacristina De Nardi show that 1 percent of Americans now own about one-third of the country's wealth.[2]

Economists Thomas Piketty and Emmanuel Saez document how income concentration has risen over the past century. Figure 1-1 charts the share of pre-tax income accounted for by the top 1 percent of earners from 1913 to 2012.[3] In 1928, the year before the Great Depression, that group garnered 21.1 percent of all income in the United States. Over the next 50 years, that percentage dropped to a low of 8.3 percent in 1976, then rose to 21.5 percent in 2007. It dropped to 18.8 percent in 2011 following the Great Recession, then rose again to 19.6 percent in 2012.[4] Those figures show that income concentration today is similar to what it was in the 1920s

FIGURE 1-1. Pre-Tax Income Received by Top One Percent, 1913–2012

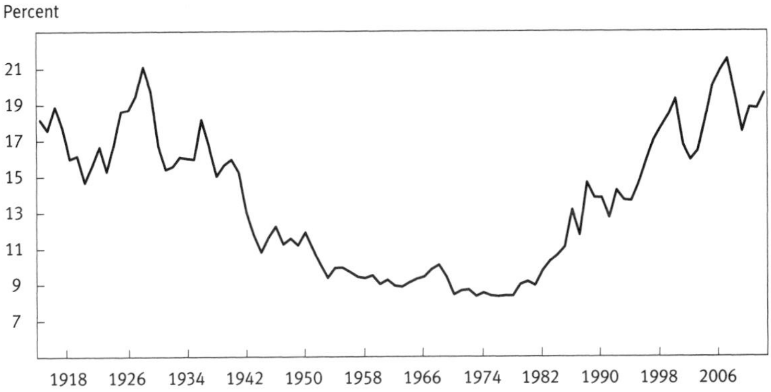

Percent

Source: Thomas Piketty and Emmanuel Saez, "Income Inequality in the United States, 1913–1998," *Quarterly Journal of Economics*, vol. 118 (2003), pp. 1–39. For 1999 to 2012 numbers, see the web page of Emmanuel Saez (http://emlab.berkeley.edu/users/saez).

and is more than double the degree during the post–World War II period.

More detailed statistics demonstrate that after-tax income stagnated for most workers from 1979 to 2009 but rose dramatically for the top 1 percent. Charting the percent change in real after-tax income for four groups of workers shows that during those 30 years, earnings rose 155 percent for the top 1 percent of earners, 58 percent for the next 19 percent of earners, 45 percent for the middle 60 percent, and 37 percent for the bottom 20 percent.[5] And if a recent book by Thomas Piketty, *Capital in the Twenty-First Century,* is correct, money is likely to become even more concentrated in the future. Drawing on data from several countries over the past 200 years, he argues that the appreciation of capital outpaces that of the economy at large and of wages in particular. That benefits the people who already hold a lot of financial resources and increases the overall concentration of wealth.[6]

Still another way to look at the income gap relies on the Gini coefficient, an economic measure developed in 1912 by the Italian sociologist Corrado Gini that is used to express inequality among different income levels. It runs from 0 to 1; 0 indicates that everyone has the same income, and 1 indicates that one person has all the income. The Gini coefficient for the United States was around .38 in 1950, dropped to .35 around 1970, and rose to .45 in 2010,[7] demonstrating that financial inequality has increased substantially over the past 60 years.

Alex Cobham and Andy Sumner of the Center for Global Development have proposed a new metric that they call the Palma ratio, after economist Gabriel Palma, who argues that it is important that the "middle 50 percent" remain stable to ensure a society's social, economic, and political well-being. The Palma ratio compares the share of national income held by the top 10 percent of households with the share held by the bottom 40 percent. The authors find that the United States ranks forty-fourth among 86 countries in terms of inequality, a rank that makes U.S. inequality worse than that of virtually every other developed nation.[8]

As a sign of how profound income divisions have become, increasing inequality has widened the gaps between different social groups. Over the past 25 years, the financial gulf between whites and blacks has nearly tripled. In 1984, the difference in wealth between the races was $85,000; by 2009, it had increased to $236,500. The gaps in homeownership, education level, and financial inheritance are responsible for most of these differences; for example, according to researchers, the "home ownership rate for whites is 28 percent higher than that of blacks."[9] As Jennifer Hochschild and her collaborators at Harvard University point out, policymakers need to think seriously about the impact of these trends on social cohesion and political representation.[10]

Financial concentration has increased not just in the United States but in many other countries around the globe. Research by Thomas Piketty and Gabriel Zucman finds that wealth has risen much more rapidly than incomes in eight developed nations: the United States, Britain, France, Germany, Italy, Canada, Australia, and Japan. They find that "wealth-to-income ratios in these nations climbed from a range of 200 to 300 percent in 1970 to a range of 400 to 600 percent in 2010"—a doubling of the wealth concentration over that time period.[11]

The reality of inequality has generated considerable attention in many countries. In Russia and Eastern Europe, the super wealthy, who profited enormously from the cheap sell-off of state-owned enterprises following the fall of communism, are derided as "oligarchs." In China, the children of prominent Communist Party leaders, who are able to accumulate extensive wealth by using their family connections, are known as "princelings." A study undertaken by the China Family Panel Studies program at Peking University that examined 14,960 households in five leading Chinese provinces found that the top 5 percent earned 23 percent of the nation's total income. In addition, the top 25 percent in those provinces earned 59 percent of total income while the bottom quarter earned only 3.9 percent. That gave those areas a Gini coefficient of .49.[12] *PRC*

Despite those numbers, one Chinese billionaire downplays the dangers of income differentials. "We don't need to solve the problem of the rich-poor gap, we need to solve the problem of common prosperity," said Zong Qinghou, one of the richest men in China. He has a great fortune, which he earned from companies that sell soft drinks, milk for babies, and children's clothing. "If we had egalitarianism, we wouldn't have enough to eat," he said. In an argument that would resonate with many conservative politicians in the United States, he claimed that the best way to create wealth in China is to lower taxes in order to stimulate financial investment and economic growth.[13] However, at least one migrant worker in China did not take kindly to his remarks. Shortly after they were publicized in the media, Zong was attacked by a knife-wielding jobseeker in Hangzhou. Some tendons in one of Zong's hands were cut, but otherwise the billionaire was not seriously harmed.[14]

Looking at the world as a whole, the United Nations World Institute for Development Economics Research showed that in 2008, the top 1 percent of earners owned a total of 40.1 percent

FIGURE 1-2. Global Inequality, 1820–2002

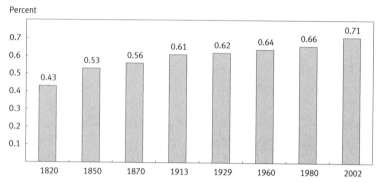

Source: Branko Milanovic, "Global Inequality and the Global Inequality Extraction Ratio: The Story of the Past Two Centuries," World Bank, September 2009 (http://elibrary.worldbank.org/doi/book/10.1596/1813-9450-5044).

of overall global wealth, a share that is larger than the one-third of national wealth owned by the top 1 percent in the United States.[15] As shown in figure 1-2, the Gini coefficient for global income has increased substantially over the past two centuries. According to World Bank economist Branko Milanovic, inequality rose from .43 in 1820, .53 in 1850, and .56 in 1870 to .61 in 1913, .62 in 1929, .64 in 1960, .66 in 1980, and .71 in 2002.[16]

Political Activism of the Wealthy

The wealthy are much more politically active than the general public. In a "first-ever" public policy survey funded by the Russell Sage Foundation of "economically successful Americans," political scientists Benjamin Page, Larry Bartels, and Jason Seawright measured the activism and beliefs of the rich. They worked with the Wealthfinder "rank A" list of the top 2 percent of American households based on wealth and supplemented it with an Execu-Reach list of high-level business executives of major companies. In order to reach their intended population, they screened for the top "1% of wealth-holders" and completed interviews with those individuals.[17] In talking with them, the researchers found that 99 percent of the wealthy said that they voted in presidential elections, almost double the rate of the general public. Most (84 percent) also reported paying close attention to politics. Two-thirds (68 percent) made campaign contributions to politicians; in stark contrast, only 14 percent of the general public does.[18]

The reason is clear. Wealthy people know that political engagement matters.[19] Being involved in politics yields benefits and enables them to express their views and influence results. Unlike the general public, which tends to be cynical about politics, believing that there is no difference between Republicans and Democrats and that politics is not a very good way to produce change, many affluent people seem to believe that politics matters and represents a way to affect national and international affairs. Indeed, a study by political scientist Lee Drutman of the top 1,000 campaign donors from 2012 (those who gave at least $134,000) found that two-thirds favored Republicans and the largest number of them came from the financial sector.[20]

Given the importance of engagement, it is not surprising that the wealthy report in this survey a large number of "high-level political contacts." When asked whether they had contacted public officials or their staffs in the last six months, 40 percent indicated that they had contacted a U.S. senator; 37 percent, a U.S. House member; 21 percent, a regulatory official; 14 percent, someone in the executive branch; and 12 percent, a White House official.[21] Those rates are much higher than the rates for the general public. A national survey undertaken at the University of Michigan documented that about 20 percent of ordinary people said that they had contacted a member of the U.S. Senate or House in the preceding four years,[22] through telephone calls, letters, or visits to legislative offices.

Distinctive Views of the Wealthy

It is important to analyze wealth in democratic systems because the super rich, as a group, hold policy views that are significantly different from those of ordinary citizens. In their survey, Page, Bartels,

TABLE 1-1. Views of the Wealthy and the General Public

Percent in agreement

View	The wealthy (top 1 percent)	General public
I favor cuts in Medicare, education, and highways to reduce budget deficits.	58	27
Government has an essential role in regulating the market.	55	71
Government should spend what is necessary to ensure that all children have good public schools.	35	87
I'm willing to pay more in taxes to provide health coverage for all.	41	59
Government should provide a decent standard of living for the unemployed.	23	50
Government should provide jobs for everyone willing to work who can't find a private sector job.	8	53

Source: Benjamin Page, Larry Bartels, and Jason Seawright, "Democracy and the Policy Preferences of Wealthy Americans," *Perspectives on Politics*, vol. 11 (March 2013).

and Seawright asked the wealthy about a range of public policy issues.[23] Comparing their opinions with those of the general public, the researchers found that top wealth holders "differ rather sharply from the American public on a number of important policies. For example, there are significant differences on issues such as taxation, economic regulation, and social welfare programs."[24] Table 1-1 summarizes the gulf in policy preferences between the top 1 percent and the general public. The wealthy are more likely than the general public to favor cuts in Medicare and education (58 percent versus 27 percent for the public), while they are less likely than the public to believe that the government has an essential role in regulating the market (55 percent versus 71 percent, respectively).

Most surprising, however, are the differences in views about social opportunities. In the abstract, it might be assumed that there would be little gap in this area. According to the Credit Suisse Global Wealth Databook, two-thirds (69 percent) of wealthy individuals came from humble origins and conceivably could favor a limited government role in the economy but still value equity of opportunity.[25] But that is not what Page, Bartels, and Seawright found in their survey. Their data show that while 87 percent of the general public believed that the government should spend whatever is necessary to ensure that all children have good public schools, only 35 percent of the top 1 percent did.[26] The wealthy also were less likely than the general public to want the government to provide jobs if private sector positions are unavailable, to believe the government should provide a decent standard of living for the unemployed, or to be willing to pay more taxes to support universal health care.

This research indicates that those with great resources are far more conservative than the public on a range of issues related to social opportunity, education, and health care. They do not support a major role for the public sector, even when government actions further economic and social opportunities for the general public. They are much more likely to favor cuts in social benefits and programs that benefit less fortunate members of society. These views of the super rich lead them to favor tax cuts—even though they reduce the financial resources to invest in education and health care— and to place more emphasis on deficit reduction than on "pump-priming" that stimulates economic growth. If politically active rich people favor tax cuts and support austerity measures, as has been the case in recent years, it is difficult to generate political support for programs that help the nation's low- and middle-income people better themselves.

The "Get a Senator" Strategy

It is no accident that the Page, Bartels, and Seawright survey of the wealthy finds them seeking influence most frequently through members of the U.S. Senate. Because of Senate rules granting unbridled authority to individual senators to block nominations through secret holds, object to "unanimous consent" motions, and engage in filibusters (that is, block action through unlimited debate), a popular tactic among those with extensive political connections is to develop a close relationship with a senator who sits on a key committee or who can exercise influence in other ways and persuade that person to block undesired nominations or bills.

Holds can be used to stop legislation that a senator doesn't like. Senator Rand Paul (R-Kentucky), for example, has been unhappy with a proposed treaty that would force Swiss banks to release the names of 22,000 wealthy Americans who have hidden an estimated $10 billion in offshore accounts. Even though the treaty likely would win the approval of the Senate as a whole, for several years he single-handedly has prevented action because he believes that the new rules would permit the invasion of people's privacy.[27]

Through what one wealthy individual described to me as the "get a senator" strategy, a person needs to obtain the support of only a single member to prevent the chamber from a taking particular action. In a system of fragmented political institutions characterized by decentralized decisionmaking and multiple veto points, having a senator who acts on one's behalf is an effective way to stymie unwanted government action or delay appointments affecting particular industries. Along with lobbyists representing businesses and other vested interests, those who are rich and connected can stop measures that they deem detrimental to their pocketbooks. For decades, if not centuries, the political ramifications of great wealth have provided cartoonists with inspiration and material, as illustrated by the *New Yorker* cartoon reprinted below.

Billionaires sometimes enlist senators to write letters to federal regulators asking for investigations of other companies. An example of this came to light in the case of hedge fund manager William Ackman, of Pershing Square Capital Management. For years, the billionaire financier has run a campaign against the nutritional

"I own one plane, two yachts, four houses and five politicians."

supplement firm Herbalife, alleging that its sales practices amount to an illegal pyramid scheme. Ackman has invested $1 billion in his belief that the company is overvalued.[28] Not content with drawing his own conclusions regarding the business practices of Herbalife, he persuaded Senator Edward Markey (D-Massachusetts) to write letters to the Securities and Exchange Commission and the Federal Trade Commission criticizing the firm and demanding a formal investigation. Ackman personally lobbied Markey's staff and hired a Markey aide to join his lobbying team. As soon as Markey's letter was made public, the Herbalife stock price dropped by 14 percent, partly achieving the billionaire's goals.

According to Princeton sociologist Martin Gilens, influence peddling is not rare. His analysis indicates that there is a strong link between "affluence and influence." Through a detailed analysis of policymaking, public opinion, and income levels, he demonstrates that "affluent Americans' preferences exhibit a substantial [positive] relationship with policy outcomes whether their preferences are shared by lower-income groups or not." He argues that there is "virtually no relationship between policy outcomes and the desires of less advantaged groups" when the preferences of the latter diverge from those of the wealthy.[29] And in a follow-up study with Benjamin Page, Gilens examined the impact of average citizens and economic elites on 1,779 policy issues over the past 30 years and concluded that ordinary people had "little or no independent influence."[30] The issue of distinctive political influence was brought home to me when I met my first billionaire at Brown University, where I taught political science. A Rhode Island businessman named John Hazen White Sr. had endowed a lecture series, and we invited legendary broadcaster Ted Turner, who had attended the university three decades earlier, to speak. Although he had been kicked out in the 1960s for disciplinary code violations involving alcohol and women, years later Brown had awarded him an honorary degree in recognition of his development of CNN, the first all-news cable network. Pleased with the honor, Turner had funded a faculty position and pledged a multimillion dollar gift to the school (he also has been a Brookings donor). That made him what Brown euphemistically called a "friend" of the university.

Accompanied by his then-wife, Jane Fonda, he came to campus in 1995 to give a lecture about the environment entitled "Our Common Future." Turner was alternately serious, funny, and outrageous. He explained the importance of the environment to the future of humanity and talked about why he was raising buffalo on his huge Montana ranch. Then, in an unexpected twist, he joked that what he really liked about living in the West was being able to "take a whiz" off his front porch. The Ivy League audience laughed uproariously.

Turning back to his broader message, he related the lessons of his life. His most difficult challenge, he said, had been making the first million dollars; after that, everything was easy. Money begets money, he bluntly observed, thereby making it possible to gain even greater wealth through social and political connections. That, of course, is the crux of the controversy about the role of billionaires in society. Wealth in and of itself is not problematic. It is how rich people convert financial might into political power for their own benefit that creates problems.

Transparency Problems

It is perfectly reasonable for rich people to express their views, lobby Congress, and attempt to influence elections as long as others are aware of what they are doing and can organize accordingly. Even if the wealthy have more money than other people, openness helps protect the general population and allows the public to assess the actions of the wealthy. The problem, however, is that many efforts to exercise influence have migrated behind the scenes and often are invisible to the news media or general public. As a result of court rulings that treat "freedom to spend" as equivalent to "freedom of speech," campaign finance has become much more secretive. Wealthy interests can fund advocacy organizations with no disclosure of their contributions required.

These kinds of judicial decisions bias the political process in favor of the ultra rich. Former GOP presidential candidate Newt Gingrich, whose super PAC received $15 million from billionaire Sheldon Adelson, notes the extraordinary importance of the rich in contemporary elections. "Whether it's the Koch brothers or Soros on the left or Sheldon, if you're going to have an election process that radically favors billionaires and is discriminating against the middle class—which we now have—then billionaires are going to get a lot of attention," he observed.[31]

Wealthy people across the political spectrum have pioneered new activist models of political involvement that combine electioneering, issue advocacy, and philanthropy. They pursue influence through interlocking networks of foundations, grassroots organizations, tax-exempt groups, and super PACs (political action committees, independent committees that can raise unlimited amounts of money). Dubbed by reporters as the "Koch model," after conservative billionaire activists Charles and David Koch, this approach now is being emulated by liberal billionaires Tom Steyer and George Soros (who also have donated to Brookings) as well as by businessman and former New York City mayor Michael Bloomberg, among others. Rich people like this approach because "it's adaptive, data-driven, and they [the Kochs] are the most propitious capital allocators in political activism."[32]

The combination of wealth and secrecy, however, is toxic to democratic systems. In the realm of political persuasion, the messenger can count as much as the message. Voters need to know who is behind particular messages so that they can assess the reliability of the information and the quality of the arguments. With lack of transparency, it is difficult for citizens and reporters to evaluate campaign discourse and advocacy efforts.

The Weakness of Countervailing Institutions

Billionaires pose another risk. They typify the combination of social, economic, and political privileges that American sociologist C. Wright Mills famously described in his book *The Power Elite*. According to Wright, the interplay of money and politics enables rich people to use their financial resources to gain special advantages. Columbia University economist Joseph Stiglitz has gone even further, arguing that some of the rich have gotten wealthy by manipulating the system. In his 2012 book, *The Price of Inequality*, Stiglitz claims that certain wealthy interests have used their financial resources to gain undue influence and thereby increase their own power.[33] Political scientists Jacob Hacker and Paul Pierson complain in their book *Winner-Take-All Politics* that the concentration of monetary resources has damaged the political process by giving the wealthy few the power to gain disproportionate benefits.[34]

Others dispute those claims and argue that many factors limit the influence of the wealthy. One is social and political divisions within the upper elite. According to this perspective, the activism of liberal billionaires balances the activism of conservative ones and entrepreneurs in different business sectors don't always agree with each other; group divisions thus prevent billionaires from coalescing into a single, monolithic class and using their wealth to impose their views on other people.

In addition, a number of countries, such as the United States, have countervailing forces that limit the power of the wealthy. If the rich gain undue advantage, according to traditional theory, politicians can use political parties and media appeals to mobilize the large number of voters whose interests are harmed. Even in the face of great wealth, investigative journalism and party organizations preserve equity in the political system. Reporters keep society informed about possible influence peddling and wrongdoing. If the wealthy deploy their money for selfish ends, the media will write negative stories about them and help other politicians curtail their influence.

In the contemporary period, however, there is considerable doubt about the ability of these forces to limit the power of the rich. On some issues, notably taxes, liberal and conservative billionaires often are united in opposing tax increases, at least for themselves. Regardless of their particular ideology, on certain issues class trumps ideology and there is no pluralistic universe of voices. It leads to what political scientist Larry Bartels calls "unequal democracy."[35]

The news media have gone through massive changes in operations and business models that have sharply diminished the quality and quantity of their public affairs coverage.[36] For example, according to the Pew Research Center's "State of the News Media" report, the transition from print to digital publications has disrupted the usual business model of newspapers. The substitution of digital advertising nickels for print ad dollars has seriously weakened corporate revenues and thereby affected the ability of reporters to cover the news. For every $16 in print ad revenue lost, it is estimated that only $1 in digital ad revenue has been gained.[37] The loss of advertising dollars has weakened the news media and led to a decline in coverage, a problem that has been especially acute at the state level. *American Journalism Review* surveys of reporters who cover state and local news have found "a staggering loss of reporting firepower in America's state capitols." Overall, the number of full-time newspaper reporters covering state government dropped from 513 in 1998, to 468 in 2003, and then to 355 in 2009 (an average of just seven reporters per state). Nearly every state in the country has witnessed additional declines since then in local reporting.[38] As a result, special interests often are able to work their will in near-secrecy at the state level.

Many political observers worry about the effectiveness of mechanisms for furthering accountability. They claim that both major parties in the United States have been so corrupted by corporate money that ordinary people cannot count on either party to represent the public interest. Both Republican and Democratic candidates are beholden to wealthy donors, and that accentuates the power of the rich over ordinary voters.[39] In recent years, money has devolved from political parties to super PACs controlled by the wealthy. According to Rob Stein, the founder of Democracy Alliance, "money is leaving the parties and going to independent expenditures groups. These now are fracturing the 'big tents' of our old two-party system into independent, narrow and well-funded wings."[40]

Globally, billionaires have short-circuited democratic accountability by purchasing major news organizations. In countries such as Australia, the Czech Republic, France, Georgia, Italy, Russia, the United Kingdom, and the United States, the ultra rich own leading newspapers, magazines, television stations, and Internet portals. They use their media control to promote particular messages and thus have weakened countervailing forces within civil society. The result has been what journalist Dean Starkman describes as watchdogs that don't bark. "One thing that everyone should realize is that overall, our reporting and fact-gathering infrastructure has been weakened far below acceptable levels, and needs to get stronger," he observed.[41]

Income Concentration and Political Polarization

Discussions about the role of the wealthy often are quite intense. In her book *Plutocrats: The Rise of the New Global Super Rich and the Fall of Everyone Else*, Canadian journalist Chrystia Freeland writes about the ramifications when a small number of people have tremendous financial resources.[42] She says that "plutocrats" deploy their considerable resources to favor policies that benefit themselves and oppose policies that create opportunities for less fortunate people. Because they have so much money, their activities skew policymaking and engender anger among others.

Activists representing poor and middle-class constituencies fear the power of the rich and employ rhetoric attacking the wealthy for having money. That makes the well-to-do feel that advocates are unfairly engaging in class warfare. Arthur Brooks, the president of the American Enterprise Institute, wrote recently about what he called the "politics of envy." Citing public opinion surveys, he claims that there is "increasing envy" in American politics and that it leads to "destructive social comparison." He says that people's fears that "the game looks rigged," combined with "increasing anxiety about income inequality and rising sympathy for income redistribution," lead to resentments that are unhealthy for the body politic.[43]

Researchers examining these claims have found a strong connection between income inequality and political polarization. Using data on U.S. House of Representatives roll-call voting and the top 1 percent's share of income from 1913 to 2008, political scientists Adam Bonica, Nolan McCarthy, Keith Poole, and Howard Rosenthal find that the two indicators rise and fall together.[44] From 1913 to the 1930s, when the top 1 percent earned a large percentage of income, political polarization was high. When their income share dropped between the 1930s and 1970s, polarization dropped. As the wealthy class's share of overall income increased over the past few decades, polarization returned to and even exceeded its levels during the early twentieth century. Part of the polarization in rhetoric and representation is driven not just by self-interested behavior but by the current system of campaign finance. A research study by political scientist Lee Drutman found that wealthy donors push candidates to the extremes, especially on the Republican side. Analyzing the campaign contributions of top donors along with data on the voting records of members of Congress, he argues that "the more Republicans depend on 1% of the 1% donors, the more conservative they tend to be." His conclusion is that wealthy donors "exert a conservative tug on American politics."[45]

The Donald Trump Encounter

A chance encounter with one well-known billionaire gave me a firsthand look at the sensitivities of the rich. Donald Trump attracted considerable attention in 2012 when he criticized President Barack Obama for raising taxes on the wealthy and, Trump insisted, for not being born in the United States. Amid all that controversy, there was talk about Trump addressing the Republican National Convention. Asked for a comment on that possibility by the D.C.-based newspaper *Politico*, I suggested, tongue in cheek, that the GOP should instead send Trump on an all-expenses-paid trip around the world because allowing him to deliver a nationally televised address would bring the party nothing but trouble.

The day my July 2012 quote was published, I received a call from Trump's assistant asking for my e-mail address. I gave it to her, and she sent me an angry missive from the billionaire himself. He pasted my media quote into his message and wrote in large, black caps: "DARRELL, YOU ARE A 'FOOL.' Best Wishes, Donald J. Trump."

The thin-skinned Trump need not have worried about my comment because there are prominent experts who publish very favorable arguments in support of the ultra rich. In a paper entitled "Defending the One Percent," Gregory Mankiw, a Harvard economist (and former economics adviser to President George W. Bush), conceded that monetary income in the very top bracket in the United States has "grown much faster than average" but argued that people should accept inequality because "these high earners have made significant economic contributions."[46] According to Mankiw, the rich have gotten wealthy because they are visionary, creative, and innovative. Since most of them are self-made individuals, he said, they are models of effective entrepreneurship who have transformed obsolete or decaying businesses into productive enterprises.

This interpretation is comparable to views expressed by Republican presidential nominee Mitt Romney. In an infamous, secretly videotaped May 17, 2012, campaign speech to a group of wealthy donors, the GOP politician distinguished "makers" from "takers." Romney said that society was divided between a small group of productive people who build companies and contribute to society and a larger set of unproductive moochers who create nothing and take money through government programs.[47] From his standpoint, income concentration is not a serious problem because those with lots of money work hard, innovate, and do things that better the lives of others. Wealth should not be criticized, but rather appreciated for the good things that it allows billionaires to accomplish. Political leaders should favor policies that promote wealth creation, such as lowering income taxes, cutting the capital gains tax, and eliminating the estate tax. Even if those policies disproportionately benefit the wealthy, they stimulate economic growth and aid other people in the long-run, according to this viewpoint.

Such arguments by Romney and others miss the risks that resource concentration raises for governance and policymaking. There are takers who make and makers who take. People with large financial resources have access to political leaders, giving them more opportunities than others have to make policy pitches. As mentioned earlier, studies suggest that the wealthy often employ direct channels to express their views at the highest levels of government and succeed in getting benefits for their businesses and themselves.

Threats to System Performance

Income differentials pose challenges to the performance of many aspects of political, social, and economic systems. When one small part of society has a disproportionate share of money, is politically active, holds distinctive policy viewpoints, and has numerous ways to make its influence felt, it is difficult for democratically elected officials to address policy problems in an even-handed fashion. Tycoons and their lobbyists are aware of veto points within the electoral, legislative, and regulatory processes and funnel considerable resources into stopping measures that they oppose and advancing ones that they support. When the general public sees these efforts by special interests—which is not always the case, since the most effective lobbying takes place behind closed doors—it feels that it is being ignored and that its interests are not being represented.

For example, the challenges of income inequality and social mobility have been discussed by many observers, but it has been difficult to produce concrete improvements in either area. The politics of so-called income "redistribution" are fraught with controversy, and advocates for programs benefiting the poor have trouble finding the money to advance their causes. Many wealthy people feel that calls for more equality punish success and are patently unfair. Less advantaged individuals complain that excessive compensation of corporate executives, unfair tax policies, and some corporate practices have pushed up the incomes of a small number of people while wages for most others have languished.[48]

Addressing inequality and addressing economic immobility involve different dynamics. Inequality is rooted in unequal distributions of financial resources; immobility refers to the inability of many workers to move up the income ladder. But the two are related in that lack of money makes it difficult for people to invest in education or training that allows them to advance economically.

As Brookings fellow Richard Reeves notes, "It seems harder to climb a ladder when the rungs are farther apart."[49]

Research by Jason DeBacker and colleagues finds that the increase in earnings inequality in the United States has developed in part because of changes in technology and required skill levels.[50] On the basis of their analysis of U.S. tax returns for 35,000 households from 1987 to 2009, they argue that some people make more money because they are among the small number of individuals who are highly skilled and much in demand. By contrast, others experience limited wage growth because they are poorly trained and not in demand. This is most apparent in the high-technology area, where some individuals with innovative ideas have gotten rich quickly by launching companies and taking them public a few years later. Those individuals parlayed their vision of new products or new services into popular enterprises and became instant billionaires, in some cases while still in their twenties or thirties. Similar things have happened in the hedge fund and private equity areas, where executives have been lavishly compensated for their investments and gotten incredibly rich through annual compensation packages in the tens or even hundreds of millions of dollars.

Demand for working-class labor, meanwhile, has been depressed by the globalization of the economy. Workers in Toledo, Ohio, now compete with those in Shanghai for wages and jobs, and there has been a "hollowing out" of the workforces in the United States and other countries once described as "industrialized." With the decline in labor unions and changes in collective bargaining, it is harder for average workers in one place to demand higher salaries for goods that could be made more cheaply elsewhere. That restricts wage growth and makes it difficult for working-class people to improve their economic fortunes.

Public policies play a substantial role in social mobility and wealth creation.[51] Governments have considerable impact on education policy, poverty programs, business operations, and tax rates. Each of these areas affects the opportunities that people have to get an education, rise out of poverty, launch businesses, and keep what they make. For the past several decades, many countries have reduced income tax rates and tilted a range of public policies to favor the affluent. In the 1980s, President Ronald Reagan cut income taxes and spurred wealth creation. That was followed in the 2000s by generous tax cuts, advocated by President George W. Bush and approved by bipartisan majorities in Congress, that gave the greatest benefits to the wealthy. The top income tax rate was reduced from 39.6 to 35 percent, while the tax on dividends dropped from 39.6 to 15 percent and the capital gains tax went from 21 to 15 percent.[52]

Education is part of the income story because of the substantial differences among groups linked to educational attainment. There are well-documented differences in income level among high school dropouts, high school graduates, college graduates, and those who have done post-graduate work. According to recent U.S. Bureau of Labor Statistics data, an American high school dropout earns, on average, an annual income of $24,492; a high school graduate earns $33,904; a college graduate earns $55,432; and those with a professional degree, such as doctors and lawyers, earn $90,220.[53] Those differences reflect a situation in which individuals trained to compete in the "knowledge economy" do well while others stagnate.

Others point to the "marriage gap" and its impact on earnings. Senior fellow Ron Haskins of the Brookings Institution noted that "between 1970 and 2010, the percentage of 35-year-old women living in married-couple families with children fell from about 78 percent to 50 percent while the percentage of women who were single and living with children more than doubled, from 9 percent to over 20 percent."[54] According to his data, those living in single-parent households are the most likely of all people to be poor. Recent research by Jeremy Greenwood and colleagues also cited marriage as a crucial factor in income inequality due to "assortative mating," that is, the tendency of well-educated people to marry one another and together earn a lot of money.[55]

Billionaires don't directly create problems of inequality or immobility. But it is difficult for those born in disadvantaged situations to move up the economic ladder when incomes are highly skewed and programs intended to advance economic opportunity are under attack. People in the middle or at the bottom of the income spectrum have trouble raising the funds to invest in education and health care. Economist Julia Isaacs found that those who grow up in the bottom quintile of family income have only a 6 percent chance of earning an income in the top quintile while those who start out wealthy have a 39 percent chance.[56]

Dangers in the Developing World

The developing world exhibits greater inequity than developed nations and therefore has more of the political and social problems associated with great wealth. Latin American nations have the highest level of inequality, with a Gini coefficient of .48, followed by Sub-Saharan Africa (.44), Asia (.40), the Middle East and North Africa (.39), Eastern Europe and Central Asia (.35), and high-income countries (.31). Within the developed world, however, there is considerable variation. Countries such as the United States and the United Kingdom are at the high end of inequality (with Gini coefficients of .37 and .34, respectively), while Denmark (.22), Finland (.25), and the Netherlands (.25) are at the low end.[57]

Many poor nations have weak rule of law. They do not have strong electoral or governance systems that can help balance the political demands of those with great wealth and the interests of the general public. For example, the Electoral Integrity Project at the University of Sydney, Australia, reports that the "lack of a level playing field in political finance and campaign media was seen by experts as the most serious risk to integrity worldwide."[58] In some cases, typically authoritarian regimes and military dictatorships, there is a nearly perfect union between economic resources and political power. The "strong man" and his relatives amass tremendous fortunes while the people languish in extreme poverty. This arrangement is most evident in African nations, along with some in the Middle East, Asia, and Latin America. The dramatic contrast between rich and poor in those countries destroys opportunity, makes citizens cynical about their government, and inhibits overall economic and political development.

These problems are aggravated when a country's legal system makes it easy to transfer wealth across generational lines, whether through customary practices in which money stays within the family or public policies on taxes and estates that facilitate large wealth transfers. Such situations raise tremendous risks in terms of inequality, poor governance, and limited opportunities for mobility. The riskiest situation arises when possession of great economic and political resources combines with easy transfer of wealth across generations. That combination creates a regime in which social mobility is stifled and hereditary forces dictate the distribution of wealth. In the worst cases, family lineage becomes far more important than talent, creativity, and ability to innovate. That is the case in many parts of the Middle East and in nations ruled by autocrats. The least risky case exists in nations such as Scandinavia and some others in Europe, where political power and economic resources are more separate and it is hard to transfer financial resources across generations. In such situations, it is difficult for any single group to dominate consistently over time, and that promotes the type of healthy societal competition that rewards merit and excellence.

Allowing oligarchs, tycoons, magnates, or princelings to dominate a society by means of their own wealth or hereditary transfer of privilege—as in too many places in Africa, the Middle East, Latin America, and Asia—frays a country's social, economic, and political fabric. When I visited Bahrain several years ago, for example, local residents told me that they needed the emir's official approval to buy personal property; it was not possible for private individuals there to buy or sell homes and businesses independently. Bahrain represents an extreme example of a modern-day feudal system that is a perfect environment for corruption and insider dealing. But even in less extreme cases, common in the developing world, formal and informal restraints on economic mobility engender public cynicism and destroy hopes for future advancement. People feel that even if they have good ideas, there is little chance that they will be able to pursue their vision or have a decent shot at developing their own business.

One already sees worrisome signs of cynicism and despair in developed nations such as the United States. A 2013 survey of the American public found that 70 percent believed that "the income gap between the rich and poor has gotten larger during the past 10 years."[59] Even more troubling, many believe that the "American Dream" is fading. Fifty-two percent of respondents thought that their generation is better off financially than their children's generation will be, and only 18 percent anticipated that their children will have the same level of prosperity that they have. It is hard to imagine that those who live in some parts of the developing world feel much better about opportunities within their societies.

Plan of the Book

The plan of the book is as follows. In chapter 2, I discuss how billionaires influence candidate elections. They do this either indirectly through campaign finance or directly by running for office themselves. I present an analysis of the 2012 presidential election and the fundraising role that billionaires played and case studies of the electoral campaigns of two billionaires who sought elective office: Michael Bloomberg's New York City mayoral campaigns and Meg Whitman's gubernatorial run in California. I argue that billionaires can't easily buy office when there is extensive media coverage, robust party organizations, and opportunities for opposing forces to organize voters. But money is influential in how campaigns unfold and in what kind of policy arguments get made. In addition, there were idiosyncratic conditions that allowed Barack Obama to triumph over Mitt Romney, and there are no guarantees that conservative billionaires who backed the GOP nominee will lose the next time around. If they find a better candidate, adjust their advertising appeals, and build a stronger field operation, they will be in a stronger position to win, even if Democrats rail against them.

In chapter 3, I look at a series of advocacy campaigns at the state and local level bankrolled by wealthy individuals. They include campaigns against gun violence, health care reform, climate change legislation, and higher taxes on the wealthy and campaigns in favor of marijuana legalization, pension reform, same-sex marriage, and stadium renovations. At a time of declining press coverage of state government, much spending has been done below the radar of the electorate and has impacted several policy debates. Referendums and policy campaigns have become a major target for a number of billionaires, and they have been successful in influencing the debate over marijuana legalization, same-sex marriage, public pension reform, and taxes. In campaigns in which they have been influential, there generally has been one-sided electoral discourse and limited media coverage.

Chapter 4 examines the new activism in philanthropy. Many observers rightfully point out that people benefit from the giving of others. By funding charitable foundations and supporting particular causes, rich people make generous contributions to society as a whole. Yet researchers need to examine new models of gift giving. Increasingly, certain activist billionaires are combining philanthropy with electioneering and policy advocacy. Because of these new forms of philanthropy, the country needs to think about better disclosure and transparency regulations, particularly in regard to tax-exempt organizations that participate in election campaigns.

Chapter 5 looks at politics and elections abroad. Billionaires such as Silvio Berlusconi in Italy, Bidzina Ivanishvili in Georgia, Serge Dassault in France, Zac Goldsmith in the United Kingdom, Frank Stronach in Austria, Clive Palmer in Australia, Petro Poroshenko in Ukraine, Thaksin Shinawatra in Thailand, Vijay Mallya and Nandan Nilekani in India, Najib Mikati and the late Rafiq Hariri of Lebanon, Manuel Villar of the Philippines, and Mikhail

Prokhorov, Andrei Guriev, and Sergei Pugachyou in Russia have run for office, and most have won. Many of them have been accused of buying votes, influence peddling, and overt corruption. The manner in which they have used their abundant financial resources raises serious questions about the ties between money and politics.

The background and manner in which billionaires make money are relevant in policy and political debates concerning the super rich. It matters for public policy whether the wealthy earn their fortunes through their own innovations or become affluent at least in part through public investment and tax policies. In looking at wealth formation, I argue that in many cases it takes a village to make a fortune. The role of societal forces in wealth creation suggests that billionaires have responsibilities to the country as a whole and should help promote opportunities for other people.

Chapter 6 presents a demographic, geographic, and industry profile of global billionaires. Using data from the 1,645 people on the *Forbes* billionaires list, I show that they are overwhelmingly white, male, and older and that many benefited from public investments and decisions that aided their sector. Chapter 7 analyzes how several prominent billionaires earned their fortunes. Many of them, dissatisfied with the status quo, displayed considerable skill in developing new products, services, or market niches that were not well-served by existing firms. While such vision is important, chapter 8 demonstrates how wealth creation also is facilitated by infrastructure investment, public investment in research and education, favorable tax policies, and social networking.

In chapters 9 and 10, I summarize the arguments about "wealthification" and call for policies that help others move ahead. It is crucial to adopt policies that promote transparency, accountability, governance, and opportunity; accordingly, I outline a number of policy actions that can improve the democratic process and extend social well-being to a broader range of people.

PART I

BILLIONAIRE ACTIVISM

2 Can Rich Dudes Buy an Election?

BILLIONAIRES DAVID AND CHARLES KOCH spent vast sums seeking to defeat President Barack Obama in the 2012 election. Through a nonprofit organization called Americans for Prosperity and related conservative groups, they spent hundreds of millions of dollars on television ads and outreach activities accusing the president and his Democratic allies of poor leadership and weak performance.[1] As described by Kenneth Vogel of *Politico*, Americans for Prosperity had a field staff of more than 100 organizers and worked with a variety of like-minded groups. Together they funded electoral data mining through a group called Themis, argued for federal budget cuts through an organization known as Public Notice, engaged in youth outreach with Generation Opportunity, emphasized job creation through tax cuts with Americans for Job Security, pushed for what they called effective leadership through Americans for Responsible Leadership, focused on senior citizens through the 60 Plus Association, and promoted the mobilization of conservative Hispanic voters through the Libre Initiative.[2]

All of the Koch brothers' activities emphasized educating the public, beating Obama in the general election, and producing a Republican majority in the U.S. Senate. Their efforts, along with those of other mega-wealthy individuals, led *CNN Money* to run an article by Charles Riley entitled "Can 46 Rich Dudes Buy an Election?"[3] At that early stage in the election cycle, in March 2012, Riley noted that forty-six wealthy individuals had contributed $67 million of the total $112 million raised by election super PACs, the funding entities that can spend an unlimited amount as long as the activities are not formally coordinated with those of specific candidates. Each person had given at least $500,000 to groups that for the most part were active on the Republican side.

In addition to the Kochs, Las Vegas Sands CEO Sheldon Adelson contributed $15 million to Winning Our Future, Newt Gingrich's super PAC, plus another $78 million to other Republicans. Harold Simmons, the Dallas billionaire who died in December 2013, gave $26.9 million to various conservative political action committees for the 2012 elections. PayPal founder Peter Thiel contributed $2.6 million to Revolution, Ron Paul's super PAC. Hedge fund manager John Paulson gave $1 million to Restore Our Future, the super PAC of Republican presidential candidate Mitt Romney.

Of course, not all the wealthy donors supported conservatives. Hollywood producer Jeffrey Katzenberg gave $3 million to Priorities USA Action, President Obama's super PAC. Comedian Bill Maher contributed $1 million, and fund manager Jim Simons, entrepreneur Fred Eychaner, and trial lawyer Steve Mostyn donated large sums to support the president's campaign. But much more of the largesse in 2012 went to the Republican end of the political spectrum. Overall, Priorities USA Action raised only $75 million, far below the amount raised by top GOP super PACs.[4]

Obama was able to triumph, but there were particular factors that allowed him to survive against a well-funded opponent. His campaign as well as those of billionaire candidates Michael Bloomberg and Meg Whitman reveal interesting details about money and politics and the electoral conditions under which wealth is decisive. Rich people can't automatically buy American elections, but money has a crucial impact on problem definition and campaign dialogue.

Declining Transparency and Accountability in U.S. Elections

Before the infamous Watergate scandal, the U.S. system of campaign finance had three basic features: weak disclosure rules; no limits on contributions, giving great clout to the wealthy; and unlimited spending based on whatever amounts candidates could raise.[5] In all these respects, current campaign finance rules are remarkably similar to the loose rules that existed prior to Watergate.

Secrecy and large amounts of money were key ingredients in the Watergate scandal. Worried that Democrats would triumph in 1972, President Richard Nixon and his aides formed the "plumbers unit," which investigated Democratic candidates, played dirty tricks designed to embarrass the opposition, and conducted a break-in at the headquarters of the Democratic National Committee in the hope of uncovering sensitive information. The operation was funded by secret cash donations from wealthy donors. When the break-in was discovered by security officers at the Watergate complex, the operation unraveled, and Nixon was forced from office—not quite two years after winning re-election.

Public disgust with the Watergate abuses produced dramatic changes in campaign finance rules. Within a few years, Congress passed and Nixon's successor, Gerald Ford, signed into law a massive overhaul, much of which was ratified by the Supreme Court in its 1976 landmark case, *Buckley* v. *Valeo*. The reforms emphasized four new features: strong disclosure laws designed to outlaw secrecy in fundraising; caps on contributions at $1,000 per individual and $5,000 per political action committee, which sharply reduced the ability of the wealthy to fund individual candidates; voluntary spending limits on presidential campaigns in exchange for public subsidies; and the creation of a new federal agency, the Federal Election Commission, with sweeping enforcement powers.

Even more important than the legal changes in the rules of campaign finance was a shift in the underlying view of electoral competition. Although both legislators and Supreme Court justices explained the reforms primarily in terms of avoiding the reality or perception of corruption in the political system, a perusal of the changes implemented during this period reveals a far more wide-reaching transformation of fundraising. For the first time in U.S. history, the ability of the wealthy to fund individual candidates was sharply limited. The rich still could spend substantial sums of money, but they had to scatter their resources among a large number of candidates. And the parties were placed on identical footing in terms of the amounts that they were able to raise and spend if their presidential candidates voluntarily accepted public subsidies to fund their campaigns.

Contributions to political candidates had to be disclosed in quarterly reports filed with the Federal Election Commission. The idea was that secrecy compromised the electoral process and therefore that voters should be made aware of who was financing a campaign. In politics, the messenger often is as important as the message. It matters who is financing particular messages and what individuals and groups are behind campaign communications.[6] Given the possible corrupting impact of money in politics, citizens need basic information on contributors and expenditures. Without meaningful transparency, it is very difficult to have fair elections.

The $1,000 limit on individual contributions to a single candidate was designed to address the fear in earlier elections that wealthy interests could buy influence by donating hundreds of thousands of dollars to particular candidates. The potential for abuse in this area—which had been demonstrated vividly by the Watergate scandal—led reformers to impose a clear limit on contributions and insist that wealthy people not funnel large sums of money to individual candidates. At the same time, overall spending limits made the playing field more equal for candidates in presidential elections. In return for accepting public subsidies to help finance the nominating and general election campaigns, candidates had to abide by caps on how much they could spend on their campaigns. In 1976, for example, during the first presidential campaign after Watergate, candidates Jimmy Carter and Gerald Ford were given the identical amount of $22 million each to contest the general election.

Nonetheless, many of the Watergate-inspired laws turned out to be rather porous in their ability to restrict spending by the wealthy. The combination of subsequent court rulings, creative political strategies, and closely contested elections led to the restoration of key pre-Watergate features. Notably, these include weak disclosure, secret spending, the reemergence of large contributors, and spending imbalances in presidential politics.

In later rulings, a number of loopholes emerged, such as through the mechanism of "independent" expenditures. Because the Supreme Court did not want to limit freedom of expression, groups that are truly independent of candidates were allowed to spend unlimited amounts of money on direct electoral advocacy. It was a decision that would have remarkable consequences for presidential campaigns. The spending by candidates who voluntarily chose to accept public funding for their campaigns obviously would be limited, but not that of outside groups that supported or opposed them. Another loophole emerged in what came to be known as "issue advocacy." The courts have allowed interest groups or political parties to run public education appeals that promote ideas but do not expressly oppose or support the election of specific candidates. Under legal interpretations dating back to *Buckley* v. *Valeo* in 1976, groups are considered to be engaged in electioneering only if they run ads or produce material including phrases like "vote for/against Representative Smith."

Supreme Court justices sought to distinguish three categories of political activism: lobbying government officials directly, which could be regulated; electioneering, which would be subject to post-Watergate rules on disclosure, contribution limits, and voluntary spending limits (for presidential candidates); and public education activities, which would face few restrictions or disclosure requirements owing to First Amendment concerns about freedom of speech. In regard to the latter, groups would not be required to register as political action committees unless they explicitly used the so-called "magic words," such as "vote for," "support," "elect," or "defeat."[7] The obvious problem with the distinction is that there are many ways to convey the instruction to vote for or against a candidate without ever using those words. With recent advances in television, video, and digital productions, it is relatively easy to employ audio voice-overs, music, text, images, color, editing, and code words to communicate powerful, election-oriented messages to the general public.[8] Indeed, it takes little ingenuity to produce a public education appeal that complies with the Buckley court decision yet still tells people that they should vote for or against a particular candidate for office.

In 2010, the Supreme Court issued a landmark ruling in *Citizens United* v. *Federal Election Commission* that upended the remaining vestiges of the post-Watergate campaign finance system. Deciding the case of a nonprofit organization that aired a documentary critical of Hillary Clinton, justices voted five to four to strike down major pieces of the Bipartisan Campaign Reform Act. Passed in 2002, that act—better known as the McCain-Feingold Act after its Senate sponsors, John McCain (R-Arizona), and Russ Feingold (D-Wisconsin)—sought to limit the use of so-called "soft money" by political parties and issue advocacy ads just before elections. Specifically, the Court's ruling allowed individuals, businesses, and unions to contribute large amounts of money to super PACS, which could broadcast ads and otherwise seek to influence elections. This ruling allowed wealthy individuals and corporations—and other groups such as labor unions—to contribute millions of dollars to finance a torrent of largely negative advertisements in support of particular candidates. Most recently, nonprofit groups have sought tax-exempt status under Internal Revenue Service sections 501(c)(3) and 501(c)(4), legal categories that allow organizations that conduct public education campaigns to influence the election.[9] Since the 2010 decision, there has been a proliferation of groups that engage in electoral activity in the guise of "social welfare" organizations.

In 2014, the Court followed up with another controversial decision in *McCutcheon* v. *Federal Election Commission*. In a 5-to-4 decision, the justices struck down restrictions on the total amount that donors could give to candidates for federal office as well as to political parties. National laws had previously capped total contributions at $48,600 for all federal candidates and $74,600 for parties and political action committees.[10] Critics lambasted the ruling for enabling wealthy individuals to pour larger amounts of money into congressional and presidential elections. In his dissenting opinion for the Court minority, Justice Stephen Breyer wrote a scathing rebuttal: "Its conclusion rests upon its own, not a record-based, view of the facts. Its legal analysis is faulty: It misconstrues the nature of the competing constitutional interests at stake. It understates the importance of protecting the political integrity of our governmental institutions. It creates a loophole that will allow a single individual to contribute millions of dollars to a political party or to a candidate's campaign. Taken together with *Citizens United* v. *Federal Election Commission*, today's decision eviscerates our Nation's campaign finance laws, leaving a remnant incapable of dealing with the grave problems of democratic legitimacy that those laws were intended to resolve."[11]

Through these and other loopholes, court rulings have effectively gutted the post-Watergate system of campaign finance. The result is that a variety of interests have been able to finance and engage in electioneering activities designed to influence the public without disclosing their campaign donors. The growth of secret electioneering masquerading as public education creates huge opportunities for clandestine political action. The United States now has a system in which political dialogue is funded secretly, thereby upending the post-Watergate efforts to promote transparency and accountability.[12]

The problem is not just a question of a broken U.S. campaign finance system. Political scientists Alfred Stepan and Juan Linz have written that the United States "is now the most unequal longstanding democracy in a developed country in the world."[13] The nation faces serious challenges in terms of fragmented institutions, poor public deliberation, limited political participation, and voter suppression. When unequal monetary resources are combined with porous campaign finance laws and secret financing, the result is what Harvard University's Lawrence Lessig describes as a *Republic, Lost.*[14]

Does Obama's Victory Prove That the Rich Can't Buy Elections?

A few billionaires took advantage of these changes in campaign finance to attempt to defeat President Obama in 2012. Individuals such as Charles and David Koch spent well over $100 million on a variety of conservative causes.[15] Casino magnate Sheldon Adelson spent $93 million on opposing Obama. Meanwhile, Karl Rove's super PAC devoted $300 million to unseat Obama and elect what Romney's supporters hoped would become a Republican majority in the Senate. Of the top ten contributors to super PACs in 2012, six supported Republican candidates, to the tune of $166 million, while four favored Democrats, for a total of $42 million. Overall, *the top 100 contributors to super PACs accounted for 73 percent of all the money donated in 2012 to these organizations.* That demonstrates the major loophole that super PACs have become for super-wealthy individuals who want to fund their preferred candidates.[16]

Nonetheless, Obama won reelection. On the surface, his triumph over a small group of the super wealthy appears to support the proposition that the rich can't buy elections. The hundreds of millions that came from these sources appears to have had little impact on the election outcome. Obama won with 51 percent of the vote, and he scored a resounding 332–206 victory in the Electoral College. Despite all the spending by conservative business leaders, Democrats actually gained two seats in the Senate, to achieve a 55–45 majority. Even Donald Trump piled on against Karl Rove's poor showing. In a tweet after the election, Trump said, "Congrats to @KarlRove on blowing $400 million this cycle. Every race @CrossroadsGPS ran ads in, the Republicans lost. What a waste of money." The ability of Obama to mobilize voters, expand the electorate, generate favorable publicity, and appeal to basic fairness on the part of the general public helped him win the campaign. The president played to public preferences regarding fairness and argued that he would fight for the middle class against wealthy interests.

The 2012 results thus raise the interesting question of whether Obama's victory was an exception that proved the rule regarding the dangers of super wealth in U.S. elections. Obama's triumph does not necessarily mean that those supporting greater fairness will always beat a small number of well-funded and well-organized rich people. Obama had a substantial advantage over Romney with respect to his personal likeability, perceived concern about ordinary people, and ability to protect the middle class. But not every presidential election will unfold that way.

Over the summer, the president ran an ad saying that his opponent would raise taxes on middle-class families. During the ad, a male narrator says, "You work hard. Stretch every penny. But chances are you pay a higher tax rate than him. Mitt Romney made $20 million in 2010 but paid only 14 percent in taxes, probably less than you. Now he has a plan that would give millionaires another tax break, and raises taxes on middle-class families by up to $2,000 a year."[17] This ad was effective because, as Northwestern University sociologist Leslie McCall has pointed out, Americans have become more aware of income inequality and its corrosive impact on the country.[18]

In many respects, Romney was the perfect target for Obama's attacks on unfairness and out-of-touch rich people. The GOP candidate had bank accounts in Switzerland, the Cayman Islands, Luxembourg, and Bermuda, and he refused for much of the year to release details from his tax returns. Brad Malt, who served as Romney's personal lawyer, revealed dramatic tone deafness when he defended the nominee's portfolio in the following manner: "I don't care whether it's the Caymans or Mars, if it's organized in the Netherlands Antilles or the Jersey Islands. That means nothing to me. All I care about is whether it's a good fund or a bad fund."[19]

Following Romney's inept political responses, Democrats aggressively painted their Republican opponent as an out-of-touch plutocrat who did not represent the values of ordinary Americans. One Obama commercial made this claim quite starkly with the tagline "Mitt Romney: Not one of us." Public opinion polls showed that these political attacks had the desired impact. In July, a national survey conducted by the *New York Times* and CBS News found that 53 percent of registered voters believed that Romney's policies favored the rich while only 11 percent thought that they favored the middle class. In contrast, only 21 percent felt that Obama's policies favored the rich and 22 percent believed that they favored the middle class.[20]

Ironically, some of the liberal billionaires who had backed Democrats in earlier races sat on the campaign finance sidelines for much of 2012. For example, there was little spending on behalf of the president by George Soros, who had devoted tens of millions of dollars in 2004 and 2008 through MoveOn and other liberal organizations to finance media advertisements, fund get-out-the-vote drives, and help build strong grassroots organizations. In 2012, Soros made few political contributions, other than to support some grassroots organizations. It was not until the end of September, when it was reasonably clear that Obama was going to win, that Soros made a $1 million contribution to Obama's super PAC and gave $500,000 to support House Democrats.[21] His total electoral contribution that year was $2.8 million, far less than that of the top conservative billionaires. His relative silence was quite noticeable given the noisiness of his political activities in previous years.

One explanation was that Obama and Soros did not click personally. In *Double Down*, their book about the 2012 race, journalists Mark Halperin and John Heilemann recounted a jarring pre-election meeting between the men at the Waldorf Astoria in New York City, part of an effort by Obama to encourage Soros to spend freely on behalf of his campaign. Much to the president's chagrin, Soros spent 45 minutes lecturing him on the poor messaging of his economic program. According to the writers, Obama was "annoyed and bored" by the tirade. Later, he told his campaign organizers that "if we don't get anything out of him, I'm never fucking sitting with that guy again."[22] Another source explained the weak support from liberal billionaires in policy terms. "Obama continues to be a disappointment to them. While they will vote for him given the alternative, they won't be doing it with their pocketbook. The groups they are supporting are part of the progressive infrastructure as opposed to candidate Obama."[23]

The so-called black oligarchs were similarly standoffish toward Obama's re-election campaign. Oprah Winfrey provided modest financial support for Obama in 2012 but made no campaign appearances for him.[24] In contrast, in 2008 she had been a strong Obama supporter. Obama had appeared on her television show, and she had filmed a campaign ad on his behalf during his initial run. On Election Night, she stood in a prominent spot near the stage in Chicago for Obama's historic acceptance speech. But efforts by Obama's super PAC to enlist her support in 2012 went for naught. She gave only $76,000 to Obama's Victory Fund—an amount that would be large for most people, but not for her.[25] Some people I know who were close to his super PAC expressed exasperation with Winfrey and other liberal rich people. In an off-the-record conversation with me, one Democratic activist said that the Obama PAC made repeated overtures to Soros, Winfrey, and other wealthy liberals who had supported him in 2008. In a surprise to the Obama campaign, many of them declined to give money or did so at relatively low levels, given their financial capacity. Their campaign contributions were far below what a number of conservative billionaires were doing on behalf of Romney, demonstrating a clear imbalance in super-rich participation in the 2012 election.

Liberal billionaires had various reasons for staying on the sidelines in 2012, according to these insiders. Although many of them agree with Obama's political views in general, most were not enthusiastic about Obama's tax policies. Through private channels, they expressed their displeasure at the president's call to return tax rates for the rich to their Clinton administration levels. The fact that Obama wanted to raise taxes on the wealthy was a major negative in the eyes of some rich, liberal donors.

Some suggest that wealth is not a problem in U.S. elections because there are liberal billionaires who favor Democrats. According to this logic, because there is a rough parity between liberal and conservative rich people, wealth drops out as a decisive factor in presidential elections. This pluralistic chorus of wealthy people thus creates a harmony that balances power within the billionaire class and prevents wealth from dictating campaign outcomes. Yet the 2012 presidential election demonstrates that even though some rich people are liberals, they did not make the same effort on behalf of Democrats as conservative billionaires did for Republicans. Obama's tax policies moved some of his natural supporters to the political sidelines and kept them from serving as a counterweight to their conservative counterparts.

In certain respects, then, it is surprising that Obama beat the billionaires. Even so, there are no guarantees that the rich will lose future races in which they have invested a lot of money. If they come up with a more plausible candidate who is not easily portrayed as rich and out of touch, they would have a serious shot at victory.

Billionaire Candidates Michael Bloomberg and Meg Whitman

Aside from providing financial support for favored candidates, rich people sometimes seek to exercise influence by running for office themselves. In the United States, it is rare for the super wealthy to seek elective office. Most of them do not want the personal scrutiny that comes with political campaigning—especially having reporters ask endless questions regarding their motivations and self-interest. Furthermore, election campaigns create problems because of the legal requirement to disclose financial holdings and political pressure to reveal tax returns. Most people with extensive financial resources are not inclined to subject themselves to a very public examination of their business dealings. The criticism that Romney endured after he reluctantly released some of his tax filings undoubtedly will reinforce reluctance to do so on the part of other wealthy people.

But there are exceptions to that trend. In 1958, wealthy heir Nelson Rockefeller ran for office and won. He served four terms as governor of New York and later was appointed vice president under Gerald Ford. His brother Winthrop, meanwhile, was elected governor of Arkansas in 1966 and served two terms. In 1992, Texas billionaire Ross Perot campaigned for president as an independent and garnered nearly 19 percent of the vote. Other notable rich candidates include former Goldman Sachs chief executive Jon Corzine (who won terms as New Jersey governor and senator), former Hewlett-Packard chief executive Carly Fiorina (who unsuccessfully ran for the U.S. Senate in California during 2010), cosmetics heir Ronald Lauder (who ran for mayor of New York City in 1989), payroll processing company founder Tom Golisano (who ran three times for governor of New York), and New York grocery store executive John Catsimatidis (who ran for New York City mayor in 2013, taunting his opponents with the slogan "I made $3 billion. What did they do?").[26] Billionaire Penny Pritzker did not run for office, but she was appointed secretary of commerce by Obama in 2013. That put her in a position to speak about trade and business development, both in the United States and abroad.

However, as the super rich boost their political activism, it is instructive to examine more closely two recent elections in which billionaires have run: Michael Bloomberg and Meg Whitman. Bloomberg was elected mayor of New York City three times; Whitman lost her attempt to become governor of California. Each contest reveals important things about wealth in politics, how the public perceives billionaires, and the probability that rich people can win democratic elections.

Bloomberg, who founded the wildly successful financial data company bearing his name, ran as an outsider who would bring business-like efficiency to government. He talked frequently about his success in building his company, adopting innovative practices, and having an effective leadership style. The policies that he espoused were designed to improve governance, education, economic opportunity, and public safety. He developed a data-driven approach to government that used performance metrics to drive decisionmaking. In education, for example, Bloomberg advocated greater accountability and innovation in public schools. He linked teacher evaluations to student performance and rewarded those instructors whose students demonstrated improvement over the course of the academic year. He argued that effective public education was crucial for long-term economic prosperity and that New York City school officials should fire incompetent teachers and make sure that all city students had a decent opportunity to better themselves. In public safety, he developed collaborations between different agencies as well as between the city and the federal government. In the aftermath of the September 11, 2001, terrorist attacks—which took place just before he first won election—he improved data sharing so that risks could quickly be assessed and resolved. He cleaned up the city and made it a safer place for people to live.

In a speech, Bloomberg described himself as a fiscal conservative who cared about people. "Being a fiscal conservative is not about slashing programs that help the poor, or improve health care, or ensure a social safety net," he noted. "It's about insisting services are provided efficiently, get to only the people that need them, and achieve the desired results. Fiscal conservatives have hearts too—but we also insist on using our brains, and that means demanding results and holding government accountable for producing them."[27]

With his emphasis on good government and improving opportunity, Bloomberg won three elections and earned strong job performance ratings throughout most of his administration. Public opinion polls regularly acknowledged his strong leadership. Voters also appreciated his philanthropy on behalf of the city. Ben Smith of *BuzzFeed* joked that Bloomberg's giving was the reverse of the typical political relationship. In most cases, Smith said, people try to bribe politicians, but in Bloomberg's case, he "bribed you, buying the silence or cooperation of individuals, cultural organizations, and social service groups with hundreds of millions of dollars spent on small personal favors—a legal payment here, a medical procedure there—and charitable contributions."[28]

A *New York Times* analysis found that Bloomberg had spent $650 million on his political campaigns, advocacy activities, and philanthropy. The three campaigns together cost him $268 million in personal money, while his charitable giving during his mayorship totaled $263 million. He also spent around $7 million on efforts to fight gun violence, $5.7 million on encouraging immigration reform, and $6.2 million on volunteerism as well as millions more on many nonprofit organizations.[29]

As he left office, politicians and media commentators debated his legacy. A city survey found mixed views regarding the impact of wealth on his public service. In a report on how New Yorkers evaluated the impact of his wealth, the *New York Times* said, "30 percent said Mr. Bloomberg's wealth had made him a better mayor; 27 percent said it had made him a worse mayor; and 35 percent said it had made no difference."[30] Democratic successor Bill de Blasio, elected in 2013, openly derided his predecessor's record. He claimed there were "two cities" and that Bloomberg was more interested in people with money than the middle class. "We cannot expect prosperity to trickle down from the top. We cannot resign ourselves to the mind-set that says rising inequality is a necessary byproduct of urban success," he declared.[31] At the same time, de Blasio softened some of his rhetoric, telling wealthy financiers that "Wall Street is our hometown industry" and that "the city's economy hinged on the health of businesses like theirs."[32] For his part, Bloomberg explained his focus on economic growth and attracting people with money to the city: "If we can find a bunch of billionaires around the world to move here, that would be a godsend, because that's where the revenue comes to take care of everybody else."[33]

Meg Whitman's storyline differed from Bloomberg's in significant ways. She had been a successful business executive at companies such as Hasbro, eBay, Proctor and Gamble, and Dreamworks, helping them increase their revenues, develop new products, and improve their financial performance. She had a reputation for strong and effective leadership. Yet when she stepped into the political arena in 2010 against a skilled opponent (Jerry Brown) who had been on the political scene for decades, she was tarred for espousing pro-rich policies. She supported across-the-board tax cuts that disproportionately benefited the wealthy. She employed a housekeeper who was an illegal immigrant. She spent $144 million of her own money on her gubernatorial race, the largest amount of money that any American had spent to self-finance a single election campaign.[34]

Her opponent, Jerry Brown, is one of the greatest survivors in California political history. He framed her as "this rich empress who lived in a bubble and couldn't relate to average Californians."[35] While the Bloomberg campaign was able to capitalize on the message that Bloomberg was too rich to be bought, Whitman was cast by Democrats as a rich person attempting to buy the election so she could enact pro-wealthy policies. She did not have Bloomberg's history of spending hundreds of millions of dollars on personal philanthropy that would shield her from self-interest criticisms.

Public opinion surveys show that Brown's attacks were effective. Voters had doubts about her motivations and policies. For example, a poll taken during the middle of the campaign revealed that many people held unfavorable views of her personally and worried that she cared more about the wealthy than the middle class. In the eyes of voters, she was viewed as a self-interested politician who would use her office to benefit a narrow slice of the electorate—the same image that would bedevil Mitt Romney just two years later. She lost her electoral bid by a decisive margin of 54 to 41 percent.

Electoral Lessons for the Future

Many factors affect the relationship between money and politics. The anwer to the question of whether rich people can buy elections is "Sometimes, but not always." President Obama won reelection despite the massive amounts spent to defeat him by conservative business leaders. He beat back their spending by having a weak opponent who was seen by voters as pro-rich and out of touch. Romney lacked the personal skills to connect with voters and persuade them that he cared about the middle class.

Clearly, then, money is not the only thing that decides election campaigns. Public opinion, media coverage, campaign strategies, and policy positions matter as well. During a time of rising campaign costs and limited public engagement in the political process, money sets the agenda, affects how the campaign develops, and shapes how particular people and policy problems get defined. It takes skilled candidates, considerable media coverage, and strong organizational efforts to offset the power of great wealth.

There are no guarantees that future Democratic candidates will replicate Obama's 2012 electoral success. The conservative financiers involved then regard the money that they spent that year as the initial down payment on a long-term investment, even if it did not immediately pay off. After the general election, Sheldon Adelson announced that he planned to "double" his investment in future races. "I happen to be in a unique business where winning and losing is the basis of the entire business. So I don't cry when I lose. There's always a new hand coming up. I know in the long run we're going to win."[36] Marc Short, one of the strategists behind the political activities of Charles and David Koch, echoed that thought: "Our members are committed to the long term, not to one individual cycle."[37]

In preparation for the long-term battle, these billionaires already have altered their campaign approach to maximize the odds of winning. After studying what went wrong with the 2012 campaign, individuals such as Adelson are aiming for a different kind of GOP nominee. According to Adelson's friend Victor Chaltiel, "he doesn't want a crazy extremist to be the nominee. He wants someone who has the chance to win the election, who is reasonable in his positions, who has convictions but is not totally crazy." Meanwhile, Republican National Committee member Shawl Steel said that Adelson has learned from the 2012 defeat: "The candidate will have to have a strong resume—no sudden lightning-new guy—will have to build a formidable fundraising apparatus and really be emotionally tethered to bringing in middle-class Latinos, Asian Pacifics, Jews and blacks like never before."[38]

Understanding the importance of the top conservative billionaires, GOP strategist and former White House press secretary Ari Fleischer said that one of the most important elements in the 2016 presidential campaign would be who would win the "Sheldon Primary." Referring to the super-wealthy benefactor, Fleischer noted that "anybody running for the Republican nomination would want to have Sheldon at his side."[39] The same is true for Charles and David Koch. With their abundant resources, grassroots network, and willingness to spend to influence elections, their role in the GOP is of utmost importance. And like Adelson, they have sought to learn from 2012 and develop new electoral strategies. From their perspective, it is crucial to adapt to the political environment and alter public outreach strategies. James Davis of Freedom Partners, a Koch-financed group, said donors must test and refine their message: "Being in the field and testing during the slower periods, and in smaller areas, allows you to refine strategy and tactics so that you can make the larger investments with confidence."[40]

For the 2014 midterm elections, Americans for Prosperity (AFP) is focusing on field operations and broadcasting ads that employ moving personal stories to deliver policy messages. Central to their approach is the idea that Obamacare is a failure and is hurting ordinary patients. "Too often, we did kind of broader statistical ads or messages, and we decided that we needed to start telling the story of how the liberals' policies, whether it's the administration or Congress, are practically impacting the lives of Americans every day," explained Tim Phillips, the president of AFP. Media expert Elizabeth Wilner of Kantar Media/CMAG noted that those kinds of ads have a greater likelihood of electoral success. "Ads that tell stories are more compelling than ads that don't," she said. "And ads that use sympathetic figures are more compelling, generally, than those that don't."[41]

With ads that have greater impact, a stronger field operation, and better candidates, conservative billionaires are likely to have greater success in the future. Worried about that possibility, Democrats have countered with a "running against the billionaires" strategy. This is a tactic that was used successfully by Barack Obama in his re-election bid. He tied his GOP opponent Mitt Romney to billionaires such as Sheldon Adelson and the Koch brothers, who were spending hundreds of millions against him. Obama appealed to basic fairness and argued that a candidate backed by the mega rich would not fight for the middle class and help ordinary people.

Senate majority leader Harry Reid (D-Nevada) has copied this approach for the 2014 elections. In a series of speeches on the Senate floor, he bemoaned the unfairness of tycoons and the millions that they are spending to defeat vulnerable Democrats in key swing states. Reid decried the radical agenda "that benefits billionaires at the expense of the middle class."[42] Continuing, he said that "the oil baron Koch brothers are very good at protecting and growing their prodigious future and fortune. There's nothing un-American about that. But what is un-American is when shadowy billionaires pour unlimited money into our democracy to rig the system to benefit themselves and the wealthiest one percent."[43]

Democratic senators under attack by Americans for Prosperity ads costing millions of dollars responded with their own ads directly targeting the Koch brothers. One spot broadcast by Alaska Democratic senator Mark Begich complained about a local oil refinery shut down by Koch Industries: "They come into town, buy our refinery, and just run it into the ground, leaving a mess. A lot of Alaskans are losing jobs, and I'm definitely concerned about the drinking water. I don't go down and tell them what to do; I expect them not to come up to Alaska and tell us what to do."[44]

Upset with these personal attacks, Charles Koch penned an article in the *Wall Street Journal* entitled "I'm Fighting to Restore a Free Society," in which he decried "collectivists [who] engage in character assassination." He said that his companies employ 60,000 Americans and that his workers have won "over 700 awards for environmental, health, and safety excellence." Continuing his self-defense, he said that "far from trying to rig the system, I have spent decades opposing cronyism and all political favors, including mandates, subsidies, and protective tariffs—even when we benefit from them. I believe that cronyism is nothing more than welfare for the rich and powerful and should be abolished."[45]

Irritated that Reid was focusing on the Kochs, Senate minority leader Mitch McConnell (R-Kentucky) said that he "wondered why he left out billionaire Tom Steyer, who plans to spend as much as $100 million pushing the issue of climate change in the 2014 election and appears positioned to rival the deep-pocketed Koch brothers."[46]

Democrats face interesting strategic decisions with respect to billionaires. For more populist-leaning candidates, the preferred approach is to attack billionaires, complain about unfairness, and criticize the lack of transparency in their electioneering activities. Other Democrats, though, have chosen a different tack. They have embraced liberal billionaires rather than running against billionaires as a general class. Their thinking is that "if you can't beat them, you should join them."

An example of that alternative comes from Democrats loosely aligned with Hillary Clinton. Thinking ahead to a possible presidential campaign in 2016, her super PAC, Ready for Hillary, has signed up George Soros as co-chair of its national finance council.[47] In contrast to his aloofness from Obama in 2012, Soros agreed to assist the group laying the groundwork for her campaign three full years before the election. Michael Vachon, the political director for the billionaire, explained Soros's early action by saying that "his support for Ready for Hillary is an extension of his long-held belief in the power of grass-roots organizing."[48] The Clinton super PAC also has received contributions from billionaire Alice Walton, one of the heirs to the Wal-Mart fortune, and Marc Benioff, the billionaire CEO of Salesforce, along with a number of other wealthy individuals.[49] Mrs. Clinton's family foundation is working with billionaire Tom Steyer on an early childhood development project.[50]

Clinton's accommodationist approach clearly reflects the pragmatic conclusion that Democrats need abundant resources to fight the conservative billionaires aligned with the Republican Party. In light of recent Supreme Court decisions opening up the big money spigot, Democrats appear to believe that they must join the arms race that now characterizes U.S. campaign finance. However, that approach comes with some pitfalls. In cozying up to billionaires, Clinton and her supporters risk alienating the populist wing of her own party and turning off voters still stewing over the Wall Street interests that they think brought down the American economy during the financial collapse. If she goes too far with this strategy, she risks facing a progressive backlash during the nominating process.

The unresolved political question is how this party division over billionaires plays out. Dividing billionaires into warring factions may be the best hope for Democrats. But that choice means that Democrats should downplay the populist rhetoric and embrace pro-growth policies. They would have to quit talking about raising taxes on the rich and endorse actions that broaden social and economic opportunity.

Even if Democrats run against conservative billionaires, they are likely to embrace moderate and liberal ones in both 2014 and 2016. The 2016 election will be a multibillion dollar battle for the future of America, and Democrats cannot compete without having ultra-rich supporters willing to spend tens of millions on their behalf.

It matters considerably to democracy as a whole how Democrats resolve this strategic and policy issue. The outcome of future elections depends in good part on whether 2016 becomes the year of conservative billionaires, liberal ones, libertarian tycoons, or a diverse set of billionaires across the political spectrum.

3 *Referendum Campaigns and Policy Advocacy*

ELECTIONS GENERATE CONSIDERABLE media attention and organizational efforts on the part of various groups. Hundreds of millions of dollars are spent on mobilizing a broad range of voters, especially during presidential elections. Congressional races also attract high levels of spending designed to persuade the electorate to vote one way or another. Along with news stories and interest group activities, candidate outreach helps voters balance competing perspectives and make up their minds. State referendum campaigns and policy advocacy efforts, on the other hand, often are less visible and, except for a few hot-button issues such as gun control and immigration reform, typically don't generate as much media coverage. In some cases, these campaigns are bankrolled much more by advocates on one side of an issue than by those on the other. This can happen when large corporate interests have a stake in a campaign or when wealthy benefactors take a special interest in an issue.

Seeing considerable opportunities for advancing their policy interests, a number of billionaires have funded advocacy campaigns and financed nonprofit organizations that take strong positions on policy issues. With the weakness in many states and localities of countervailing institutions such as competitive political parties, such actions put billionaire-advocates in a strong position to shape public perceptions of important topics. At a time of declining media coverage of state issues, the large flows of money from liberal, conservative, and libertarian billionaires have made a major difference on several policy issues, such as marijuana legalization, same-sex marriage, public pension reform, and keeping taxes low.[1]

Activism on Marijuana Legalization, Same-Sex Marriage, Immigration, and Gun Control

Referendum processes in U.S. states allow policy measures to be placed directly on the ballot to be approved or rejected by voters; if approved, a measure becomes law. This process eliminates, or at least reduces, the need for advocates to work through legislators, governors, or presidents. Twenty-seven states allow direct balloting on policy issues. In direct balloting, political persuasion is the name of the game, and people with money are focusing on such contests. Although not all advocacy campaigns have been successful, a number of them have been.

One issue on which big money has made a substantial difference is marijuana policy. The late Peter Lewis, who died in 2013, was active in referendum campaigns supporting the legalization of marijuana. Lewis, who was a Brookings donor, was running Progressive Insurance when his leg was amputated following a serious infection that he contracted at the age of 64. While he was recuperating, he used marijuana to deal with the pain and found that it eased his suffering without severely impairing his judgment.[2] Concerned about the strict criminal penalties associated with use of the drug and having been arrested for possession in New Zealand, Lewis spent millions of dollars supporting its legalization. He devoted $525,000 to support a Massachusetts ballot measure to authorize marijuana use for medicinal purposes and $200,000 to support a similar California ballot item; both ultimately succeeded. Along with tech entrepreneur Sean Parker, Lewis was a big supporter of successful referendums in Colorado and the state of Washington to legalize marijuana use. It is estimated that over the last two decades Lewis has spent between $40 and $60 million on the decriminalization and legalization of marijuana. He said that his mission was "to reduce the penalties for growing, using and selling marijuana."[3] Armed with substantial funds from the billionaire insurance executive, activists have been successful in legalizing or decriminalizing marijuana possession in several states. Lewis's expenditures on marijuana legalization have been effective because the opposition hasn't spent large amounts of money to defeat legalization. Religious organizations and law enforcement have spoken out against marijuana legalization, but generally their efforts have not been well funded. This imbalance has helped pro-legalization forces persuade the general public that legalization would not endanger social well-being, that it would increase the visibility of what currently is an underground economy, and that it would generate valuable tax revenues for beleaguered state governments. As a result, other states and public opinion at large are moving in this direction. One-sided referendums are where big money can have its greatest impact on problem definition and agenda setting.

Another area where money has played a major role is same-sex marriage. Along with Seth Klarman, Paul Singer, who founded the Elliott Associates hedge fund, has been a vocal supporter of gay marriage legislation and has fought to encourage Republican legislators to vote in favor of same-sex marriage.[4] For him, the issue is personal: he has a son who is gay. He founded a political action committee, American Unity, that spent $2 million in 2012 on congressional elections to support Republicans who were in favor of same-sex marriage. Although Singer is politically conservative, he says that his support of same-sex marriage is consistent with his basic values. "This fight is about basic equality and individual liberty—both conservative principles. But for those who remain unconvinced, state-by-state evidence that marriage equality does no harm and actually strengthens families and the institution of marriage should put doubts to rest and pave the way for more conservatives to join this growing movement."⁵ In 2014, Klarman and Singer each contributed $375,000 to the group Americans for Workplace Opportunity, which seeks to ensure passage of workplace protections for the lesbian, gay, bisexual, and transsexual community.⁶

Singer and Klarman are not the only rich people to put money behind this cause. A 2012 same-sex marriage referendum in the state of Washington elicited financial support from local billionaires Jeff Bezos, of Amazon, and Bill Gates, of Microsoft (the Bill and Melinda Gates Foundation has contributed funds to Brookings). Bezos and his wife MacKenzie gave $2.5 million while Gates contributed $100,000, helping the referendum to win voters' approval.⁷ The advocacy efforts behind this and other campaigns have helped shift public opinion toward greater sympathy for same-sex marriage. Other billionaires, including conservatives, may personally oppose same-sex marriage, but none of them has put substantial resources into opposing it. Again, the money imbalance has made it easier for some state legislatures to approve marriage reform and has contributed to changing the general political atmosphere regarding reform, which may have encouraged judges in some states to overturn legal barriers to same-sex marriage.

Other issues have experienced more balanced spending, media coverage, and political organization. In these cases, it has been more difficult for billionaire funders to drive the agenda. When they spend money supporting one side of a controversy, countervailing forces are able to push back strongly and contest their claims. Immigration policy is an example of this kind of political situation. Facebook founder Mark Zuckerberg, for example, has formed a group, FWD.us, to push for immigration reform. In conjunction with other groups in the technology area, the organization broadcast ads designed to encourage Republican legislators to support reform efforts. In one commercial, the narrator says that "our immigration system is a joke" and tells viewers that we need "to fix our broken immigration system" by strengthening border security and legalizing those who have a job, pay a fine, and learn English.[8] In a 2013 visit to Washington, Zuckerberg explained his political involvement by saying that the United States doesn't have "enough talented people" and needs immigrants to strengthen the knowledge economy. He has put together various funds that reach out to Republicans, Democrats, and the country at large. "We want to be there to help those who need to take challenging positions on immigration," he said, noting that his organization was rare because it funded both Republican and Democratic legislators.

So far, however, this advocacy effort has not been successful. Strong political forces oppose immigration reform, and they have been vocal in fighting the legalization of undocumented immigrants. The U.S. Senate passed a comprehensive immigration reform bill, but legislation has languished in the House of Representatives. Speaker John Boehner (R-Ohio) has not managed to wrangle much Republican support for reform, despite Zuckerberg's efforts to target GOP legislators specifically. To prod lawmakers, a group affiliated with Zuckerberg's advocacy organization ran an ad in 2014 blaming Republicans for the congressional gridlock. "No one debates we need to fix our broken immigration system. Republican leaders know it. They've even said so time and again. So why are House Republicans cooling, retreating and even privately saying they'd rather do nothing this year," intones the spot's narrator.[9]

Gun control is another hot-button issue that has raised strong forces on different sides. Michael Bloomberg supports several groups devoted to fighting gun violence: Mayors against Illegal Guns, Moms Demand Action for Gun Sense in America, and Everytown for Gun Safety. The first organization has enlisted 889 mayors and 1.2 million other supporters to back its "Demand a Plan" proposal. Working in state capitals as well as Washington, the group seeks to convince legislators to strengthen background checks on gun purchasers and reduce the ability of people to buy high-magazine automatic weapons. Along with a super PAC active in this area, the group has targeted legislators who earn high ratings from the National Rifle Association.[10] Bloomberg has said that he planned to spend $50 million in 2014 fighting gun violence and that his goal was "to make them afraid of us."[11] The organization has experienced some wins and losses in its endeavor. In fall 2012, it spent more than $9 million to unseat pro-gun legislators. One of its targets was U.S. Representative Joe Baca, a Democrat from California who opposed gun control and had strong support from gun rights organizations. Bloomberg's organization ran ads criticizing the incumbent and suggesting that he was out of touch with ordinary voters.[12] In this case, Bloomberg's effort was successful: Baca lost the election by a 56-to-44 percent margin. Bloomberg also ran commercials in an Illinois primary election condemning a candidate, Debbie Halvorson, who received an "A" rating from the NRA, and supporting Robin Kelly, an anti–gun violence contender who favored Bloomberg's point of view on gun control.[13] Kelly triumphed over Halvorson by a two-to-one margin.

Bloomberg's organization was less successful in 2013 when it provided $350,000 (along with $250,000 from California billionaire Eli Broad) to support two Colorado legislators at risk in recall elections launched by gun defenders following the state's adoption of strict gun control laws. John Morse, the president of the Colorado senate, and Angela Giron, a Pueblo senator, were targeted by the National Rifle Association for supporting gun restrictions. The NRA spent around $2 million on the election, about the same amount as the supporters of the senators. A Bloomberg spokesperson justified the expenditure by noting that the mayor "has said he is going to support officials across the country who are willing to stand up to the N.R.A. and Washington gun lobby to support sane gun laws that will keep guns out of the hands of criminals."[14] Despite Bloomberg's efforts, the two were recalled by Colorado voters. Opposition forces took a page out of the Obama "run against the billionaires" strategy and derided Mayor Bloomberg's out-of-state intervention. Referring to his anti-obesity campaign, they retaliated with "in Colorado, we don't need some New York billionaire telling us what size soft drinks we can have, how much salt to put on our food, or the size of the ammunition magazines on our guns."[15]

In 2013, his last year in office as New York mayor, Bloomberg put considerable resources into successful efforts to elect a few candidates who pushed for pragmatic problem solving. Amid fears late in the campaign that Newark, New Jersey, mayor Cory Booker's poll numbers were slipping in Booker's bid for the U.S. Senate, Bloomberg launched a million-dollar ad buy through his super PAC, Independence USA, during the two weeks before the Senate special election. His argument was that Booker "is a solutions guy rather than an ideologue."[16] Booker won by 55 to 44 percent.

Also in 2013, Bloomberg funded similar ads totaling $1.1 million on behalf of Virginia Democratic gubernatorial candidate Terry McAuliffe, who won his race. One spot said that Republican candidate "Ken Cuccinelli opposed closing the gun show loophole—against comprehensive background checks at gun shows for criminals and the dangerously mentally ill. Siding with the NRA and undermining law enforcement. No wonder the *Washington Post* calls Cuccinelli polarizing, provocative, and partisan." The ad closed with the tagline: "Too extreme for Virginia."[17]

Richard Cullen, the communications director for Cuccinelli, complained. He argued that "Terry McAuliffe and his allies are spending tens of millions of dollars in an attempt to buy Virginia's governor's mansion and impose an ideological agenda that will severely restrict Virginia's Second Amendment rights, hike energy prices for Virginia families, and undermine our right-to-work laws."[18] Bloomberg did not apologize for his political activism. He pointed to the freedom that his wealth provides for political action. "A lot of elected officials are afraid to back controversial things. I'm not afraid of that. You're not going to hurt my business, and if you are, I don't care. I take great pride in being willing to stand up."[19]

In short, several billionaires have been effective in supporting certain referendum campaigns or otherwise pushing their views on policy issues. They approached their policy advocacy as a political campaign and used polling, advertising, and direct mail to communicate their point of view. Judging from the recent adoption in some states of laws that have legalized same-sex marriage or marijuana use, several of those billionaires have helped reform efforts gain traction. When there are strong organizational or financial forces on the other side of the issue, however, it is more difficult for wealthy activists to shape the public debate decisively. The political use of their wealth is less effective when there is a well-funded opposition and abundant media coverage of the policy issue.

Activism on Government Spending, Pension Reform, Obamacare, and Entitlements

In North Carolina, multimillionaire Art Pope, the chief executive officer of Variety Wholesalers, has spent millions of dollars on state legislative races, helping Republicans gain full control of the legislature for the first time since 1870. Three-quarters of the campaign funds spent by pro-Republican outside groups such as Real Jobs NC and Civitas Action came from Pope.[20] That investment paid off: the state now is controlled by Republicans, and it has passed a number of conservative bills cutting spending. With a GOP governor and a GOP-controlled House and Senate, North Carolina also has virtually eliminated teacher tenure in K-12 schools, enacted laws requiring voter identification, and cut the number of days for early voting. Pope serves as the state government's budget director, and he has used his position to set the agenda in favor of eliminating graduated state individual income taxes in favor of a flat tax.[21]

Scaling back public employee pensions is another area in which billionaires have been influential, particularly John and Laura Arnold, who are passionate about the cause. Arnold is a former trader for Enron Corporation, the energy company that went spectacularly bankrupt in December 2001. He made his fortune through that company as well as by managing Centaurus, a Houston hedge fund focused on energy. The couple have devoted considerable resources to studying public pensions and pushing for what they view as greater fiscal responsibility at the state and local government levels. Concerned about unfunded government liabilities and their impact on state budgets, the two have spent millions on reform initiatives.[22]

Through campaign contributions, super PAC gifts, issue advocacy, the group Action Now Initiative, and public policy research (including a grant to Brookings to study state reform efforts), the Arnolds have been successful in getting lawmakers in several states (such as Illinois, New Jersey, Rhode Island, and Utah) to reduce pension benefits and shift costs to employees. When asked why he funded research and advocacy, John Arnold noted that "organized labor spent \$4.4 billion" between 2005 and 2012 to "resist any reform efforts. We are happy to provide a very small counterbalance to the well-funded advocacy operation of organized labor. We support candidates of both parties who have the conviction and the political will to address one of society's most difficult problems. Unlike virtually every other actor in the debate on pension reform, we have absolutely no financial interest in the outcome."[23] In a article written for *The Chronicle of Philanthropy*, he said that "attacks and vitriol will not deter me from supporting fixes to public policy."[24]

Members of public employee unions and progressive organizations, however, complain that the Arnolds have a partisan agenda and buy influence through their advocacy efforts. The Institute for America's Future, for example, published a scathing report entitled "The Plot against Pensions" that criticized the Arnolds and claimed that "conservative activists are manufacturing the perception of a public pension crisis in order to both slash modest retiree benefits and preserve expensive corporate subsidies and tax breaks."[25]

Health care has become another popular issue for political mobilization. Unhappy with President Obama's health care reform, Americans for Prosperity, a nonprofit group funded by Charles and David Koch, has been running ads against Obamacare. In 2013, the group devoted more than $1 million to running online as well as television ads asking people to test their "Obamacare risk factors." In one of the spots, a young mother asks, "How do I know my family is going to get the care they need? Can I really trust the folks in Washington with my family's health care?"[26] Organizations funded by the brothers have encouraged healthy young people not to enroll in Obamacare, criticized poorly functioning health information exchanges, and pushed Republican lawmakers to demand "defunding" of the president's health care initiative—a position that resulted in a two-week shutdown of most of the federal government in October 2013.[27] Between 2010, when President Obama signed the Affordable Care Act into law, and 2013, the Campaign Media Analysis Group, a division of Kantar Media, found that $500 million was spent on ads concerning health care reform and that the commercials ran five-to-one against the president's legislation. Researchers project that another $500 million will be spent between 2013 and 2015.[28] Such ad campaigns have reinforced public doubts about Obamacare and helped keep support for it well under 50 percent in opinion surveys.

In the lead-up to the U.S. 2014 midterm elections, Americans for Prosperity has targeted a number of vulnerable Democratic senators, such as Mark Begich of Alaska, Mary Landrieu of Louisiana, Mark Pryor of Arkansas, and Kay Hagan of North Carolina, and several House members who supported Obamacare. In the first three months of the campaign, the group spent more than $30 million on television ads saying "health care isn't about politics. It's not about a website that doesn't work. It's not about poll numbers or approval ratings. It's about people. And millions of people have lost their health insurance." Interviewed about the spots, Tim Phillips, the president of the organization, said in late 2013 that "we want to make sure Obamacare is the No. 1 issue they're thinking about. We believe repealing Obamacare is a long-term effort, and a key part of that effort is keeping it in front of the American people night and day."[29]

In 2013, Americans for Prosperity branched out into other issues in school board, mayoral, and city council races across the country. For example, the Douglas County School District, just outside Denver, has been a model of conservative experimentation. It abolished teacher tenure, instituted a school voucher program, refused to bargain with the local teachers union, and adopted merit pay for math and science teachers. When four of the seven board seats came up for election in 2013, the American Federation of Teachers spent $150,000 in an effort to defeat the board members who had approved the changes. In response, Americans for Prosperity spent $350,000 to defend the incumbents and support their market-based policy actions. With total spending of more than $800,000, this race became the most expensive school board election in the country.[30] All four of the candidates backed by Americans for Prosperity won.

The group also has supported property tax reduction in Iowa, Kansas, Ohio, and Texas. It broadcast ads condemning Tennessee Republicans who fought the repeal of a 6 percent capital gains tax on stocks and dividends.[31] It also has waged campaigns in local communities where anti-tax views are dominant. In Coralville, Iowa, for example, it mailed fliers and ran newspaper advertisements calling for fiscal restraint in establishing budgets and property tax rates and supported local candidates for mayor and city council who shared its views on keeping tax rates low. Tim Phillips explained the organization's motivations, saying that the reason that "we fight local issue battles is because they result in good policy outcomes, generally promoting economic freedom via less taxes, less government spending."[32] In most of these places, the anti-tax position has triumphed.

One issue on which billionaires have not gained much traction is "entitlement reform," focused on restraining spending on Social Security and Medicare. For example, Stanley Druckenmiller, founder of the hedge fund firm Duquesne Capital Management, has traveled across the country telling young people that they need to push for cuts in Social Security so that the government will have enough money to deal with issues of concern to their generation. According to Druckenmiller, because of the money spent on Social Security and Medicare, members of Generations X, Y, and Z have been ripped off and therefore must demand that elected officials stop such "generational theft" and support a grand bargain on the federal budget.[33] So far, this effort has not been successful. Congress has not embraced cuts in programs for seniors or enacted any of Druckenmiller's proposals for reducing long-term spending.

Blackstone Group co-founder Peter Peterson, a Brookings donor, also has devoted millions of his private equity earnings to addressing what he considers the problems of fiscal irresponsibility and excessive national debt.[34] Through his foundation, he has argued that the United States needs to make changes in its entitlement programs to reduce the debt. Peterson has generously funded organizations that work in this area, such as Fix the Debt and the Committee for a Responsible Federal Budget. Although the federal budget deficit has declined, there has been little progress on addressing long-term debt.

Gambling is another issue that has attracted advocacy money, but the jury is out regarding its impact. Casino magnate Sheldon Adelson attracted attention in 2013 when he started a new campaign to ban online gambling through his group Coalition to Stop Internet Gambling. His spokesperson said that Adelson had hired two dozen experts—pollsters, lobbyists, and communications experts—to focus on this advocacy effort, which seeks to influence federal and state legislation in order to protect Adelson's casinos from online competition. "In my 15 years of working with him, I don't think I have ever seen him this passionate about any issue," commented Andy Abboud, his political adviser.[35] However, as with nearly everything that Adelson has done, both in business and public advocacy, this effort generated considerable controversy. His opponents included large competitors in the gambling industry, such as MGM Resorts and Caesars Entertainment, which argued that Internet gambling was important to economic development. John Pappas, the executive director of the Poker Players Alliance, warned that "we don't make a habit of picking fights with billionaires. But in this case, I think we'll win, because millions of Americans who want to play online will oppose this legislation."[36] In short, billionaires don't always win policy debates. Their success depends on political conditions, mobilization of other forces, media coverage, and campaign strategy. But they have been successful in pushing their views on issues such as public pension reform, keeping taxes low, and public opinion of Obamacare. Many of them have focused public attention on these topics and gotten either voters or legislators to adopt their point of view.

Tom Steyer and Climate Change

Liberals for many years have complained about conservative billionaires seeking to influence policy debates. They point to David and Charles Koch and Sheldon Adelson as poster boys for what they view as bad behavior on the part of the rich in attempting to influence the general public. Yet progressives now have their own version of those poster boys in the form of Tom Steyer, on the climate change issue. Steyer, the billionaire founder of hedge fund Farallon Capital Management, is worried about global warming and upset that politicians don't take climate change very seriously. Accordingly, he has put his wealth behind green campaigns. He has devoted a lot of money to derailing the proposed Keystone XL pipeline, which would move crude oil from Canada to the Gulf of Mexico.[37] In his eyes, the project would pump too much carbon into the atmosphere and thereby damage the planet. He has announced plans to spend $100 million during the 2014 mid-term elections to raise public awareness of climate change and help to elect legislators committed to action in this area.[38]

As a sign of his commitment to the environment, he spent $5 million in a successful effort to defeat a ballot measure undermining a landmark California law intended to curb greenhouse gas emissions. He later devoted $35 million to supporting a ballot proposition that would close a tax loophole for out-of-state companies.

He financed a get-out-the vote effort in support of Massachusetts Democrat Edward Markey's successful bid for the U.S. Senate in 2013, citing Markey's longtime activism in seeking to raise awareness of the climate change issue.[39]

Steyer also spent $8 million on television commercials, digital advertising, direct mail, and get-out-the-vote activities in the 2013 Virginia governor's race on behalf of Democrat Terry McAuliffe. Relying on political advice from Chris Lehane, a former aide to President Clinton, Steyer's NextGen Climate Action PAC works "to establish a real presence in the early states to impact the candidate and make climate a top-tier issue, whereby candidates are forced to put forth comprehensive climate policies and address the issue."[40]

In each of those activities, Steyer seeks to elevate the importance of climate change in public thinking. Referring to the climate issue in the Virginia race, he said that "there's a very clear choice on this topic between these two candidates, and I think the citizens of Virginia deserve to understand both what the truth is and what the implications of that are."[41] He was motivated to action after the 2012 election saw little public discussion about the issue that he considers most important to the future of human beings. "If you look at the 2012 campaign, climate change was like incest— something you couldn't talk about in polite company," he said.[42]

Many of his efforts fall within the category of efforts to affect long-term change. The U.S. Congress has not taken significant action to address climate change, and the public continues to rank climate issues low on the list of the nation's most important problems. But Steyer has been successful in state referendums and has helped to elect some politicians who support his views on this issue. It remains to be seen how much impact he will have on this subject in the years ahead.

Fighting Higher Taxes on the Wealthy

Fighting higher taxes has long been an important cause for wealthy individuals. For example, rich investors and industrialists fought the introduction of the federal income tax in 1895 and funded the Supreme Court case that led to its repeal. Following that action, it took nearly two decades for progressives to get a federal income tax enacted by Congress, through a constitutional amendment. Another tax initiative, Proposition 13, passed in California in 1978. The initiative reduced local property taxes and placed a 1 percent cap on real property taxation; it also mandated that annual property tax increases could not be larger than 2 percent.[43] In 1980, Massachusetts enacted Proposition 2½, which limited annual property tax increases to 2.5 percent, and in 1990 Oregon capped property taxes through Ballot Measure 5.

In more recent times, following the reduction of taxes in many states and for the country as a whole, the tax debate has shifted to raising taxes on the rich. Not surprisingly, some wealthy people are upset over such proposals and have helped fund referendum campaigns opposing them. In Oregon, for example, businessmen Tim Boyle and Phil Knight, a Brookings trustee and donor, were the largest individual contributors to an organization called Oregonians against Job-Killing Taxes, which fought ballot measures 66 and 67 in 2010. Measure 66 proposed raising income taxes on those with taxable income over $250,000 a year; measure 67 proposed increasing tax levies on corporations. Despite their financial support, both measures passed by a margin of 54 to 46 percent.[44]

Knight donated $150,000 and Boyle contributed $75,794 to Oregonians against Job-Killing Taxes, which raised $4.9 million in its losing effort.[45] There also were gifts of $280,515 from Associated General Contractors, $225,000 from the Oregon Automobile Dealers Association, and $185,900 from the Oregon Restaurant Association. With a budget of around $7.5 million, the various pro-tax organizations outspent the anti-tax organization. Much of the money for the pro-tax effort came from public employee unions and teacher organizations worried about education funding. The Oregon Education Association and the National Education Association, for example, gave $2.4 million, while Service Employees

International Union contributed $2 million. Pat McCormick, the spokesperson for Oregonians against Job-Killing Taxes, complained about the campaign, saying that "the tone and tenor was often venomous, trying to pit the haves against the have-nots."[46] Supporters of the tax increases had broadcast ads showing "well-dressed people stepping off private jets";[47] the spots also condemned the profiteering of banks and credit card companies.

Two years later, the state of Oregon smoothed some of the feathers ruffled during the referendum by enacting a bill promising not to change the way that it computes corporate taxes for 30 years. Oregon takes a "single-sales factor" approach to corporate income tax that levies taxes on "sales only within the state, not on worldwide sales, property, or payroll."[48] Nike officials promised to create at least 500 new jobs if state officials would guarantee that they would maintain that approach. On a 50-5 vote in the House of Representatives and a 22-6 vote in the Senate, the legislature approved the provision for any company within the state that promised to invest a minimum of $150 million to create new jobs.

Playing Hardball on a Football Stadium Renovation

Professional football is a big business in many cities around the country. On Sundays in the fall, it attracts huge crowds and extensive media coverage, and fans, debating the virtues of different players, avidly track the ups and downs of their favorite teams. Stephen Ross, the owner of the Miami Dolphins, has a net worth of several billion dollars. Concerned about the poor condition of Sun Life Stadium, where his team played, he wanted a public referendum on a proposal for taxpayer funding of up to $289 million for its renovation. "Miami is about big events," he noted. "The biggest industry down here is still tourism and bringing people here. Having a first-class facility in a city that right now [is] the most [desirable] city in the world . . . I think it really demands it. From an economic development perspective, I don't think there could be anything more important."[49]

Yet when state legislative leaders held up the request, he formed a political organization that, according to local news accounts, sent "attack mailers against lawmakers who scuttled his stadium plans."[50] He didn't understand why lawmakers would oppose a public subsidy that would benefit his football team—in spite of the fact that a number of economic studies have found that sports stadiums rarely generate enough jobs or tax revenues to justify the huge amount of tax dollars that local governments have invested in building and maintaining them.[51]

After legislators stopped the referendum, Ross generated considerable criticism in Florida when he announced a $200 million gift to his alma mater, the University of Michigan. According to press reports, the contribution would go toward the Stephen M. Ross School of Business and the Stephen M. Ross Athletic Campus.[52] People in the Miami community found it ironic that he would donate such a large sum to an out-of-state university while demanding a similar amount from taxpayers for his stadium renovation. When asked to justify the large charitable gift in light of his request for public funding for his stadium, Ross explained that "to compare giving a gift to the University of Michigan and say I'm taking something away from this community, that I find hard to believe. My commitment to this community is just as great as it was then. In fact, it's greater."[53]

Assessing Policy Activism by the Super Rich

Political advocacy by the super rich raises several questions, among them the following: How transparent are the expenditures? How one-sided is the campaign dialogue? How do news organizations cover the campaign? From the standpoint of free and fair democratic elections, political participation of the super wealthy is not problematic as long as there is reasonable transparency and alternative perspectives are well-covered during the campaign.

In some of the cases discussed in this chapter, one-sided referendum campaigns were conducted by advocates on either the left or the right and were effective. Wealthy individuals helped to push marijuana legalization (or decriminalization) and same-sex marriage to the forefront. Others sought to keep taxes low and roll back public pensions in various states and local communities. In looking at advocacy campaigns, there is not a consistent liberal or conservative bias in what is funded or what works. In some cases, a liberal was willing to fund action on a particular issue, while in others, it was a moderate, conservative, or libertarian. But sometimes the spending has been lopsided and the cause favored by the tycoon has triumphed due to the lack of a well-funded or well-organized opposition. As noted by Nick Nyhart, president and CEO of Public Campaign, a campaign finance reform organization, "When politics is a proxy war for billionaires, you've lost democracy."[54]

Policy advocacy becomes challenging when there is lack of transparency in campaign finance or one-sidedness in the electoral dialogue. For that reason, states and localities need to make sure that they have adequate disclosure rules governing policy referendums so that voters can see who is behind particular advocacy efforts. With declining media coverage of state and local issues, it is important that there be strong transparency in these kinds of campaigns. Open disclosure helps reporters and voters judge the exercise of wealth and the relevance of various policy arguments.

4   New Models of Philanthropy

MICHAEL BLOOMBERG IS ONE of the leading practitioners of a new approach to philanthropy. As described by Mike Allen of *Politico*, the former New York City mayor intends to "dive in on an unprecedented plan to combine the forces of philanthropy, political advocacy and business. Bloomberg's ambitions: to be the only force on the globe to blend all three on a huge scale."[1] Crucial to this reported strategy is the integration of several parts of his financial empire. According to Allen, Bloomberg wants Bloomberg Philanthropies to focus on charitable giving directed at "public health; education; the environment; the arts; and urban innovation." Bloomberg also supports research and advocacy in these areas.

Yet he believes that charity alone is not sufficient. Some important issues such as gun control and immigration require political muscle, so he uses his Independence USA super PAC for electoral advocacy and nonprofit organizations such as Mayors against Illegal Guns to fight for long-term change on gun control. Additional advocacy is coordinated through the opinion page of his Bloomberg media company, which provides a high-profile outlet for the former mayor's news commentary and editorializing.

In his work outside the United States, Bloomberg focuses on health and well-being. For example, he has devoted more than $100 million to fighting polio in Afghanistan, Nigeria, and Pakistan and $100 million seeking to "genetically engineer a better mosquito, in the hopes of eliminating malaria." In explaining his interest in that issue, Bloomberg noted that "I want to do things that nobody else is doing."[2]

Part of his international efforts, however, go beyond traditional philanthropy to issue advocacy and consulting. In Mexico, he spent $10 million for anti-obesity research and public advertising. That helped him to improve awareness of the obesity problem and eventually secure passage of legislation that raised taxes on soft drinks and junk food.[3] He hopes that the effort will become a model for action elsewhere on obesity, smoking, and other issues. In addition, his consulting firm, Bloomberg Associates, provides practical advice to local governments around the world on urban problems.[4]

Many observers rightfully point to philanthropy as an area in which society benefits from great wealth. This is especially the case in the United States, which relies much more heavily on private philanthropy than do most other countries. By funding charitable foundations and supporting the arts, education, health care, and other causes, the super rich make enormous positive contributions to society as a whole. Yet what should people make of the new breed of activist billionaires, who combine traditional philanthropy with issue advocacy and electioneering? Most of them have backgrounds in business or finance. Being results oriented, they focus on concrete objectives, and they want demonstrable impact for their money. In essence, they treat their spending on causes the same way that they would a business investment. Increasingly, some have clear partisan points of view on major issues. This new type of activism needs to be examined, to determine what issues it raises and how others might judge its societal impact.

The Traditional Model of Philanthropy

For many years, philanthropists have followed a familiar model of gift-giving. They outlined their top priorities, found projects to fund, and gave money to universities, libraries, hospitals, and other non-profit organizations to execute the projects—often prominently displaying their names. Typically, they were not partisan in how they thought about their causes. They hoped to provide public services they deemed important or improve public action in specific areas.

Real estate developer A. Alfred Taubman is an example of someone who has been generous and nonpartisan in his giving to many different organizations, among them the University of Michigan, Harvard University, Brown University, the Illinois Institute of Design, and the Brookings Institution, including the Governance Studies program, which I direct. As a businessman, Taubman has owned enterprises as diverse as shopping malls, a professional football team, and auction houses. His attempt to reinvent the venerable auction house Sotheby's, however, led to a conviction on price-fixing charges.

As a philanthropist, Taubman worked for a number of years with an economist named William Haber. Haber, an adviser to President Franklin Roosevelt, had chaired the Federal Advisory Council on Unemployment, and during World War II he had worked with the War Manpower Commission and the Office of War Mobilization and Reconversion. After his government service, he became a professor of economics at the University of Michigan and eventually was named department chair and dean of the school's College of Literature, Sciences, and the Arts.

Haber wrote books on labor relations, industrial arbitration, and post-war economic recovery. He taught a popular course known around Ann Arbor as "Labor by Haber." Among the legions of individuals who monitored the course was Taubman. The two men became lifelong friends, socialized together, and shared many interests in politics, economics, and philanthropy. In one of their conversations, Haber and Taubman talked about launching a new program at Michigan. The two had an idea for a university initiative on public policy and American institutions that would look at the intersection of the public and private sectors in the United States and bring together experts from different disciplines to study pressing economic and political problems. Taubman agreed to fund the program, and it was a big success. It blended academic expertise and real-world issues in ways that were novel and innovative, and both students and faculty loved its interdisciplinary focus and practical efforts to solve problems. Other schools sought to emulate the exciting new initiative. When Taubman told Brown University's president, Howard Swearer, about his new program in Ann Arbor, Swearer liked the idea. He asked whether Taubman would support a similar program at Brown. The shopping mall magnate said yes and agreed to fund it generously.

Launched in the 1980s, the A. Alfred Taubman Center for Public Policy and American Institutions ran a successful undergraduate program and funded faculty research on major public policy issues; eventually it added a graduate program.[5] The center attracted high-quality students and faculty and put on high-profile lectures. It brought leading speakers to campus, including such notable individuals as then-senator Barack Obama (D-Illinois), Senator John Kerry (D-Massachusetts), Secretary of Housing and Urban Development Andrew Cuomo, New York governor George Pataki, and New Jersey governor Christine Todd Whitman, among others.

In taking this approach, Taubman followed a long line of philanthropists in the United States. He did not push a particular ideological line in giving his gifts; instead, he sought out good people and worked with them to make their programs effective. He emphasized broad-based research, civic education, and raising public awareness.

U.S. Philanthropy over the Years

In his book *Why Philanthropy Matters*, Zoltan Acs noted that pragmatic problem solving is a vital part of American culture.[6] Individuals honestly believe that they can make a difference by giving of their time, money, and ideas. Moreover, philanthropy—a way for those with money to help people less fortunate than themselves, promote social opportunity, and strengthen society as a whole—is consistent with common moral and religious imperatives.

According to the National Philanthropic Trust, 88 percent of American households give to charity. In 2011, total giving amounted to $298 billion. Of that, individuals gave $218 billion, foundations donated $42 billion, corporations contributed $14 billion, and other entities were responsible for $24 billion. The trust noted that "the majority of charitable dollars went to religion" (32 percent), followed by education (13 percent), human services (12 percent), and grant-making foundations (9 percent). Overall, these gifts constituted 2 percent of the country's gross domestic product.[7]

In the contemporary period, a number of billionaires have been especially generous in supporting specific institutions or causes. Among the largest donors in recent years have been Mark Zuckerberg, who gave $990 million to the Silicon Valley Community Foundations (including $100 million to support education reform in Newark, New Jersey); Phil Knight, who donated $500 million to the University of Oregon for cancer research and $125 million for a cardiovascular institute; Paul Allen, who contributed $300 million for brain research; Mort Zuckerman, another Brookings donor, who donated $200 million to Columbia University; Fred Fields, who gave $150 million to the Oregon Community Foundation for arts and education; Carl Icahn, who gave $150 million to the Mount Sinai School of Medicine; Ken Griffin, who contributed $150 million to Harvard University for student financial aid; David Gundlach, who contributed $140 million to the Elkhart County Community Foundation; Charles Johnson, who gave $250 million to Yale University; Stephen Ross, who gave $200 million to the University of Michigan; John McCall MacBain, who contributed $120 million to the Rhodes Trust; Frank McCourt, who gave $100 million to Georgetown University for a school of public policy; and David Geffen, who provided $100 million to UCLA for medical school scholarships.[8]

Some of these and other individuals have become major funders of "private science." At a time of declining government support for the sciences, they have launched initiatives devoted to brain science (Paul Allen), stem cell research (Alfred Taubman), anti-aging (Lawrence Ellison), prostate cancer (David Koch and Michael Milken), space travel (Jeff Bezos, Elon Musk, and Richard Branson), Parkinson's disease (Sergey Brin and Ronald Perelman), oceanography (Eric Schmidt), and astronomy (Gordon Moore), among others.[9]

In 2013, Michael Bloomberg pledged $350 million to Johns Hopkins University. Bloomberg graduated from the school in 1964, and the following year, he made a $5 donation. Since then, his philanthropy has skyrocketed. As his wealth has grown, he has funded a school of public health, a center for physics and astronomy, and a children's center. He also has endowed chairs and student scholarships. Overall, his giving to a variety of organizations, including Johns Hopkins, has now topped $2.5 billion.[10]

Brown University, meanwhile, secured its largest-ever gift of $100 million from liquor magnate Sidney Frank. President Ruth Simmons used the money to build a new life sciences building and provide scholarships to needy students. Indeed, the money allowed the school to adopt a "need blind" admissions policy, which meant that the ability to pay its high tuition would not be a factor in undergraduate admissions.

Cultivating wealthy individuals requires considerable tact, persistence, personal contacts, and know-how. For example, to persuade Frank to give that sum of money, Simmons spent long hours wooing the reclusive and somewhat eccentric older gentleman. He did not like to get dressed up, preferring instead to lounge around his residence wearing pajamas. On occasion, he would invite her into his bedroom to watch his favorite movie videos. While he lay on the bed in his pajamas, she sat in a chair, praying that the film wouldn't last too long.

David Rubenstein, co-founder of the Carlyle Group, a private equity investment firm, practices what he calls "patriotic philanthropy." Rubenstein, who is co-chair of the Brookings Institution board of trustees, engages in charitable activities that emphasize "providing support or help to parts of the government where help is needed and the federal government is not able any longer to provide that support." He believes that "those who have been fortunate in society have a responsibility to give back to that society."[11] It was for that reason that he purchased a copy of the Magna Carta for $21.3 million in 2007 and loaned it permanently to the National Archives. He wanted to preserve it for posterity because it "is one of the founding documents of Western law, human rights and personal freedoms."[12] He also bought the Emancipation Proclamation for the White House and an original version of the Declaration of Independence for the State Department.

Most recently, Rubenstein paid $14.2 million for the Bay Psalm Book, the first book printed in the United States (in 1640). He explained the gift by saying, "I thought it was important to keep this historic American book in the country, and I also thought I could expose more Americans to its significance—and the importance of books to our country—by having it displayed throughout the country at libraries that might not otherwise have a chance to display something quite so old and rare."[13] When asked what guides his philanthropy, Rubenstein said, "I look for things that were helpful to me in my life and things that wouldn't happen if I didn't give the money."[14]

Another way people that engage in philanthropy is by establishing foundations, which often carry their names. Sixty-seven charitable foundations have assets of $1 billion or more.[15] Charitable foundations provide valuable support for a wide range of organizations in the United States. The nonprofit sector accounts for about 9 percent of all the wages and salaries paid in the country.[16] Employees and volunteers at nonprofits engage in research, education, communications, and advocacy in virtually every walk of life.

The Rise of Activist Philanthropy

The activities of Michael Bloomberg and others illustrate a relatively recent trend: some wealthy donors are engaging in a new, activist style of philanthropy that Matthew Bishop and Michael Green describe as "philanthrocapitalism."[17] Using this approach, magnates bring skills and tools from the business world to philanthropy and push nonprofit organizations to focus, in some cases for the first time, on specific outcomes of their work and on performance metrics. In so doing, donors are dramatically changing the ways in which charities function.

In her book *Giving 2.0*, Stanford University professor Laura Arrillaga-Andreessen describes this new philanthropy as being based on learning, improvement, and innovation.[18] Instead of feel-good investments with uncertain impact, the new breed of business-oriented philanthropists emphasizes a clear statement of goals, an impact strategy, performance metrics, and evaluation research. Their hope is that treating philanthropy in a more business-like manner will encourage nonprofit organizations to become more systematic about evaluating their own effectiveness and thus to have more impact.

Making a discernible difference is a key motivation for the new-style philanthropists, who choose to employ what Paul Brest and Hal Harvey refer to as "impact investment."[19] These wealthy benefactors are strategic in their thinking and focused on achieving tremendous impact. In their own foundations, they have fostered a new emphasis on the actual results from charitable giving—for example, on whether a charity's work actually is improving the lives of the people that it serves. In response to these emerging trends, Charity Navigator, a nonprofit watchdog, has updated its ratings to include measures of results. "How clearly do you identify the problem that you're trying to solve and how well do you have measures to know that you're on the road to solving that problem?" asked the firm's chief executive officer, Ken Berger.[20] Philanthropists assess results by asking beneficiaries what they are doing that makes a difference and relying on business school–type metrics that measure impact.

One of the big supporters of this approach was the William and Flora Hewlett Foundation, where Brest previously served as president. But in 2014, foundation officials announced that the foundation was ending its funding for this kind of impact assessment and investment and no longer supporting organizations such as GuideStar, Charity Navigator, and GiveWell that publish financial performance data on charitable organizations. The foundation still funds research on impact strategies, but it found that few donors relied on the information produced in making their philanthropic decisions.[21]

Unlike other donors who have given money for traditional projects such as buildings, professorships, or organizational support, Bill and Melinda Gates focus on practical results. The Bill and Melinda Gates Foundation, which they cofounded in 2000, now has around $40 billion in assets. In recent years, the foundation has provided annual grants totaling $3.4 billion.[22] Famed investor Warren Buffet has joined forces with the Gates Foundation to support its philanthropic activities. Starting in 2006, he pledged 10 million Berkshire Hathaway Class B shares to the foundation. He noted that in order to claim the pledged amount, Bill or Melinda Gates must be alive and active in the administration of the foundation, it must continue to qualify as a charity, and each year it must give away an amount equal to the previous year's Berkshire gift, plus another 5 percent of net assets. The first year, Buffet gave more than 600,000 shares with a valuation of $1.5 billion and said he would make similar donations each year thereafter.[23] Eventually, the Gates Foundation will receive $58 billion of Buffet's Berkshire Hathaway stock, with the proviso that all the money be spent in the decade following the gift.[24] The matching of these two billionaires will make the Gates Foundation the most important institutional player in the field of private philanthropy in the world.

According to *Harvard Magazine*, Bill and Melinda Gates, plus Buffet, "pursue research-driven, strategic, and measurable solutions to global problems: eradicating diseases; enhancing the effectiveness of K-12 education; improving disadvantaged students' access to and chances of success in obtaining higher education; and promoting economic development in underdeveloped nations (through investments in healthcare, education, nutrition, sanitation, and agricultural productivity)."[25]

In a 2013 interview with *Bloomberg Businessweek*, Bill Gates explained that, among other priorities, his foundation had set the goal of eradicating polio in the subsequent five years and committed $1.8 billion toward a $5.5 billion project to rid the world of the crippling disease by 2018. From his standpoint, health officials have made tremendous strides toward that objective. "By getting new vaccines out, we've had more progress in the last decade than ever before," he pointed out.[26] Speaking at the Clinton Global Initiative in 2013, the billionaire argued that "philanthropy should be taking much bigger risks than business." Donors should not be investing in maintaining the status quo; instead, they should seek bold and innovative approaches with the potential to resolve complex issues and transform the lives of future generations. He pointed to his foundation's work in fighting malaria as an example of an initiative that was having tremendous success.[27]

The Combination of Philanthropy and Advocacy

Other benefactors have pushed the boundaries of activism even further by combining philanthropy with direct advocacy. In addition to the Bloomberg example noted earlier, individuals such as Charles and David Koch on the right and George Soros and Tom Steyer on the left have become poster boys for activist philanthropy. They have clear policy objectives and work closely with nonprofit organizations that help them achieve their goals. They do not shy away from taking strong stances and often align themselves with partisan advocacy organizations that work at the grassroots level.

In the past, philanthropists such as John D. Rockefeller, Henry Ford, and Andrew Carnegie saw their mission as financing buildings, funding libraries, or providing gifts to organizations (including foundations that they established) to figure out the best approach to solving problems. Now, the new breed of benefactors focuses on specific remedies and discernible impact. Some modern-day philanthropists are aggressive in wanting to influence public policy—not just the work of charities—and are quite pointed in how they think about social change.

In a provocative article entitled "Can Billionaire Philanthropists Replace the Federal Government?" writer Amy Schiller noted that some conservative billionaires are pursuing an antigovernment approach in their philanthropy. Citing the activism of Laura and John Arnold on curtailing state pensions, she accused them of financing an "aggressive anti-government edge of megaphilanthropy."[28] Yet Schiller made no mention of billionaires who support environmental causes or the super wealthy who finance campaigns for same-sex marriage equality. Analysts need to think about the power of money regardless of whether they agree personally with the particular causes being supported.

A key consideration in evaluating this kind of activism is its transparency or lack thereof. The public should know who is supporting particular causes that affect people and how money is being deployed. Is all the big money flowing into one side of a debate, or is it supporting a pluralistic universe of perspectives? That is a key question in assessing the impact of the philanthropic and social activism of the new breed of super-wealthy individuals.

The combination of philanthropy and advocacy raises other problems. Many people do not trust politicians and worry about the influence of big money in elections. Yet they have confidence in the nonprofit sector and admire people who are seeking to solve pressing social problems. The risk of blending the two domains is that political mistrust and hyperpartisanship will infiltrate the nonprofit world and taint the entire sector. Rather than becoming a model for pragmatic problem solving, the nonprofit world may fragment into armed camps funded by feuding billionaires, thus politicizing efforts to deal with the problems traditionally handled by charities as well as public policy issues.

With the blurring of the lines, some donors are becoming more interventionist and seeking more direct control over the people and groups that they fund. The disagreement between Peter Lewis and the Guggenheim Museum in New York City provides an example. Lewis, who contributed $77 million to the museum, grew upset when the institution's director wanted to develop international branches in other countries and run new programs devoted to architecture. Lewis resigned from the board in protest and blasted the museum's management.[29] Lewis also had a contentious relationship with Case Western Reserve University in Cleveland, where his business was based. He donated $36.9 million for a new management school building but complained about cost overruns and mismanagement. As a result of his dissatisfaction with the university, he announced a philanthropic boycott of all Cleveland-based institutions. He pledged not to contribute to any organizations in that area until his grievances were addressed, and for several years, he refused to fund groups located there.[30]

These are not isolated problems. The Los Angeles Museum of Contemporary Art (MOCA) has had disputes with its large donors over management style, spending, and artistic vision, among other things. Billionaire Eli Broad withheld his gifts of art and then later announced that he was opening his own museum across the street from MOCA. Eventually, the director, Jeffrey Deitch, stepped down amid the turmoil.[31] If contentiousness becomes a common practice in the world of philanthropy, it would undermine the independence of nonprofit organizations and damage the sector as a whole.

The University Connection

An example of the new philanthropy in action was seen at Georgetown University near the end of 2013. The NextGen Climate

Action group, run by billionaire Tom Steyer, organized a forum there entitled "Can Keystone Pass the President's Climate Test?" The forum presented information on "whether the proposed pipeline would increase greenhouse gas emissions."[32] This was an issue near and dear to the heart of Steyer, who has spent freely to elevate public awareness of climate change. The event opened with six ministers and priests— each a leader in efforts to mobilize churchgoers against climate change—gathering around Steyer and putting their hands on his torso as they begin to pray for "divine help in shaping public opinion: 'Soften them. . . . Open them to you . . . for your purpose. . . . Claim the promise made to Moses."[33]

One of the tycoon's spokesmen, Mike Casey, explained the rationale behind the forum. Part of the controversy surrounding the Keystone pipeline is that it will create both jobs and carbon pollution, he noted. The forum would present several experts who would analyze the pipeline's environmental impact. "If the company has been truthful with investors and public officials all along, why is it now so twitchy about the top experts in North America examining their project's pollution footprint?" Casey asked.[34]

In an effort to present a balance of points of view, the university invited Russ Girling, the president of the pipeline builder, Trans-Canada, and Gary Doer, the U.S. ambassador to Canada. However, neither agreed to speak at the forum because of concern about Steyer's well-known advocacy on the topic. "We won't support in any way this gentleman's political grandstanding as he builds his profile to make a run for office," said TransCanada press representative James Millar.[35]

With colleges and universities increasingly drawn into divisive policy controversies, it is becoming harder to separate academic philanthropy from advocacy. Many donors who have a strong point of view want educational institutions to hold events, publish reports, or even offer courses that address the subjects of interest to them. Such demands can put the academy, which tries to be nonpartisan as an institution, in a difficult position.

I saw firsthand the volatile combination of money and politics when I was running the Public Opinion Laboratory at the Taubman Center for Public Policy at Brown University, which conducted regular state surveys of public views on various officials and issues facing Rhode Island. The surveys covered job approval ratings, right- and wrong-track questions, and views about the economy and political issues. To honor the first decade anniversary of the center, the university invited Taubman to a 1994 party commemorating its creation. There were panels showcasing center faculty and students and a social gathering for people in the community. As the director of the center's Public Opinion Laboratory, I attended the party. Rhode Island governor Bruce Sundlun showed up. A wealthy man in his own right, his personal popularity had dropped to 16 percent in one of our state surveys that year due to a lingering recession and an unprecedented banking crisis that had closed many credit unions across the state.[36]

Seeing Taubman at my side, he made a beeline for the two of us. Sundlun was a blunt man who always came immediately to the point; he never bothered with small talk or social niceties. That week, he was extremely irritated with me because, when asked in a recent news interview about his reelection prospects, I intemperately had replied that his political prospects were so poor that if "Mickey Mouse were on the ballot, the mouse would win." Understanding the importance of philanthropy to the center's operations, he turned to Taubman and declared, "You no longer should fund the Taubman Center." Glaring, Sundlun then pointed to me and told our leading donor, "This guy doesn't know what he's doing." The governor figured that the best way to shut me up was to cut off our money supply.

Fortunately, there were no dire consequences. Taubman, who saw the center as a place for nonpartisan education, was unmoved by the governor's demand. Nonetheless, the episode illustrates the risky environment surrounding philanthropy. Had Taubman been susceptible to political pressure or had he held a strong point of view concerning local politics, as is the case with certain benefactors today, that episode would have created major problems for the center and me personally.

In the current climate, in which activist philanthropists have clear objectives and partisan goals, the political risks have risen dramatically. There is a much greater chance of a donation going wrong, from the donor's perspective, by not being aligned with the donor's intentions. The good old days when wealthy individuals gave money and let universities or nonprofits figure out the best way to use it to solve problems has too often given way to interventionism and a focus on achieving specified goals.

Philanthropy outside the United States

Most other countries have weak traditions of private giving. Even in Europe, people are less likely to make charitable contributions, and when they do give, they typically contribute a smaller percentage of their financial assets to philanthropy than Americans do. For example, Bill Gates and Warren Buffett organized a dinner in China in 2013 to encourage fifty local billionaires to sign the "Giving Pledge" and donate at least half their fortunes to philanthropy. But no one agreed to the pledge. According to Indian philanthropist Sonu Shivdasani, "China's billionaires are at a different stage in their wealth cycle and their money is frequently tied up with businesses and family dynasties. . . . Many wealthy Chinese individuals may shy away from addressing social problems directly for fear of stepping on the toes of the state."[37]

To get a sense of global philanthropy, the British Charities Aid Foundation publishes the World Giving Index, which asks people about their charitable actions. Its 2012 survey found that only 28 percent of people polled in 146 nations said that they had donated money that year, less than one-third the American level of nearly 90 percent. This research has been undertaken for a number of years, and that percentage has remained consistent over time.[38]

There are reasons why people in many nations donate money at far lower levels than those in the United States. In many countries, for example, there is more of a culture of supporting the public sector through tax dollars and having the government—rather than private individuals—take the primary responsibility for subsidizing education, health care, arts, music, and culture. That is the case in many European countries, where the public sector supports operas, theaters, and museums and provides heavily subsidized health care and higher education. The result is that on a per capita basis, "American citizens contribute to charity nearly seven times as much as their German counterparts" (Germany is the richest European nation).[39] The trade-off is that most Europeans pay higher taxes than Americans do.

Americans are unusual in their preference for supporting arts and culture through private giving rather than taxation. According to John Micklethwait and Adrian Wooldridge, "Americans much prefer to give away their money themselves, rather than let their government do it. . . . This tradition of philanthropy encourages America to tackle its social problems without building a European-style welfare state."[40]

However, that does not mean that other countries lack billionaires and other wealthy people who are generous in their private giving. There are numerous examples of super-wealthy people outside the United States who give large sums, either individually or through charitable organizations. For example, Mexican billionaire Carlos Slim—who, through a wide range of business interests, has become one of the world's wealthiest men—incorporated the Carlos Slim Foundation in 1986. The foundation has an endowment of $5.5 billion, and another Slim foundation, the Telmex Foundation, has an endowment of $2.5 billion. His foundations focus on "non-lucrative projects in education, health, justice and personal and community development by contributing human and financial resources to equip Mexican society with the necessary tools to succeed professionally and socially."[41] These charities have contributed

$100 million to eradicate global polio, provided scholarships for the National Autonomous University, funded broadband access for underprivileged areas, and supported food production research, among other gifts. Following major floods along the western coast of Mexico, Telmex donated more than 140 tons of aid to areas that were hard hit.[42]

Aliko Dangote, the richest businessman in Africa, has endowed his Dangote Foundation with N200 billion (around $1.2 billion). Among the issues it is addressing are the empowerment of youth and women, polio eradication, poverty alleviation, and disaster relief. Speaking about his charitable work, Dangote explained that "I personally want to take it very seriously. I want to be much more aggressive than what we have had in the past."[43]

Swedish billionaire Stefan Persson, son of the founder of the fashion company H&M, has donated 2.2 billion Swedish krona (around $322 million) to the Erling-Persson Family Foundation, which funds scientific research, education, and the care and upbringing of children. The organization has been generous in supporting research on various diseases, such as Parkinson's, Alzheimer's, diabetes, and gastrointestinal disorders.

Li Ka-shing of China established the Li Ka-shing Foundation in 1980. He has pledged to donate one-third of his financial assets to this organization, which focuses on "strategic contributions to education and medical care projects in Hong Kong and mainland China." So far, he has given 13 billion in Hong Kong dollars, which is around $1.66 billion.

Spain's Rosalia Mera made a fortune through the retail apparel chain Zara. Her 7 percent ownership stake allowed her to set up the Paideia Foundation, which promotes education reform and helps those who suffer from mental or physical disabilities. In addition to its charitable work in these areas, the foundation works to improve public understanding of major policy issues and to support policy change.[44] Since Mera's death in 2013, her daughter Sandra Ortega

Mera, who inherited $5 billion, has continued her mother's philanthropic work.[45]

Foundations and Advocacy in the Developing World

In many parts of the world, charitable foundations and nongovernmental organizations work closely with political leaders. Government officials view those with financial resources as people that they should keep within their orbit. If the wealthy seek to influence public policy, politicians fear that they will exercise disproportionate influence or that the super rich will finance projects that undermine official policies. Such fears are especially strong when organizations receive financial support from outside a country's borders.

Under President Vladimir Putin, for example, the Russian government has cracked down on nongovernmental organizations financed with Western funds, whether from the private or government sectors. Russian authorities are concerned that foreign money distorts their society and gives power over Russian life to outsiders who do not understand national sensitivities. They cite the Open Society Foundations, run by George Soros, as an example, claiming that they support local dissidents and seek to undermine Russia. As a result, the Russian parliament enacted legislation requiring groups funded by foreign entities to register as "foreign agents" and disclose details regarding their budgets, personnel, and activities. Critics complain that the new rules threaten independence and funding and undermine the Russian economy.[46]

In other places, charitable foundations have thrived by keeping some distance between themselves and political authorities. Mo Ibrahim, the Sudan-born billionaire who founded the telecommunications company Celtel, sold the firm for $3.4 billion in 2005 and used the money to establish the Mo Ibrahim Foundation, which focuses on supporting good governance in Africa. The foundation has created the Ibrahim Prize for Achievement in African Leadership, which awards $5 million plus a $200,000 annual payment for life to African heads of state who help their constituents and voluntarily transfer power through democratic means to their successors.[47] This award is a way to provide a financial incentive for political leaders to hand power over to others without suffering financial deprivation themselves. The hope is that the prize will lead to fewer coup d'états and war-based transitions

So far, three political leaders have received Ibrahim's African Leadership Prize. In 2007, Joaquim Chissano received the award for voluntarily leaving office in 2005 and thereby helping Mozambique make the transition to peace and democracy.[48] In 2008, Festus Mogae won the prize for vacating the presidency of Botswana and also for helping his country deal with an HIV/AIDS pandemic.[49] In 2011, Pedro Pires received the award for giving up the national leadership of Cape Verde and thereby enabling the country to make a peaceful political transition.[50]

The Ibrahim Foundation illustrates the good ways that wealth can be used to support desirable public policies. Across the African continent, dozens of countries have been harmed by civil wars, military takeovers, or corrupt, authoritarian regimes, and weak political institutions make it difficult for governments to address pressing problems. Ibrahim's charitable organization has made good governance an important priority and has provided money to help several countries handle the transition from one political leader to another.

5 Elections Abroad

IN THE FORMER Soviet republic of Georgia, billionaire Bidzina "Boris" Ivanishvili has a net worth equal to one-third of his country's $15.8 billion gross domestic product, according to *Forbes*. He made his fortune early on in Russia by investing in financial institutions, factories, and mines. Along with his business partner, Vitaly Malkin, he set up Rossiyskiy Kredit Bank in 1990 and bought a number of firms cheaply during Russia's mad dash to privatization during the 1990s. After selling those companies, he invested in a Russian drugstore chain called Doctor Stoletov and also in the Hotel Lux, along with a number of firms in Georgia.[1]

He came into politics following major policy disagreements with Georgian president Mikheil Saakashvili. Saakashvili, who was elected in 2008 on an anticorruption platform, pursued pro-Western and pro-NATO policies and sought membership in NATO and the European Union. Russian leaders were upset with those moves, and after talks failed, they sent military troops into Georgia in 2008 to support separatists in the region of South Ossetia.

Following alleged legal violations by Ivanishvili, the Georgian government in 2011 attempted to strip the billionaire of his citizenship. That prompted him to form a new political organization, the Georgian Dream party, to fight Saakashvili and his policies. The next year, members of Ivanishvili's party sought seats in the parliament and won against Saakashvili's supporters. Ivanishvili was named prime minister of Georgia, serving in an awkward arrangement with Saakashvili remaining as president.[2] In the aftermath of his electoral triumph, Ivanishvili arrested the previous prime minister, brought his own people into government, and charged the previous regime with corruption and graft. He says that he gets "no pleasure from politics, it's not in my character." His only goal, he claims, is "keeping tabs on the government."[3]

In 2013, the parliament enacted constitutional changes limiting the powers of the president. Ivanishvili chose a little-known candidate, Giorgi Margvelashvili, to run for the presidency against a candidate representing the party of Saakashvili, who was prohibited by law from seeking a third term. Margvelashvili won overwhelmingly, with 67 percent of the vote.[4] Following this victory, Ivanishvili left the prime minister's seat and chose his interior minister, Irakli Garibashvili to take his place. The billionaire also launched a nongovernmental organization called Citizen with the stated goal of strengthening civil society within Georgia.[5] In an interview, however, Ivanishvili admitted that he planned to remain the power behind the throne. "I will control the government which I leave behind. I would prefer not to reveal the mechanism for now, the way in which I will act," he said.[6] These sentiments made it clear that he did not plan to give up any of his newly won political power.[7]

For his part, Saakashvili worried about what he saw as the threat facing his country from the new regime. "We are back to the Wild West of some kind of post-Soviet politics," he argued. "The prime minister envisions for me either prison or exile."[8] In December 2013 Saakashvili accepted a position as lecturer and "senior statesman" at Tufts University, near Boston.

Ivanishvili provides an example of how electoral activism on the part of the super wealthy is becoming increasingly common around the globe. Instead of simply influencing public policy from the sidelines, billionaires have sought public office in thirteen countries during the past decade. In addition to Ivanishvili in Georgia and Michael Bloomberg in the United States, billionaires such as Silvio Berlusconi, in Italy; Serge Dassault, in France; Frank Stronach, in Austria; Clive Palmer, in Australia; Zac Goldsmith, in the United Kingdom; Petro Poroshenko, in Ukraine; Thaksin Shinawatra, in Thailand; Manuel Villar, in the Philippines; Najib Mikati and the late Rafiq Hariri, in Lebanon; Vijay Mallya and Nandan Nilekani, in India; and Mikhail Prokhorov, Andrei Guriev, and Sergei Pugachyou, in Russia have run for office. Most of them have won. The increasing prominence of billionaire politicians raises questions about the link between financial and political power. As seen in this chapter, the fusion of economic and political influence creates reasons for concern about its potential impact on democratic elections and social opportunity. Some billionaire leaders have been accused of vote buying, influence peddling, and even having gained their wealth through outright corruption. Whatever the truth of such charges in each case, the involvement of extremely wealthy people in politics can increase citizen cynicism and make ordinary people feel that the system is rigged in favor of the rich.

The Case of Berlusconi

Silvio Berlusconi is one of the world's most prominent and most controversial billionaires-turned-politicians. He started his business career in residential construction, building Milano Due, an upscale suburb of Milan, in the 1970s, and he used the profits to launch a small cable television company. The profitability of that venture led to his formation of the Fininvest media group and a national network of local TV stations. With the help of a favorable government ruling from his friend, then–prime minister Bettino Craxi, his stations were allowed to broadcast nationwide, and Berlusconi thereby amassed a great fortune. Armed with a major media platform, he went into elective politics and quickly won control of government.

He was elected to the Chamber of Deputies in 1994, and as the leader of Forza Italia, the parliamentary party that he founded, he was named prime minister. He served just one year as prime minister but returned to office again from 2001 to 2006 and from 2008 to 2011. His built his elective career on alliances with other center-right political parties. In several contests, he campaigned on a platform of job creation, citing his business background. Along with his efforts to strengthen the Italian economy, he sought to simplify his nation's tax code, launch a massive public works project, and fight crime. In each of his elections, Berlusconi spent large amounts of his own money on campaign advertisements. With his background in media and advertising, he ran compelling ads that connected him to average voters. That helped him survive politically during a time of political gridlock and a struggling economy at home.

In 2011, Berlusconi lost his prime ministership following personal scandals and an indictment on tax fraud charges. His flamboyant lifestyle also led to charges of having sex with young girls and not paying taxes on all of his income. Following conviction on the tax fraud charges in October 2012, Berlusconi was stripped of his seat in parliament and lost the right to hold Italian elective office for two years. The court sentenced him to four years in prison but later reduced the punishment to ten months of community service in a Catholic nursing home.[9]

Through it all, Berlusconi has proclaimed his innocence and promised to stay in the public limelight. Early in 2014, he announced his intention to run for the European Parliament on a platform criticizing a "Germanised Europe." Upset with German chancellor Angela Merkel's criticism of Italian economic policies under his watch, his supporters complained that Germany "was enriching northern Europe at the expense of the south."[10] He also has criticized U.S. and European moves to impose sanctions on Russia following its annexation of Crimea. Berlusconi's latest political ambitions appeared to be quashed in March 2014, however, when Italy's highest court upheld his conviction.[11] Despite his conviction, Berlusconi's ability to remain in the political limelight demonstrates that billionaire politicians have great staying power and often are able to overcome scandals that would have more quickly destroyed the careers of nonwealthy politicians.

Billionaires Running for Office

When billionaires run for public office, they almost always are criticized for using their abundant financial resources to win elections, and once they are in office, observers worry whether they are abusing their positions to further their own social and economic interests. Given the wide-ranging business interests of most politicians who are very wealthy, conflicts of interest are almost inevitable unless they place their holdings in blind trusts or otherwise credibly remove themselves from active involvement in their businesses.

In France, billionaire Serge Dassault, the owner of the conservative newspaper *Le Figaro,* was elected mayor in 1995 of a small town east of Paris called Corbeil-Essonnes. He served for a number of years but has been under investigation for violence and intimidation linked to electoral corruption. Authorities say that the mayor exchanged cash for votes in 2008, 2009, and 2010 and orchestrated physical attacks to keep people quiet about his vote buying. He was stripped of his mayoral position after a French court found him guilty of "cash gifts to voters."[12] But he also continued to serve as a senator and to be protected from criminal prosecution until the senate stripped him of parliamentary immunity early in 2014.[13] Dassault has admitted paying people and groups in Corbeil but says that the money was for philanthropy, not vote buying.

Clive Palmer, who made most of his money in the mining industry, is one of the wealthiest people in Australia. He attracted considerable public attention by designing a dinosaur park in Queensland and building a replica of the *Titanic* ocean liner. Using money from his business ventures, he won a senate seat in 2013 by 53 votes, representing the center-right party bearing his name, Palmer United. As is typical with many activist billionaires, the party was little more than a personal vehicle to advance Palmer's electoral aspirations. Along with $2.3 million in public funding, he financed the party, served as its public spokesperson, and used his election campaign to push conservative ideas about the future. Opponents, however, charged him with unfair campaign practices. In Australia, candidates are not allowed to publish their opponent's name or picture in ads without the opponent's consent. Palmer's party appeared to violate this rule when it ran a newspaper ad showing Liberal Party leaders as the "Three Amigos."[14]

In his short political career, however, he has displayed a tin ear regarding public opinion. When asked about possible conflicts of interest with his commercial ventures, Palmer downplayed the risks, explaining that "I've got more money than you could ever dream of. What's the conflict of interest?"[15] After a public outcry following those comments, Palmer altered his stance and acknowledged possible conflicts with the seventy-four mining, refinery, and tourism companies in which he had investments. When legislation to repeal the country's landmark carbon tax came before parliament in November 2013, he did not attend the policy debate or cast a vote. However, members of his legislative party did vote in favor of repeal, which remained pending early in 2014.[16]

Billionaire Frank Stronach, founder of the auto parts company Magna International, is a Canadian of Austrian origin who won a place in the Austrian parliament in September 2013 when his rightist party, Team Stronach, garnered 5.9 percent of the vote. Employing populist attacks on incumbent officials, his party cleared the 4 percent threshold for gaining seats. Stronach used the race to call for reform of taxes, health care, and education. He also criticized Austria's participation in the European Monetary Union but was vague about whether the country should abandon the euro.

More controversially, he "warned of the danger of Chinese troops marching into Austria and voiced support for the death penalty," according to one news account.[17] He campaigned as a strong leader who would emphasize "truth, fairness, and transparency." He complained vociferously about the cozy nature of Austrian national politics and condemned the "unholy" alliance of the center-left and center-right parties that had long dominated Austrian politics. Election observers said that the party spent around $41 million on the campaign, much more than any of the other parties.[18] This was unprecedented in Austrian politics and led to accusations that he was seeking to buy the office. But even after spending that amount, his party did not do as well as Stronach had hoped. Following his disappointing electoral performance, Stronach announced that he was leaving politics and returning to life as a businessman. The unease of some Austrian voters with the combination of his wealth and policy prescriptions likely persuaded him that he did not have a bright political future in his native land.

In India, billionaire Nandan Nilekani ran for elective office in Bangalore South. A cofounder of outsourcing company Infosys, he sought the district on the Congress Party ticket in 2014. Since leaving his company board in 2009, he has run the Unique Identification Authority of India, a government agency responsible for the country's mammoth new project of issuing every citizen or resident a unique identity card.[19] His work on that issue brought him to the attention of Congress Party leaders, thereby enabling his campaign for the national parliament. Seeking to appeal to citizens upset with the corruption of government officials, he campaigned by saying, "I am not in politics to make money. I have already made money the honest way; I am incorruptible."[20] After voters cast their ballots in 2014, however, Nilekani lost when his Congress Party suffered an overwhelming defeat.

Wealth and Politics in Thailand and France

Thaksin Shinawatra founded Advanced Info Service, a mobile phone services company in Thailand. Having a near-monopoly on the market, the firm was able to grow rapidly, and it became Thailand's dominant mobile operator. Eventually, Shinawatra moved into politics and was named foreign minister. In 2001, he became prime minister after his Thai Rak Thai (Thais Love Thais) party won a major electoral victory. Although a billionaire, Shinawatra built his political career by appealing to the country's poor, especially those in rural areas who believed that they had been ignored by the national elite. He served for five years before being removed from power in a military coup.[21]

While he was in office, opponents accused him of engaging in corruption and tax evasion and using his position to enrich himself and his family. Critics pointed to favorable tax breaks given to his Shin Satellite firm and regulatory decisions that gave advantages to his Shin Corp airline company. The military government convicted him on "policy corruption" charges, finding that he had used the levers of government to make decisions that favored his businesses. Later, the Assets Examination Committee charged him and his wife with profiteering related to land purchases and illegal stock trading. He was found guilty in 2008 and forced to leave the country to avoid imprisonment.

Former Thai foreign minister Kasit Piromya, noting Shinawatra's ethical lapses, remarked that "we have come to the point where we want to get rid of Al Capone."[22] Meanwhile, political analyst Voranai Vanijaka of the *Bangkok Post* noted that "we understand that everybody takes a little bite of the apple. The problem with Thaksin is that he put a sign on the whole apple tree saying 'property of the Shinawatra family.'"[23]

But like many billionaire politicians, Shinawatra has demonstrated amazing staying power in politics. The military government had stripped more than $1.3 billion from his fortune, but according to *Forbes*, he retains $1.6 billion and keeps in touch with ruling party leaders on a regular basis.[24] Despite the controversy surrounding him, his sister Yingluck Shinawatra became prime minister. Opposition figures and some commentators claim that Shinawatra ran the country through his sister, despite living in political exile. Indeed, his absence from Thailand has not quelled dissatisfaction surrounding the family's rule; protestors called for his sister's ouster as prime minister and threatened to impeach her if she did not resign. In May 2014 she was removed from office by the Constitutional Court for abuse of power, and the military took over in a coup. The main opposition organization, the Democrat Party, boycotted a 2014 election on grounds that it was unfair and not held in an orderly manner. The discontent in Thailand shows how volatile national politics can be when dominated by billionaires.[25]

Rather than seek elective office, some billionaires opt for working through political patrons. This allows them to gain influence behind the scenes and avoid the media spotlight that comes with holding office themselves.

An example can be seen in France, which for years has had spirited debates about the appropriate role of government and level of taxation. Liliane Bettencourt, daughter of the founder of the L'Oreal cosmetics firm, is a French billionaire concerned about taxes and public spending. At one point in 2010, she was heard on tape discussing a possible job for the wife of Budget Minister Eric Woerth. What caused controversy was that Woerth was in charge of the initiative to identify tax evaders, and Bettencourt had been accused of hiding assets in a secret Swiss bank account. During a meeting with Bettencourt, Woerth sought to have his wife be given the position of manager of the billionaire's portfolio, something that would have been a blatant conflict of interest. The recording of their conversation also indicated that Bettencourt had provided 150,000 euros in cash for the initial campaign of then-president Nicolas Sarkozy, in violation of French campaign finance rules.[26] When billionaires seek to circumvent finance or other government regulations through large and secret cash contributions, accountability and transparency are weakened.

Forming a New Party in the Czech Republic

Andre Babis is one of the richest people in the Czech Republic. He initially made his fortune through an agribusiness firm called Agrofert and then built greater wealth with diversified stakes in agriculture, food production, and chemicals. As a businessman, he was disturbed by government corruption. In 2013, he bought MAFRA, which operates two major newspapers, *Lidové noviny* and *Mladá fronta Dnes*, giving him substantial ownership of some of the country's most prominent media companies. These newspapers helped him launch a grassroots organization with the assistance of an American public relations firm that specialized in public communications.[27] "We have a pseudo-democracy," Babis complained, "in which you can go to elections once in four years, select four names from the list of candidates, and that's it. After the election, the politicians disappear and all they care about is themselves."[28]

He fought this problem by forming a political party ANO ("Yes") and contesting parliamentary elections in 2013. His party focused on fighting political corruption and streamlining government operations. Its candidates argued that there should be no tax increases to close the budget deficit and that the country should invest in transportation infrastructure as opposed to social benefits. To the surprise of many, his party won 18.7 percent of the popular vote and finished second among Czech political parties. It ended up with 47 legislators in the 200-seat parliament, which was a terrific showing for a new political organization.[29]

Through this strong electoral showing, Babis's party joined the Social Democrat–led ruling coalition, and he was named finance minister. Among the issues that he pushed were privatizing government pensions, eliminating the minimum wage, and cutting value-added taxes.[30] Critics dubbed him the "Czech Berlusconi" and pointed out possible conflicts of interest through his empire of 200 companies.[31] This is a refrain that often arises in regard to many billionaire politicians.[32] Nearly all of them have extensive business holdings, and once they are in government it is difficult to disentangle public decisions from private interests. Many decisions that they make in government have ramifications for their commercial interests.

Prime Minister Bohuslav Sobotka publicly called for Babis to sell Agrofert in order to "eliminate questions about any conflict of interest." But Babis refused to do so and told the premier that "he could dismiss him or find another coalition partner if he is bothered by his ownership of Agrofert." The two also clashed over budgetary policy. Babis has opposed raising hospital payments and also fought Sobotka's proposal to provide government assistance to a coal mine that provides thousands of jobs. "The Social Democrats only want money," Babis complained. "They don't know what it means to save money or how to function rationally."[33]

A year before the parliamentary elections, I had a phone conversation with Babis about his anticorruption work. Billionaires who live in nations with a weak rule of law have discovered that their wealth can be in danger when there are few constitutional protections against the actions of corrupt officials armed with the power of the state. He told me that corruption was the most pressing public sector challenge in many countries and that it was vital to improve government performance. I was not surprised when he went into politics.

Other billionaires in the Czech Republic also are working to address what they consider major public policy problems—for example, Czech billionaire Zdenek Bakala. Bakala came to the United States at the age of 19 with $50 in his pocket. After washing dishes in a Lake Tahoe casino, he earned a B.A. at the University of California at Berkeley and an MBA at Dartmouth College. He formed a private equity firm, RPG Industries, and conducted a leveraged buyout of a Czech coal mining conglomerate. Indeed, his company owns the coal mine that is the object of political contention between Sobotka and Babis. Bakala took his company, New World Resources, public in 2008 and gained $2.1 billion in the process.[34]

In 2013, Bakala spent a half-million crowns (around $25,000) to support reform-minded presidential candidate Karel Schwarzenberg, an outside leader who fought political corruption and pledged to clean things up if elected.[35] Although Schwarzenberg lost his bid, the campaign and Bakala's support for it raised public awareness of corruption in Czech politics and pushed leaders to improve the political process.[36] Unlike Babis, Bakala has not expressed interest in forming a party or running for office. He has stayed out of the political limelight and limited his activities to trying to make what he considers improvements in government and backing others who choose to run. Like many other billionaires, he has purchased a media platform—the publishing company Ekonomia, which prints a weekly magazine called *Respekt* and a major daily, *Hospodarske noviny*—to help get his message across to the public.

The Case of Russia

Ever since the chaotic days following the collapse of the Soviet Union at the end of 1991, money has been a powerful tool for influencing politics in Russia. Political leaders use their control of government enterprises and procurement contracts to reward friends and punish enemies. A small number of men with inside connections, known as the "oligarchs," became fabulously wealthy in the 1990s by purchasing government-owned enterprises at fire-sale prices and building then into viable businesses. In turn, some of the oligarchs have used their newfound wealth to help politicians win elections and retain influence.

For example, billionaires Arkady Rotenberg, Yuri Kovalchuk, Vladimir Litvinenko, and Gennady Timchenko helped fund Vladimir Putin's 2012 presidential election campaign. Each of them had become wealthy through business deals with state-owned enterprises. Rotenberg made money by selling pipes to Gazprom, a government-owned oil and gas firm. Timchenko co-owns a commodity company that specializes in oil and gas trading through Rosneft, another Russian oil company.[37] Kovalchuk, who also benefited from inside connections at Gazprom, built a small St. Petersburg bank into a financial powerhouse. In 2013, Kovalchuk parlayed his political connections with Putin into a purchase of one-half of Tele2, a Russian wireless carrier. The acquisition helped the billionaire expand his empire beyond banking and natural gas into mobile communications and video. He has known Putin since their days together in St. Petersburg during the 1990s, when Putin worked for the local government while serving in the agency that succeeded the KGB, the Soviet secret service.[38]

Such arrangements have generated a great deal of criticism in Russia. One opponent of the relationship between money and politics is opposition political leader Vladimir Bilov. He notes that "certain personal close friends of Putin who were people of relatively moderate means before Putin came to power all of a sudden turned out to be billionaires."[39] As part of the alleged quid pro quo of this relationship, Putin's financial backers secured a lucrative business deal to construct a large resort. Following the president's 2012 reelection, his wealthy supporters announced that they would build a multibillion dollar resort on the Black Sea in Sochi for the 2014 Winter Olympics.

More recently, billionaire Mikhail Prokhorov has attracted attention in Russia by fielding a slate of local candidates under the pro-business Civic Platform party. In an effort to position himself as a presidential candidate down the road, Prokhorov is supporting thirty individuals running for mayor and city council in various areas around the country.[40] With an estimated net worth in the billions, Prokhorov sees opportunities for political gain. "A process of schisms in the elite is under way today. In the Kremlin, in the government, in Parliament, in the regions, and at the end of the day, in the kitchens of this country, politics has returned to Russia," he said. Prokhorov garnered 7 percent of the presidential vote in 2012 and hopes to build a significant platform for future campaigns.[41]

Crony Capitalism in the Developing World

Close connections between wealth and politics are common in many places around the world. *The Economist* publishes a "crony capitalism index" that ranks nations on the wealth of billionaires as a percentage of GDP. The countries with the highest percentage of billionaire wealth are Hong Kong (around 60 percent of GDP),

Russia (20 percent), Malaysia (18 percent), Ukraine (16 percent), and Singapore (15 percent).[42]

India, which ranks ninth on *The Economist*'s crony capitalism index, is one of many countries plagued by widespread corruption. It is not unusual for business people in India to use political connections to build wealth and for politicians to draw financial support from those seeking government favors. A company linked to one Indian billionaire, Kumar Mangalam Birla, is being investigated for insider dealing. The offices of his company, Hindalco, were raided in 2013 by law enforcement officials as part of an investigation into how the government allocates the right to mine coal deposits to private companies. During the raid, authorities found $4 million in cash, while Hindalco executives "expressed surprise at the discovery."[43]

Some African business leaders also have used preferential political treatment to grow rich. Nigerian billionaire Aliko Dangote is one example. Through his company, the Dangote Group, he has earned a fortune in cement and food production and today is worth an estimated $11.2 billion. Dangote is a close ally of former Nigerian president Olusegun Obasanjo. While president from 1999 to 2007, Obasanjo banned imports of cement, rice, and sugar, giving Dangote a near-monopoly in those lucrative areas. In return, Dangote put large amounts of money into Obasanjo's political campaigns and helped him build public support for his leadership.[44]

Early in 2014, when Russia sent troops into the Ukrainian peninsula of Crimea after the fall of the pro-Russian president, Ukrainian authorities responded by appointing two billionaires, Sergei Taruta of Donetsk and Ihor Kolomoysky of Dnipropetrovsk, as governors of eastern provinces also at risk of a Russian takeover. According to Brookings senior fellow Steven Pifer, "the government is doing what it can to avoid provoking any internal divisions. They need people who have credibility in eastern Ukraine." Since billionaires form a "shadow government" in Ukraine, political authorities hoped that naming the magnates governors would stabilize the political situation and ease the tension.[45] In another example of the close ties between weath and politics, one of the leading presidential candidates in Ukraine is billionaire Petro Poroshenko, who owns a company that produces chocolate candy. Poroshenko supports close ties between Ukraine and the European Union.[46]

In China, so-called "princelings"—sons and daughters of high government officials and Communist Party leaders—have used their family political connections to create great wealth. For example, Wen Yunsong, the son of former prime minister Wen Jiabao, runs a large satellite communications company. Jiang Mianheng, the son of former leader Jiang Zemin, heads an investment company with stakes in semiconductor manufacturing, film studios, and telecommunications companies. Hu Haifeng, the son of the most recent former president, Hu Jintao, runs a company that sells security scanners to Chinese airports. Li Ziaolin, the daughter of former prime minister Li Peng, runs China Power International, one of the country's top utility companies.[47]

In a series of reports in 2013, the *New York Times* estimated that various relatives of Wen Jiabao control over $2.7 billion in corporate assets. Their holdings include "a villa development project in Beijing; a tire factory in northern China; a company that helped build some of Beijing's Olympic stadiums, including the well-known 'Bird's Nest'; and Ping An Insurance, one of the world's biggest financial services companies."[48] The *Times* reported that when Wen Jiabao was running the government, the State Council awarded millions of dollars in government contracts to companies run by his relatives and exempted some of those firms from onerous regulations. For example, Ping An Insurance benefited considerably from favorable government rulings. In the aftermath of the 1999 Asian financial crisis, efforts were under way to break up large financial services companies. The fear was that they had grown too large, threatening long-term market stability. Yet when Chinese regulators set their sights on Ping An, its chair, Ma Mingzhe, asked Wen Jiabao, then the vice premier, to "lead and coordinate the matter from a higher level."[49] The result was that three competing companies were broken up, but this particular company was allowed to stay intact. Following that ruling, Ping An grew into a $50 billion behemoth. Undisclosed at the time was the fact the Jiabao's relatives held substantial shares in the company.

Bulat Utemuratov became rich after Kazakhstan president Nursultan Nazarbayev asked him in 1992 to open a trading firm. Right after the collapse of the Soviet Union, Utemuratov was sent to Vienna to negotiate with European firms needing zinc and copper. While trading on behalf of his government, Utemuratov set up his own business. According to industry observer Kate Mallinson, "as in many other nations globally, public officials in Kazakhstan historically had access to significant public funds and strategic energy resources as well as the knowledge and ability to control budgets, public companies, and contracts with fellow government officials."[50] Utemuratov invested in mining, telecommunications, and resorts, among other areas, and built a multibillion dollar fortune. He remains close to the country's political leaders and assists them in their policy activities.

The Risks of Political Advocacy in Russia and China

In some countries, political advocacy by the wealthy can be hazardous to their personal well-being. One Russian billionaire, Mikhail Khodorkovsky, paid a heavy price for his political involvement. Khodorkovsky, who controlled the energy company Yukos, was once the richest man in Russia. However, he ran into trouble with the Kremlin when he funded opposition political parties contesting parliamentary elections in 2003. In what was widely seen as a politically motivated case, he was convicted of tax evasion in 2003 and thrown into prison. President Putin released Khodorkovsky from prison in 2014, with the understanding that he stay out of politics. He left the country with just a fraction of his previous wealth.

In China, billionaire Wang Gongquan has spoken out about his desire for greater citizen involvement in his country's decisionmaking. After making a fortune in real estate, he now distributes what he calls "citizen pins" and "citizen stamps." These trinkets included engraved images of the Chinese flag and references to the Chinese constitution and Chinese citizens. He has attended meetings of the Open Constitution Initiative and favored migrant rights to education and housing.[51] In 2013, Wang was arrested in Beijing on charges of "assembling a crowd to disrupt order in a public place." More than twenty police officers went to his personal residence, searched his home, removed a computer for possible evidence against him, and took him to the police station. Along with other Chinese activists, Wang has asked political leaders to respect the Chinese constitution and provide more liberal social policies for its people.

His friend Liu Suli said that "one of the main reasons for arresting Wang Gongquan was that he was using money to support public interest causes."[52] He is one of the few super-wealthy individuals in China to speak out on political issues, and that clearly worries Chinese authorities. In this case, they shut down his political activities, apparently hoping that doing so would have a deterrent effect on the activism of other Chinese billionaires. Government officials did not want to end up with an oligarch, such as Khodorkovsky, whose political advocacy might represent a major threat to the regime.

In light of this action, other Chinese tycoons made sure that they were not seen as oppositional figures. For example, Jack Ma, a billionaire who earned his fortune through the e-commerce firm Alibaba Group Holding, has set up a charitable trust with an estimated $3 billion in assets to work on the environment and health care. Ma is concerned about environmental pollution in China. "Somebody has to do something," he said. "Our job is to wake people up." Yet he was cognizant of the political risks facing Chinese billionaire advocates. In announcing his venture, he was careful to reassure government authorities about his long-term intentions. "I'm not political," he noted. "We don't want to confront [the government]; we want to sit down and work with them."[53]

The Chinese and Russian cases demonstrate that political involvement by the super rich is not always cost free. In places with weak rule of law, it can be risky for the wealthy to attempt to influence political developments. Rather than seeing the involvement of wealthy business owners as an opportunity to reap personal rewards for themselves—as has been the case in some countries—authorities may crack down in fear that billionaires have too much power, are seeking to disrupt existing power alignments, or are contemplating antigovernment actions.

In most places, however, it is more common for wealthy individuals to seek to influence high-level officials or to control public policies of interest to them rather than challenge a regime. In some cases, billionaires use their wealth to promote their political views, often those on taxes or government regulations affecting their businesses. In other cases, the wealthy, or those seeking wealth, hope to use the government's ability to grant contracts or award licenses to make money for themselves and their businesses. No matter how it is done, over time a type of systemic corruption can result from the involvement of very wealthy people in government, breeding great cynicism among the general population. Ordinary people come to believe that politicians and the wealthy are in cahoots and that they use their power to benefit themselves to the detriment of everyone else. Figuring out how to address these issues is the major governance challenge in many nations.

PART II

IT TAKES A VILLAGE
TO MAKE A FORTUNE

6   The Global 1,645

IF BILL GATES WERE a country, he would be the sixty-fifth richest nation in the world. At an estimated $76 billion, his fortune is larger than the gross domestic product of countries such as Costa Rica, Lebanon, Tunisia, Uruguay, Slovenia, Kenya, Panama, and Bolivia.[1] If Microsoft stock had performed better over the last decade, Gates might have had much more than that, but the value of the company's stock fell from $601 billion in 2000 to $270 billion in mid-2013.[2] Gates cofounded the company with Paul Allen after dropping out of Harvard University, and eventually the two made billions selling the Windows operating system and other software products.

Back in 1974, over the Christmas holiday break, Gates and Allen spent eight weeks writing intensive BASIC code to develop the first commercial software package that could run on a home computer, the Altair, which had an Intel 8080 microprocessor. Commandeering the school's Digital Equipment Company PDP-10 mainframe computer, they tested the software. When it worked, Allen flew to Albuquerque to demonstrate it for Altair's designer, Ed Roberts. The software booted up the machine, and Roberts offered Allen a contract on the spot to oversee software development for the Altair.[3]

The only glitch in their plan occurred when auditors for the U.S. Department of Defense checked the use of the mainframe that it was funding at Harvard's Howard Aiken lab. They discovered that most of the computer time was being used by a college sophomore known as W. H. Gates and that he had shared his password with a nonstudent, Paul Allen, who attended Washington State University. Harvard brought Gates up for disciplinary action and reprimanded him for the security breach. That, however, represented only a minor setback on what became the young men's road to riches.[4]

Seizing on the invention of the personal computer, Gates, his Microsoft collaborators, and the companies that he bought developed software that allowed those without a computer background to use the machines. Users did not have to be mathematicians or computer scientists to benefit—even novices could purchase programs that enabled them to write documents, compile spreadsheets, and perform complex statistical computations. Gates's genius did not lie in inventing new things. Others were better at writing code, for example, and building devices. His talent lay in recognizing the skills of other people and incorporating their creations into the Microsoft product line. He was an adept businessman who established market domination in a particular niche and used his market power to make billions of dollars.

In 1998, however, the U.S. Department of Justice brought a lawsuit against Microsoft alleging antitrust abuses. At issue was the company's "bundling" of its Internet Explorer web browser with the Windows operating system. According to the federal government, the company employed predatory business practices that took advantage of its operating system monopoly to shut out competing browsers, especially Netscape. After a trial, the federal judge found the firm guilty of unfair business practices. That ruling, however, was overturned by the Washington D.C. Circuit Court of Appeals, and in 2001, Microsoft and the Department of Justice signed an agreement to settle the case. Microsoft pledged to share its software code with other firms and in turn was allowed to provide its browser along with its operating system.[5] The manner in which billionaires make their money is relevant for controversies concerning the rich. Their backgrounds and personal narratives affect how others see them and the way in which people think about policy issues affecting the wealthy. The mix of personal, social, and government assistance that billionaires received in accumulating their wealth influences what others think about taxes, regulation, and the role of government. Learning more about billionaires' backgrounds and how they built their businesses therefore is necessary for evaluating their impact on society as a whole.

Estimating Wealth

Measuring a person's wealth is not a simple matter, even when the person is a billionaire. Often, financial information on significant portions of an individual's personal assets is not publicly available. It is not always clear what percentage of an asset is owned by a particular person, especially when multiple family members or business associates are involved. In addition, financial assets are not amenable to precise measurement if they are illiquid (such as real estate) or privately held. Finally, it is hard to know how to assess debt. In many cases, personal debt levels are not known unless information on such obligations is publicly available, as it is, for example, on mortgages.

Various sources calculate wealth differently. *Bloomberg Businessweek,* which inaugurated its Billionaires Index in 2012, shows that as of March 2014, the wealthiest individuals in the world were Bill Gates ($77.8 billion), Carlos Slim Helu ($63.5 billion), Warren Buffet ($59.7 billion), Amancio Ortega ($57.7 billion), and Ingvar Kamprad ($51 billion). It updates its rankings daily. According to the magazine, its measurements are

based on changes in markets, the economy and *Bloomberg* reporting. . . . Stakes in publicly traded companies are valued using the share's most recent closing price. Valuations are converted to U.S. dollars at current exchanges rates. Closely held companies are valued in several ways, such as by comparing the enterprise value-to-Ebitda or price-to-earnings ratios of similar public companies. The criteria used depend on the company's industry and size. Calculations of closely held company debt are based on the net debt-to-Ebitda ratios of comparable peers.[6]

In the case of illiquid assets, *Bloomberg Businessweek* says that it employs a "5 percent discount [that] is applied to most closely held companies where assets may be hard to sell. . . . In some instances, a country risk discount is also applied, based on a person's concentration of assets and ease of selling them in a given geography. A country's risk is assessed based on Standard & Poor's sovereign debt ratings."[7]

Because there are tremendous country-to-country variations in tax laws and enforcement, one of the hardest things to measure is how national taxation affects income. According to *Bloomberg Businessweek*, "taxes are deducted based on prevailing income, dividend and capital gains tax rates in a billionaire's country of residence. Taxes are applied at the highest rate unless there is evidence to support a lower percentage."[8] *Bloomberg* notes that "no assumptions are made about personal debt."

In 2012, a service called Wealth-X and UBS Financial Services launched a competing analysis that identified 2,170 billionaires based on criteria and metrics different from those used by other services.[9] Using a "global census," it did not rank specific individuals (apart from identifying the four richest individuals as Bill Gates, Carlos Slim, Amancio Ortega, and Warren Buffet); instead, it aggregated data on wealth collected between July 2012 and June 2013 for billionaires as a whole. The Wealth-X/UBS report indicates that the total wealth of global billionaires increased by 5.3 percent over the preceding year to a total of $6.5 trillion. According to this assessment, 60 percent of the wealth of billionaires is self-made, not inherited[10] and 42 percent is in private holdings.[11] The census is based on paid, open source, online, and in-print valuation information. The firm employs a proprietary model that assesses "all asset holdings, including privately and publicly held businesses and investible assets, inclusive of real estate, private aviation, yachts, artwork and collectibles to develop a net worth valuation for ultra high net worth individuals."[12]

The Knight Frank property consultancy also publishes its "Wealth Report" each year. In 2014, it estimated that there were 1,682 billionaires, up 80 percent over the preceding decade. Its most recent analysis found that the wealthy invest 30 percent of their money in real estate but that increasingly they are devoting their money to things such as vineyards, art, expensive cars, and vintage wine. The 2014 Knight Frank report identified 167,000 individuals throughout the world with total assets of at least $30 million.[13]

Another source of data is *Forbes* magazine, which has been measuring the wealth of billionaires annually for three decades, first the wealth of billionaires in the United States and then of others around the world. Forbes says that it compiles net worth by valuing "individuals' assets—including stakes in public and private companies, real estate, yachts, art and cash—and take into account estimates for debt. . . . We also consult an array of outside experts in various fields."[14] The magazine does not include "royal family members or dictators who derive their fortunes entirely as a result of their position of power, nor do we include royalty who, often with large families, control the riches in trust for their nation." That means that the list does not incorporate some very wealthy individuals who fall outside the magazine's scope of analysis.

In China, a developer, Star River Property, publishes the "Hurun Global Rich List." Its February 2014 list estimated that there were 1,867 billionaires around the world, more than the 1,645 on the Forbes list. It is not clear exactly what leads to different numbers across the ranking services. But in this case, there is a striking difference in regard to China: while Forbes counts 152 billionaires in China, Hurun counts 358.[15]

In at least one unusual case, a wealth assessment sparked legal action. Saudi prince Alwaleed bin Talal sued *Forbes* in 2013 over the net worth estimate that it gave for him. He said that the publication was "deliberately biased" against him when it published his net worth at $20 billion; in reality, he claimed, his assets totaled $30 billion. Part of the discrepancy was due to variations in the valuation of his holdings in the social media company Twitter. For most of 2013, before it went public, Twitter was privately held, and therefore it was difficult to produce a precise measure of the prince's fortune.[16] There also is uncertainty about the worth of Kingdom Holding, the prince's stock holding company. Through it, Alwaleed invests in stocks, real estate, and other assets. Its value rises and falls in reaction to perceptions about or financial moves undertaken by the Saudi royal family. *Forbes* does not rely entirely on prices coming from the Tadawul stock exchange in Saudi Arabia because it does not fully understand its pricing mechanisms and has had problems validating the value of the prince's portfolio.[17] For example, there have been times in recent years when the value of Kingdom Holdings rose while one of its major stocks (Citi) plummeted by 90 percent.[18] According to news reports, the prince feels that there should be more consistent treatment of stock exchanges, regardless of geographic region.

The Wealthiest Individuals

After Bill Gates, the *Forbes* ranks Carlos Slim Helu of Mexico as the second-richest person in the world. Slim, of Lebanese origin, oversees a telecommunications, finance, and retail empire of extraordinary reach through his conglomerate Grupo Carso. He is the chief executive officer of America Movil, the largest mobile firm in Latin America, and Telmex, a monopoly that controls 80 percent of Mexico's landlines. He purchased his first stock shares at 12 years of age and later invested in real estate, construction, and mining companies, making an enormous amount of money with considerable help from public authorities. That wealth allowed him to acquire greater resources in other areas. His big financial break came during the early 1980s, when a devaluation of the peso and a deep recession allowed him to buy several businesses at low prices and thereby increase his fortune. Recently, however, the Mexican government has moved to break up America Movil on the grounds that it is a "preponderant economic agent" and the country needs more competition in telecommunications.[19] If the company is broken up, Slim's fortune could be diminished.

Amancio Ortega, who left school at age 12 to work as a delivery boy, is number 3 on the 2014 *Forbes* list. Ortega made his fortune through the Spanish fashion retailing company Inditex. He originally sold shirts and used the proceeds to launch a company that made bathrobes. He and Rosalia Mera, who was then his wife, made robes, gowns, and lingerie in their living room; they launched their first retail outlet in A Coruña, Spain, in 1975. From that start, he was able to build a clothing company called Zara and open a chain of stores throughout Spain. The company specialized in "affordable imitations of catwalk designs that can move from drawing-board to stores within two weeks."[20] Zara puts new styles on display in thousands of outlets before they are replaced by even newer designs. The company operates 6,000 stores in around 90 countries around the world, and it distributes 840 million garments each year.

Having amassed billions in wealth, Warren Buffet, number 4 on the *Forbes* list, is widely considered the greatest investor of recent times. He visited the New York Stock Exchange for the first time at 10 years of age and began investing at age 11 using the $120 he had saved from his paper delivery route. He has noted that "you don't need 20 [investment] decisions to get very rich. Four or five will probably do it over time."[21] Following the financial principles of David Dodd and Benjamin Graham, he launched a series of investment partnerships that proved quite lucrative. In the 1960s, he merged those holdings into Berkshire Hathaway, through which he bought shares in companies such as Coca-Cola, the *Washington Post*, General Re, ABC News, Goldman Sachs, and General Electric.

Number 5, Larry Ellison, is the chief executive officer of Oracle, an enterprise software company that sells software packages enabling businesses and other users to share and analyze large databases. He had an early interest in computers and worked for various database companies. One of his first employers, Ampex Corporation, had a government client (the Central Intelligence Agency) that needed a relational database, so Ellison designed a program to meet its needs. After developing expertise in the area, he launched his own company in 1977 and eventually renamed it Oracle, after its leading product at that time. As the computer era flourished, the success of his enterprise software put him near the top of the global financial elite. In recent years, he has moved into cloud computing and worked with companies to migrate them from enterprise software to cloud-based storage solutions.[22]

Charles and David Koch, tied at number 6, are co-owners of Koch Industries, which they inherited from their father, Fred Koch. The family business is diversified among a number of sectors, including oil, minerals, transportation, consumer products, and commodity trading. The privately held firm is run on what the family calls "market-based management" principles.[23] David Koch suffered what could have been a fatal accident on February 1, 1991, when he was aboard USAir flight 1493 to Los Angeles, which hit another airplane on landing and burst into flames. Twenty-two people on the plane died, but he survived.[24] Koch ran as the vice presidential candidate of the Libertarian Party in 1980. In recent years the brothers have become well-known as major financial backers of conservative Republican candidates for public office.

Sheldon Adelson, next on the *Forbes* list at number 8, heads the Las Vegas Sands Corporation and through it owns hotels and operates casinos in countries such as the United States, Macau, and Singapore. Much of his business is based on government licenses to operate gambling facilities. A self-professed risk-taker, he has won and lost billions of dollars at various points in his life. His companies rise and fall with the overall economy and the amount of discretionary spending that consumers undertake. In 2009, for example, it is estimated that he lost $25 billion when the global economy plunged. This moved his net worth from $30 billion to under $5 billion.[25] As the economy recovered, however, he made all of his losses back and became even richer than before. He owns a daily newspaper in Israel called *Israel HaYom*, which he uses to support the conservative government of Prime Minister Benjamin Netanyahu.

Christy Walton, number 9, is the widow of John Walton, one of the sons of Wal-Mart founder Sam Walton, while Jim Walton, number 10, is the founder's youngest son. Christy inherited her husband's fortune after he died.[26] Jim replaced John on the Wal-Mart board of directors in 2005. Wal-Mart is the largest retailer in the world. Launched in Bentonville, Arkansas, in 1962, the company has expanded to more than 11,000 stores in 27 countries. It employs more than 2 million people and has had a dramatic impact on the retail sector due to its huge scale, large labor force, and administrative innovations.[27] Including relatives Alice Walton (number 13) and Robson Walton (number 14), this extended family is one of the richest ones in America.[28]

This review of the wealthiest figures on the Forbes list shows that most billionaires possess significant entrepreneurial talent. They have tremendous ability to identify market niches and build firms that satisfy consumer needs. But a number of them made their fortunes with the help of favorable government policies and regulatory decisions, public procurement, or government connections of one sort or another. An analysis by *The Economist* found that state involvement is especially important for wealth creation in many fields of business,[29] including areas such as casinos, coal, timber, defense, finance, infrastructure, oil, gas, chemicals, ports, real estate, construction, steel, mining, public utilities, and telecommunications. In these sectors, governments play a disproportionate role in business operations and public officials can facilitate the acquisition of wealth through their decisions regarding licenses, business permits, contracts, and tax policies.

Demographic Characteristics and National Origins

The top billionaires on the *Forbes* list represent only a small segment of the super wealthy. According to *Forbes*, there are 492 billionaires in the United States and another 1,153 around the world.[30] Together, these 1,645 people control around $6.4 trillion.[31]

Tabulating data from the *Forbes* global billionaires list, I found that 90 percent of the billionaires are male, 65 percent are white, and 60 percent are 60 years of age or older. Just 26 percent are of Asian ancestry, only 10 percent are female, and only 2 percent are under the age of 40. The average age is 63 years.[32] Thirty-three percent of billionaires live in North America, 28 percent are from Europe, 27 percent reside in Asia, 3 percent are from the Middle East, 6 percent live in South or Central America, 2 percent come from Australia and New Zealand, and 1 percent are from Africa.

The United States has nearly one-third of the known billionaires and eight of the top ten wealthiest people in the world. As the Industrial Revolution swept over the country in the nineteenth century, great fortunes were created in the steel, finance, automobile, mining, energy, communications, and real estate industries. Today, owners of computer software, general business investments, and retail firms are at the top of the list. Of the American billionaires, 26 percent live in the East, 23 percent in the South, 17 percent in the Midwest, and 34 percent in the West. Forty states have billionaires, with the largest numbers coming from California (111), New York (88), Texas (50), Florida (34), and Illinois (19). (See appendix table A-2 for the number by state).[33]

With 492 billionaires, the United States has more super-rich people than any other country, followed by China (152), Russia (111), Germany (85), Brazil (65), India (56), the United Kingdom (47), Hong Kong (45), France (43), Italy (35), Canada (32), Australia

(29), Taiwan (28), Japan (27), and South Korea (27). (See appendix table A-1 for the full distribution by country.) Overall, sixty-nine nations, representing one-third of all the countries in the world, have billionaires; two-thirds of nations have none. Most of the countries without billionaires are found in Africa, South America, and parts of Asia and the Middle East.

As the country with the world's fastest-growing major economy, China is rapidly generating remarkably wealthy individuals. One of its richest is billionaire Robin Li, who earned a fortune through digital technology. Li studied computer science at the State University of New York at Buffalo. After getting his master's degree, he went to work for IDD Information Services, a subsidiary of Dow Jones and Company, and while there he helped develop a search algorithm that ranked web pages. He used the patent on that innovation to build his Chinese search engine firm, Baidu, and serves as its chief executive officer.[34]

Another Chinese billionaire is Ren Zhengfei, the founder of the telecommunications equipment and services company Huawei. The firm, which has more than $32 billion in annual sales, is owned by its employees. Ren is described in news accounts as reclusive because he generally does not seek media coverage (an unusual trait among billionaires), yet when I met him at a 2013 technology conference, he was charming, articulate, and funny. With more than 140,000 employees worldwide and partnerships with most of the globe's telecommunications operators, his company is growing at a rapid rate and turning out many products.

Li Ka-shing is a Hong Kong businessman who owns companies that invest in container terminals, electricity, telecommunications, real estate, construction, hotels, and health and beauty stores. His initial success came with a plastics manufacturing company, which he launched with money borrowed from family members and friends; in the early days, he sold plastic flowers. After riots in 1967, he purchased several real estate properties at bargain basement prices and benefited later when the value of the city's real estate shot up dramatically. In recent years, he has diversified into waste processing. In 2013, he paid $1.3 billion for AVR Afvalver-werking, a Dutch company, after purchasing New Zealand's Enviro-Waste. His company's managing director, Kam Hing Lam, noted that "with waste treatment being an imminent issue in most places around the world, we see good growth potential in this business."[35]

One of the richest Russian billionaires is Alisher Usmanov, who built his fortune through government contracts in mining and lumber. He is the largest shareholder in a firm called Metalloinvest, which helps to run the metallurgy business of the government-owned oil and gas company, Gazprom.[36] With money earned through his investments, he has diversified into technology and is a large investor in Russia's second-largest mobile company, MegaFon, and also is part-owner of the largest Internet firm in Russia, Mail.ru.

In India, one of the richest men is business executive Mukesh Ambani, the chair and CEO of Reliance Industries (Ambani supported the opening of Brookings India). Through this Mumbai-based holding company, he has stakes in oil, gas, refining, and retail outlets. He and his wife reside in what is thought to be the most expensive private home in the world: a twenty-seven-floor building called the Antilia that has an estimated value of $1 billion.[37]

Sir Richard Branson of Great Britain displayed entrepreneurial flair during his twenties. While he was awaiting the last flight of a commercial airline to the Virgin Islands, the flight was cancelled, stranding him and a number of other travelers in England. Desperately wanting to reach his destination in order to see a young woman, he chartered an airplane and, hoping to attract other stranded passengers, held up a sign advertising "Virgin Airlines: $29." He filled the flight and thereby paid for the trip. That gave him the idea to form an airline, which has been very successful.[38] Now, he is a pioneer in privately financed spaceflight through his company Virgin Galactic.

French billionaire Bernard Arnault built his wealth through the luxury goods firm LVMH. He started in his father's construction business in France and branched out into real estate and luxury condominiums. He was named CEO of Financière Agache, a luxury goods firm, and acquired Christian Dior. LVMH was formed in 1987 as a merger of Louis Vuitton and Moët Hennessy. The firm sells luxury clothing, luggage, liquor, and perfumes, among other things. Arnault later purchased a major stake in Carrefour, the world's second-largest retail chain. His foundation supports the arts and has funded a young creator award for students.

One of the most dramatic drops in a billionaire's fortune befell Eike Batista, a Brazilian businessman who owns several oil, gas, and mining companies. His father was minister of mines and energy during two presidential administrations in Brazil. The son's early activities focused on gold and diamond trading, but he soon developed a gold mining operation in the Amazon, which made him millions of dollars. From that, he branched out into mining in Canada and Chile and built a global energy empire. He started 2012 with $30 billion, but financial calamity struck as the year progressed. His wealth shrank to $300 million after one of his companies, OGX, announced that it was ceasing oil production due to "unexpectedly challenging geology" in the valuable Blue Shark oil and gas field. Without the revenues from that operation, Batista's wealth dwindled to a fraction of its previous total and the company declared bankruptcy after failing to meet a bond obligation.[39] Its default made Batista's financial collapse one of the biggest and most dramatic in the history of the super wealthy.[40]

While most rich people are older white men, a rapidly increasing number are not. Around half of the world's female billionaires live in China, and most of them are self-made women with rags-to-riches stories. Zhang Xin, for example, worked in Hong Kong factories. During the Cultural Revolution, her parents were sent to rural "re-education camps," and she grew up poor. However, she learned English and got a scholarship to Cambridge University. After working at Goldman Sachs in New York City, she returned to China and launched SOHO China with her husband Pan Shiyi. Their company constructs commercial buildings in Beijing and Shanghai, and the couple has made a fortune. "I think women of our generation went through [the] Cultural Revolution, went through hardship, coming from nowhere, and suddenly see China's amazing opportunity. So women just seized the opportunity," she explained.[41]

Chen Lihua, on the other hand, was a high school dropout who ran a furniture repair shop. But she saved enough money to start a furniture factory and eventually founded Fu Wah, a Beijing conglomerate. She became a successful real estate developer and built the first private museum, the Red Sandalwood Museum, which has furniture from the Ming and Qing dynasties.[42] Women like her succeeded on the strength of their own hard work and ingenuity, often outside male-dominated networks.[43]

One of the wealthiest American members of a minority is Patrick Soon-Shiong. He was born in South Africa to parents who had migrated from China in the 1940s. He later came to the United States, where he earned much of his wealth through the pharmaceutical firms American Pharma Partners and Abraxis BioScience. A surgeon, he has performed islet of Langerhans (pancreatic) transplants, and he invented the first FDA-approved technology for inserting protein nanoparticles into patients suffering from breast cancer.[44] Abraxane, one of the drugs that he developed for cancer therapy, is used in more than forty countries. He devotes much of his current efforts to personalizing medical therapies based on a patient's genetic structure. His goal is to use medical "Big Data" centers to determine which treatments work best for particular individuals.[45]

Jennifer Pritzker, formerly known as James, is the first transgender billionaire. Her family made its fortune through ownership of Hyatt Hotels and the industrial group known as Marmon Holdings, which it sold to Berkshire Hathaway for $4.5 billion in 2007. Pritzker, a former lieutenant in the U.S. Army, has devoted herself to transgender studies. In 2013, she donated $1.35 million to the Palm Center to support the Transgender Military Service Initiative, whose goal is to provide "state-of-the-art scholarship on transgender military service, and to enhance the quality of public dialogue" in that area. She hopes to improve public understanding and knowledge of transgender behavior.[46] Overall, seven of the world's billionaires are openly gay or transgender, including Domenico Dolce, Stefano Gabbana, Michael Kors, David Geffen, Jon Stryker, and Peter Thiel.[47]

Business Sectors

Not all businesses are equally likely to generate large amounts of money. The leading areas for wealth creation, as determined by my tabulation of the percentage of the *Forbes* billionaires in various sectors, are as follows: diversified companies (18 percent of all billionaires); real estate, construction, and hotels (15 percent); retail and consumer goods (14 percent); finance and banking (9 percent); technology (8 percent); energy and mining (7 percent); manufacturing (7 percent); food and beverages (7 percent); health and medical care (5 percent); and business services (5 percent).

The technology field has been the most lucrative in recent decades. It has spawned a number of wealthy individuals known as "technopreneuers."[48] Billionaires in that sector have assets averaging $5.6 billion, followed by those in energy and mining ($4.7 billion), retail ($4.7 billion), diversified companies ($4.1 billion), business services ($3.7 billion), media ($3.4 billion), food and beverages ($3.4 billion), finance ($3.3 billion), manufacturing ($3 billion), real estate and hotels ($2.7 billion), and health care ($2.6 billion).

Younger billionaires are most likely to have earned their fortunes in high technology. As shown in table 6-1, 42 percent of the world's billionaires who are 40 years old or younger made their money in computer software and other technology fields, while 16 percent did so in real estate and hotels, 10 percent in finance and banking, 6 percent in retail, and 3 percent in energy and mining. One of the most prominent young technology entrepreneurs is Mark Zuckerberg, who, along with others, launched the social media firm Facebook in 2004 while he was a student at Harvard University. Seeing

TABLE 6-1. Percent of Billionaires Who Earned Their Fortune in
Selected Business Sectors, by Age of Billionaire

Source	20–39 years	40–59 years	60 or older
Technology	42	12	5
Real estate and hotels	16	14	15
Finance and banking	10	11	9
Energy and mining	3	7	7
Retail	6	10	17
Media	6	3	4
Food and beverages	6	4	7
Manufacturing	6	10	8
Diversified	3	19	17
Health care	0	4	6
Business services	0	5	5

Source: Author's tabulations based on data from Forbes, "The World's Billionaires" (www.forbes.com).

opportunities to connect friends by developing a platform for sharing pictures, life events, and news items, he organized a network initially aimed at college students. It later spread to other areas and became an all-encompassing social media platform.[49]

This pattern contrasts with how those aged 60 or more generated their money. The wealth of older billionaires is most likely to have been earned in real estate and finance (15 percent), retail (17 percent), finance and banking (9 percent), food and beverages (7 percent), and energy and mining (7 percent). Only 5 percent of older billionaires earned their financial fortune through technology companies.

7 Innovative Ideas

SUCCESSFUL ENTREPRENEURS OFTEN are dissatisfied with the status quo and recognize when current companies are not providing needed services or products or are failing to understand broader trends that affect their markets. These individuals excel at anticipating new trends and have the remarkable ability to see around corners. They offer consumers new products or services that align with broader trends unfolding at the time—or they anticipate trends that no one else has considered. Through innovative ideas, they transform entire segments of the market and can become quite rich in the process. In this chapter, I look at the personal visions and societal developments that propelled the creation of great fortunes. Focusing on particular individuals, I examine how they built wealth. A review of their stories demonstrates the range of factors that further wealth creation.

Dissatisfaction with the Status Quo

One of the most common personal characteristics of successful business leaders is dissatisfaction with the status quo. Many of them recognize when existing firms are not meeting current or even potential market demands. That was the case with retail stores in the United States in the 1950s.

Alfred Taubman struggled with dyslexia while he was growing up. Reading was difficult for him, and occasionally he was chastised by his teachers for not keeping up with the other students. Yet he had an unusual talent for design and creative business merchandising. As is often the case with dyslexic students, he could recognize patterns that other people missed, and he could foresee actions several steps down the road. While attending the University of Michigan, Taubman had a number of part-time jobs, including one as an assistant at an Ann Arbor shoe store. One of his responsibilities was to display samples in campus sorority houses and take orders. With a quick glance, he could judge a woman's shoe size from a distance to a remarkably accurate degree. And it wasn't just shoe sizes that he could estimate correctly—he had an innate ability to see what customers wanted even before they made their selections. It was a skill that would help him imagine a very different way of selling shoes and ultimately a wide range of retail products.

In the 1950s, Taubman worked for a construction company that designed and built spaces for small retail establishments in Michigan. As he got involved in various projects, he could see that things were changing for retail companies around Detroit. In the post–World War II era, the automobile and new highway systems were transforming the landscape. People were using cars to gain greater freedom and mobility. They were living farther away from where they worked, and commutes of five or ten miles were becoming more common. The United States was in the early stages of what urban planners eventually would christen the era of suburbanization. However, the people who were moving to the suburbs were not a microcosm of the American public. They had increasing leisure time and discretionary income. As cities became more crowded, dirty, and crime filled, middle-class residents were voting with their feet, buying larger homes on bigger plots of land farther out and pursuing a different lifestyle.

But something was missing. Adequate shopping options did not exist outside of downtown areas, and shoppers had to head there to purchase goods and services. During this period, many of the big department stores were located only in the urban core, and with their significant political power, store executives made it difficult for new chains to enter local markets.

The people who moved to the suburbs had time, money, and mobility, but they were not being well served by the retail configurations or infrastructure of the time. Surveying the changing urban landscape, Taubman believed that it was possible to attract a critical mass of retail outlets to locations closer to suburban households, with convenient access from the new highways that were shrinking drive times and expanding trade areas. And because he could design these "shopping centers" from scratch, he could create an ideal environment for both shopper and merchant.

In his book, *Threshold Resistance*, Taubman noted the importance of design to retail shopping. Stores had to be welcoming, offering easy access to products in order to break down the natural resistance that some shoppers have to making purchases. Retailers had to work hard to encourage people to come into their shops and present them with goods that would make them want to buy. Studying the strengths and shortcomings of traditional urban marketplaces to find ways to lower this so-called "threshold resistance," Taubman decided that he could do better. For example, rather than have store entrances face the street and force customers walk from store to store outside, exposed to traffic and bad weather, stores could open into an indoor pedestrian mall and people could browse in comfort.[1] Whether it was July or January, the shopping experience would be consistent and predictable from season to season.

Taubman had still another idea for how to reduce consumer resistance to purchasing. Rather than have a three-foot-wide front door that had to be physically opened by each customer, stores could be designed to be doorless, completely open at the front, and customers could walk in and out at their leisure. The beauty of the idea was that if stores with open storefronts were built in an indoor mall, people could walk easily and quickly from store to store. Customers would enjoy a pleasant shopping experience, and barriers to consumption would thereby be reduced.

The influential author Malcolm Gladwell wrote an article in the *New Yorker* magazine that detailed the retail innovations that Al Taubman helped to launch.[2] Gladwell extolled Taubman's virtues as a retailer and the creative manner in which he built his shopping centers. He reviewed how the development of malls fit broader trends taking place in society, such as suburbanization, infrastructure development, and highway construction. Out of Taubman's forward-looking observations would come the modern shopping mall, which would transform the city landscape and consumer shopping experience in the years that followed. Taubman would go on to build and operate many high-end shopping malls with some of the highest sales per square foot of any retail establishments in the world.

Taubman Centers, the firm that he founded, became a dominant player in retailing. The developer expanded into department stores and auction houses such as Sotheby's. He also became a donor to many institutions, including the University of Michigan, Harvard University, Brown University, the Illinois Institute of Design, and the Brookings Institution. I got to know him because he had endowed the public policy center that I directed at Brown University. From my dealings with him, I saw that he was someone who could recognize long-term trends as they were unfolding and envision new retail models. Although he was not alone in seeing the rise of suburbanization and the transformative impact of automobiles on housing, employment, and leisure activities, he was a pioneer in understanding the limits of downtown department stores and the value of building large shopping malls in the suburbs, closer to where people with disposable income lived.

In conversations with me, Taubman emphasized the importance of building relationships to succeeding in business. Accomplished people needed to be hard-headed, pragmatic, and action-oriented, and they had to have the connections to bring together a wide range of private and public sector leaders. Completing a major project like a shopping mall requires navigating a detailed permitting process involving zoning, environmental, and traffic officials, as well as negotiating with department stores, small retailers, financial institutions, and political leaders. Government is very involved in the permitting process, and local decisions affect how long it takes to build particular developments and, to some extent, how successful the project is. Making money through malls is not a solo action but one that is affected by societal and government decisions.

Instant Financial Information

A couple of decades after Taubman got his start with malls, another innovator was thinking about the information needs of businesses. The United States, the world's economic superpower, was growing, and executives needed real-time data on market and business conditions. However, in the early 1980s—long before the Internet, blogs, tweets, and social media would become commonplace—it was hard to find market news and real-time information on stock performance.

At the time, Michael Bloomberg was working at the Wall Street securities firm Salomon Brothers. He saw that investment companies and other businesses required immediate market data—waiting minutes, hours, or days for information to be reported in daily newspapers or during evening television newscasts was not sufficient. Delayed reporting made it difficult for investors to act quickly when conditions changed or new information came to light, and lucrative opportunities could be lost before an executive had time to respond.

Bloomberg's opportunity to act on that insight came in 1981, when he was laid off by Salomon. Using his $10 million severance package, Bloomberg launched a new company called Innovative Market Solutions. The company provided corporate clients with financial terminals that provided instantaneous financial data, charted unfolding market trends, and gave investors immediate access to fast-breaking financial news. He leased his first terminals to Merrill Lynch; by 1990, 8,000 terminals were in service. Within 30 years, his company (later renamed Bloomberg L.P.) would install 315,000 terminals around the globe at a cost of $24,000 per device.[3] These machines would take advantage of the Internet network that was then emerging. Through the digitization of information and the growing reach of the finance sector, Bloomberg's idea propelled him to tremendous wealth. He ran for mayor of New York City in 2001 in a largely self-funded campaign and served three terms. Bloomberg Philanthropies, the foundation that he set up, has become one of the largest in the world. He gained renown as a committed yet hard-headed leader who brought a penchant for pragmatic and data-driven decisionmaking to the public sector.

I met Bloomberg at Gracie Mansion one morning in 2010 for a session on immigration reform. He had assembled a group of local government and business executives from around the country for a discussion of why immigration reform was vital to long-term innovation and economic prosperity. Along with pollster Frank Luntz, I gave a talk on the links between immigration and economic development and why it was important to reform current U.S. immigration laws.

As Bloomberg guided the discussion, I could see the qualities that had made him successful. He is very focused on his core priorities and persistent in following through on them; unlike some leaders, he does not get distracted by side issues or trivial considerations. His persistence in pursuing his long-term vision is one of the qualities that have made him enormously successful in both business and public service. Bloomberg's idea for data terminals had fit nicely into the information economy that was emerging. Interviewed later by reporters about the qualities that helped him become rich, Bloomberg said that his secret recipe was "arrive early, stay late, eat lunch at your desk. Oh, and don't go to the bathroom so much." Although some commentators derided this last suggestion as "mind over bladder," an aide pinpointed his boss's strong work ethic as a key attribute of his success.[4]

Making Software Easy to Use

In 1972, on the other side of the country from Bloomberg's New York, Charles Simonyi was working at the Xerox Corporation's Palo Alto Research Center. His task was to help people make sense of the newly emerging technology of computers. Until that point, using a computer required detailed programming skills. A person could not just turn on a computer and get down to the business at hand; he or she first had to learn complex, challenging programming languages. It took considerable effort to master FORTRAN and COBOL, the computer languages that were popular then. I learned this firsthand in 1975 when I took a course on FORTRAN at Miami University in Ohio and discovered how hard it was to write computer instructions. My programs kept getting stuck in endless "do" loops and would not execute the desired commands. Even as an interested undergraduate, I found it very hard to understand FORTRAN, and I ended up getting a C in the class.

Fortunately, there were programmers like Simonyi who understood that for computers to gain wider acceptance, consumers needed an interface that was easy to use. Without some means of language translation, these new electronic gadgets would have remained a product with a limited market, such as universities, large businesses, and scientific users with highly sophisticated programming skills. To meet the needs of other users, during the 1970s Simonyi helped create the first WYSIWYG ("What you see is what you get") text editor, known as Bravo. This software allowed ordinary people to type in text with embedded commands for formatting, margins, and fonts that a preexisting computer language could convert into digital instructions. It represented a huge advance over the previous requirements for using computers.[5]

In 1982, Simonyi was hired by Microsoft, where he became director of application development, chief architect, and distinguished engineer. Simonyi built on his work in Palo Alto and computing advances funded by the federal government to find ways to develop computer software. While at the company, he directed teams that developed key software packages in the Microsoft Office Suite, including the word processing program known as Word and a data-entry and analysis program called Excel.

Those breakthroughs in information processing would make Simonyi extremely wealthy. He would endow professorships at the University of Oxford and Princeton University and support a variety of charitable enterprises in Seattle, Washington. He would marry a Swedish woman named Lisa Persdotter. I met him one day in 2011 at his Bellevue office just outside of Seattle. His personal story intrigued me. He had been born in Hungary and came to the United States in 1968 to get a master's degree in engineering, mathematics, and statistics. He attended graduate school at Stanford University and worked at Xerox before joining Microsoft.

In my conversations with him, he displayed an unususal combination of traits, being both analytical and intuitive. Many smart people are good on one of those dimensions, but it is rare for an individual to have both talents. The ability to combine clever design with technical capacity at the dawn of the Internet era was a special gift. Innovators who saw the match between computer infrastructure development and consumer usability made tremendous fortunes.

Envisioning a Lifestyle Industry

Following graduation from the University of Oregon in 1959, Phil Knight was searching for his way in life. As was common among members of his generation, he spent a year in the army; he then enrolled in the Stanford Graduate School of Business. While there, he took a life-altering course on small business management. Inspired by Frank Shallenberger's discussion of entrepreneurs, he wrote a paper entitled "Can Japanese Sports Shoes Do to German Sports Shoes What Japanese Cameras Did to German Cameras?"

Knight had been a member of the track team at Oregon, and he wanted high-quality running shoes. At the time, however, it was difficult to find them. There did not appear to be much consumer demand for running shoes, and American companies were not targeting that segment of the market. U.S. shoe sellers were staid enterprises that offered few options and did little to promote leisure running or a healthy lifestyle among the general population. Then, during a 1962 information-gathering visit to Japan, Knight saw athletic shoes that were made in Kobe by the Onitsuka company. On the spot, he decided to visit the firm to see the owner. Knight so impressed the Japanese businessman that he won distribution rights to the company's "Tiger" running shoes for the western part of the United States.[6]

It took a year before the footwear was shipped to Knight, but after it arrived, one of his first stops was to see his former Oregon track coach, Bill Bowerman. The coach loved the shoes and placed an order. He then expressed his interest in forming a new company with Knight, and in 1964, the two cofounded Blue Ribbon Sports to fill the then-tiny niche for athletic footwear. A few years later, the company was renamed Nike, after the winged Greek goddess of victory. Over the decades, the company would revolutionize the running shoe business and then expand into other athletic and recreational attire, building a global brand that transformed the lifestyle of millions of people around the world. Knight became a generous supporter of many institutions, including Stanford University, the University of Oregon, and the Brookings Institution, among others.

Spotting Market Inefficiencies through Mathematics

Wealth sometimes arises from an individual's ability to anticipate new trends and create products that take advantage of the opportunities that they present. High-speed stock trading is an example of such a trend. It offered a way for investors to take the enormous processing power of computers to spot inefficiencies in the marketplace and make money out of small differentials in stock valuation.

Jim Simons was a math professor at MIT, Harvard, and the State University of New York at Stony Brook and an internationally renowned expert on multidimensional surfaces and how to measure their size. He won the American Mathematical Society's Oswald Veblen Prize in Geometry for his work on dimensionality. In 1978, while working at a public university, he saw an opportunity to apply mathematical models to the world of financial investment. Through a company called Renaissance Technologies, he developed hedge funds that employed computer-based trading. Searching for minute differentials in stock valuation, the firm executed automatic purchases when those differentials were positive and sales when they turned negative. Using mathematics was a way to make stock trading more analytical and less tied to the whims or impressions of market brokers.

Simons got in on the ground floor of the trend of taking a quantitative approach to financial investment, and his firm created huge wealth for him. Although later that approach would fill a large market niche, in the 1970s and 1980s it was used only infrequently. Critics complained that it created too much of a focus on immediate returns and thereby destroyed the long-term perspective on investing. But its adherents defended it on the grounds that they were bringing higher levels of analysis and rationality to the stock market, which often moved in response to irrational considerations.

Simons used the money from his hedge funds to support a nonprofit group known as Math for America, which emphasizes the importance of math education in the United States and the need for better-trained math instructors in K-12 schools. He also has provided generous gifts to Stony Brook University, the Institute for Advanced Study at Princeton, Brookhaven National Laboratory, and Rockefeller University.

I met him one day in his New York City office. Chain-smoking cigarettes, Simons displayed the nervousness of a scientist on an endless quest to tame the uncertainty of the universe. In the financial world, the greatest unpredictability arises in markets that are driven by rumors and irrational fears or hopes. Simons talked fast and thought out loud, in the manner of a mathematician standing at a blackboard in front of a classroom. But he had a knack for devising methods that could spot inefficiencies arising from irrational impulses. Combining the rationality of a mathematician with the entrepreneurial skills of a businessman, he launched a firm that could take advantage of people's desire for rapid market responses.

Powering the Mobile Revolution

Irwin Jacobs always was interested in engineering. Speaking at a Washington, D.C., forum in 2013 on invention and intellectual property, he related that his high school adviser in New Bedford, Massachusetts, had had doubts about his proposed career. According to the counselor, there was no future in the fields of science and engineering, and he advised the young man to enroll in the Cornell University hotel management program. After a brief detour along that path, Jacobs switched to electrical engineering to study the emerging field of information theory.

He had taught for a number of years at MIT when he began to get more and more consulting requests. When it became clear that digital technology had considerable promise for the future, he formed a company, Linkabit, with Andrew Viterbi and Leonard Kleinrock (who soon left). One of his successful products was designing a satellite terminal for the U.S. armed services that relied on software. He also designed the first analog scrambling device for HBO, which allowed the company to protect its intellectual property.

After selling Linkabit, Jacobs started a company, Qualcomm, that made no tangible products but had many ideas for new possibilities. He understood that digital and wireless technologies were becoming important and that manufacturers needed a means to communicate through mobile devices. Working with others, he came up with the idea for the "code division multiple access" (CDMA) method of accessing communication channels, which allowed others to use spectrum when people stopped talking on wireless phones. The invention proved wildly popular and became the bedrock of the wireless revolution. By solving the interference problems that arose when people used the same communication channel, he improved the efficiency of wireless communications. People could communicate wherever they wanted.

Mobile devices in the 1980s were bulky and unwieldy; researchers had not yet determined how to make the pocket-sized phones that exist today. But realizing that miniaturization was necessary to make phones practical, he and his collaborators developed integrated circuits that packed an extraordinary amount of processing power into a very tiny microchip. Critics claimed that this invention would not work. Jacobs struggled through the microchip development phase, waking up "at 4 a.m. each day to ask himself if it still made sense." Eventually, he would have the answer. His wireless advances made great sense, and they were licensed through hundreds of companies around the world. Soon cell phones and then smartphones would take off, becoming a tremendous benefit to communications, entertainment, and commerce. He would become a billionaire and later devote his time to improving education in the United States. He wanted to make sure that future generations had the same opportunities that he had been offered.

I talked with him following the D.C. event. Brookings had received a corporate gift from his company, and I was curious about his management style. Jacobs had the ability to pinpoint needs and the opportunities that flowed from them. One of the unique things about his firm is that even though it is a large and very profitable company, it has retained the feel of a startup. Jacobs said that he likes to circulate among his employees and keep communications open. Many technology companies have difficulty maintaining their success after the initial wave of innovation. They become highly bureaucratic and cannot sustain the spark of creativity that propels invention, but that does not appear to be a problem with his company.

Restructuring Companies

Companies, even successful ones, often stop operating effectively. Problems might be due to poor leadership, changing economic circumstances, or products that no longer are innovative or popular in the marketplace. For whatever reason, well-established businesses often require reinvigoration and recapitalization to thrive.

David Rubenstein was born into a working-class family in Baltimore, the son of a postal worker and a homemaker. When he was in his mid-twenties he secured a job in the Jimmy Carter White House as deputy to the president's domestic policy adviser. While there, he developed a reputation as the last guy to leave the office. He worked hard, cultivated relationships, and displayed unusual insight and curiosity for someone so young. Yet when Carter lost his reelection bid in 1980, Rubenstein was out of a job. He tried his hand at several pursuits but was not satisfied with the results. He eventually came up with the idea of starting an investment fund that would buy struggling companies, infuse them with new capital, and make them much more profitable.[7]

Rubenstein cofounded the Carlyle Group in 1987 with William Conway and Daniel D'Aniello. The partners raised money from investors and launched buyout funds to purchase the targeted companies. Charging the standard fee of 20 percent of the profits, the Carlyle Group became very successful. From its initial funding of $5 million, it grew to over $180 billion in assets; over time, it delivered over $68 billion in profits to its investors.[8] In its early period, the firm took stakes in defense, electronics, and aeronautics, among other areas. Since then, it has diversified into sectors such as energy, telecommunications, health care, and consumer retail. It has worked with companies such as Hertz, Booz Allen Hamilton, Nielson, and United Defense, helping to reorganize and recapitalize them.

Rubenstein and his partners built a financial network that was global in scope, with offices on six continents. It enlisted big-name advisers such as former president George H. W. Bush, former secretary of state James Baker, former secretary of defense Frank Carlucci, SEC chair Arthur Levitt, former British prime minister John Major, and former Philippines president Fidel Ramos. Along the way, Carlyle pioneered the use of private equity investing. "You're making companies more efficient and helping them grow and become more profitable. That success means our investors—such as public pension funds—benefit, which contributes to the economic wealth of society," Rubenstein said.[9] One of Rubenstein's most impressive traits is his inquisitiveness. I have seen him display his intellectual curiosity and ability to listen while interviewing top government and business leaders. He has a knack for asking seemingly innocuous questions that elicit interesting responses. He is an aggressive listener, one who follows up on small slips of the tongue or hesitations that reveal inner conflicts or hidden meanings. Many billionaires lose their interest in asking questions because they have made so much money that they think that they know everything they need to know. Rubenstein understands that other people have access to information that may be quite valuable to him and that he can learn by listening to what they have to say.

Learning from Short-Term Setbacks

One lesson that stands out among those offered by the careers of many billionaires is the importance of overcoming adversity and learning from short-term ups and downs. One myth about rich people is that they always succeed. In fact, many entrepreneurs suffered early, even repeated, setbacks but demonstrated resilience and went on to achieve long-term success by learning from their failures.[10] Patience and the ability to keep a lengthy time horizon in view are key qualities that distinguish the ultra wealthy from many other people.

Early in his career, for example, Jeff Bezos experienced business difficulties. He had the novel idea that the Internet could serve as a platform for a successful retail operation, and in 1994 he founded Amazon as an online bookseller. Even though people were used to walking into stores and physically touching products, Bezos thought that consumers would like the convenience of online shopping and appreciate being able to compare different products while at home.[11] Despite the seeming allure of that idea, Amazon's profits were slow to materialize. For years, investors questioned his quarterly results while critics doubted his business model and claimed that he was failing as a businessman. Some argued that the company never would make money and criticized Bezos for spending too much on digital infrastructure.[12] The negative commentary continued into the 2000s, when the company moved into cloud computing with Amazon Web Services and Kindle book readers. Outside observers questioned each decision on the grounds that it distracted from the company's strategic focus and would require expensive investments. Some prognosticators forecast permanent damage to the company.

Yet Bezos stayed focused on the long term, and his persistence paid off. Soon Amazon was earning more than $50 billion in revenue and had solidified its place as the dominant online retailer for a wide range of products. No longer was the company limited to books. Instead, consumers could purchase thousands of different items, and businesses could lease space on the Amazon cloud. Amazon became a leader in retailing and providing real-time business analytics for a number of different corporations.

Bezos explained his approach as follows: "We don't give up on things easily. Our third-party seller business is an example of that. It took us three tries to get the third-party seller business to work. We didn't give up. If you're not stubborn, you'll give up on experiments too soon," he said.[13] In his opinion, persistence was the key to his business success. Too many leaders have a short-term perspective that blinds them to long-term opportunities. Investing money and demanding a quick return is not the way to build a successful company—it often takes years for investments to pan out. Patience is a major virtue, especially in industries with strong long-term growth potential.

Following up on his success in e-commerce, Bezos surprised observers in 2013 by purchasing the *Washington Post* for $250 million. In announcing the acquisition, he explained that "journalism plays a critical role in a free society." He said that he believed that buying the paper represented a way to inform readers and improve society. Later, he added, "There's no lone genius who figures it all out and sends down the magic formula [for success]. You study, you debate, you brainstorm, and the answers start to emerge. It takes time. Nothing happens quickly in this mode."[14]

The purchase pleased those who believed that the union of newspapers and digital technology was necessary to save journalism. The past decade had been a time of great challenge for the business models of print media. With readers migrating to smartphones and tablets, print publishers were forced to reinvent themselves for the digital era. But the switch has been a painful and costly one. Having an executive with a long-term orientation offers hope for reinvention of the newspaper industry. Bezos stated recently in the *Harvard Business Review* that "one thing that I learned within the first couple of years of starting a company is that inventing and pioneering involves a willingness to be misunderstood for long periods of time."[15]

Bezos is someone who thinks big. His governing philosophy is not to bring about incremental change but to focus on large-scale transformation of business models. One of his Amazon employees noted that "for many of us, creating Earth's biggest bookstore would have been enough. Jeff's goal was a touch grander: to conquer the world." Anticipating the new challenge of owning a daily newspaper, another employee predicted that "if he goes even halfway through with his much-vaunted reinvention of journalism, there is no way he's not going to break some eggs."[16] A tendency to disrupt the status quo is a trait shared by many billionaires.

8 Not a One-Person Act

IN THE 1983 COMEDY *Trading Places*, actor Dan Aykroyd plays a rich commodities trader named Louis Winthorpe III who involuntarily switches social and economic position with a street hustler named Billy Ray Valentine, played by Eddie Murphy. Winthorpe is stripped of his privileged life, credit cards, job, and money as part of a bet by his managers, Randolph and Mortimer Duke. They do this to resolve the age-old question of whether a person's lot in life is determined by nature or nurture.[1] The wealthy trader is forced to endure the discomforts of poverty, deprivation, and social isolation while the hustler quickly thrives in his new life as a successful business executive aided by lucrative perks. The Duke brothers settle their $1 bet in favor of nurture, but Winthorpe and Valentine join forces to redress the injustice and execute a commodity trade that wins them $394 million at the expense of the Dukes.

In this chapter, I do not pretend to resolve the age-old nature-versus-nurture debate. That is a topic that goes far beyond the scope of this volume. Instead, I suggest that wealth flows from a combination of individual initiative, long-term vision, hard work, good timing, educational opportunities, social networking, and government assistance. Wealth creation often is affected by societal trends, public policy, tax rates, and social welfare programs. In

145

other words, so-called "self-made" men—and women—receive a lot of help along the way.

The Libertarian Perspective

Peter Thiel displayed tremendous foresight in cofounding PayPal, an online payment company, with Max Levchin in 1998. Thiel understood the importance of electronic commerce and the need for a payment system that would enable digital financial transactions. In a world where people increasingly were buying and selling products through the Internet and engaging in a wide variety of financial activities, both businesses and consumers required some mechanism for transferring money.

In Thiel's case, the company was more than a business that generated great wealth. He brought ideological passion to his idea. Not only did he believe in the convenience of an online payment system, he saw it as a way for people to limit government and stop unfair currency manipulation by political authorities. Speaking at a meeting, Thiel argued that "PayPal will give citizens worldwide more direct control over their currencies than they ever had before. It will be nearly impossible for corrupt governments to steal wealth from their people through their old means."[2] Eventually, he sold the firm to eBay and launched several hedge funds and venture capital funds. He purchased a 10 percent stake in Facebook when it was just starting in 2004 for $500,000 and sold most of his shares in 2012 for more than $1 billion. He has used his considerable wealth to support visionary research on anti-aging products, artificial intelligence, and "seasteading" (building new communities on the ocean, beyond the control of governments), among other initiatives.[3]

More controversially, as part of his "20 Under 20" project, Thiel offered $100,000 fellowships to young people under the age of 20 who skip college to launch business ventures instead. His idea is that a college education distracts students from creating new companies, but that notion has attracted derision from others, including, of course, those in the academic community. Speaking at the Nantucket Project, a gathering of leading thinkers to discuss new ideas, Harvard economist Larry Summers complained that the "single most misdirected bit of philanthropy in this decade is Peter Thiel's special program to bribe people to drop out of college."[4]

As a political libertarian, Thiel espouses the view that government power should be quite limited. He has helped fund the election campaigns of libertarian candidates such as Ron Paul and supported the principle that individual entrepreneurs deserve the financial fruits of their efforts. In a Cato Institute essay entitled "The Education of a Libertarian," he wrote that "I stand against confiscatory taxes" and higher taxes on the wealthy.[5] More pointedly, he declared that "the 1920s were the last decade in American history during which one could be genuinely optimistic about politics. Since 1920, the vast increase in welfare beneficiaries and the extension of the franchise to women—two constituencies that are notoriously tough for libertarians—have rendered the notion of 'capitalist democracy' into an oxymoron."[6]

Underlying Thiel's perspective—and similar complaints by some of the super rich—is that people become wealthy on the strength of their own ideas and therefore owe little to society. Certain wealthy individuals who entertain that view are unhappy about the country's "progressive" tax system, which is based on the concept that the tax rates should be higher on those most able to afford it. Some of the wealthy, although not all, favor "flatter" tax rates. They also argue that government should be kept small, with few regulations and other restrictions that they view as interference in their business operations and obstacles to innovation. But these views ignore the public investments that make wealth creation possible.[7] Without several enabling factors, it would be difficult for even the most imaginative and far-sighted individuals to profit to the extraordinary extent that some of them have.

Government Assistance through Infrastructure, Education, and Research

Not all entrepreneurs go to the "small government" extremes of Peter Thiel, but many of them oppose higher taxes on the wealthy on the grounds that creators deserve to keep the money that they make from their ideas and inventions. The irony is that many billionaires and other not-quite-so-wealthy people generated their wealth with direct or indirect government assistance. Even as they complain about government regulation and taxation, they benefit from public investment in infrastructure, education, and research. They could not have developed the products or services that they did without relying on infrastructure built by the public sector and employing people educated through public funding.[8]

For example, much of the industrial revolution was aided by infrastructure development and public education. The government built canals, railroads, highways, and dams and educated the workforce. These construction projects linked the nation and provided a means to ship products to distant sites. Men such as Andrew Carnegie, John D. Rockefeller, and Henry Ford could not have accumulated their vast fortunes without these and other kinds of public investments.

In the current era, the electronic communications networks that people now take for granted were spurred by federal infrastructure development, education funding, and research and development grants. The precursor to the Internet was a U. S. Defense Department digital network known as ARPANET, which connected computers in different geographical locations. Launched in 1969, the system allowed scientists at different universities and U.S. Defense Department officials to exchange information and post notes that could be viewed by others on common computer spaces.[9]

Unlike telephones, which require parties to be on the line at the same time in order to communicate, ARPANET allowed a person to send information asynchronously, without the other person being at the other end to receive the transmission. Scientists could transmit e-mails, access bulletin boards, or review ideas on which others were working without physically being in the same location. This type of communication proved very popular with scientists and members of the defense establishment. It was not until 1991, however, with the formation of the World Wide Web, that the Internet was created as a means of communication among the general public. The web integrated text, images, and sound, facilitating the instantaneous communication of information in several modes. Unlike past electronic systems, which required extensive technical knowledge or specialized programming, the Internet was simple to use.

Marc Andreessen and Eric Bina, both of whom were computer science students at the University of Illinois and worked at the National Center for Supercomputing Applications, created an early Internet browser known as Mosaic in 1992–93. Andreessen saw its transformative potential and cofounded the Netscape Communications Company with Jim Clark to market the product. Mosaic enabled ordinary people to access digital content from around the world. Along with Microsoft's later browser, Internet Explorer, Mosaic powered the Internet, allowing billions of people to benefit from the technology revolution. In 1999, Netscape was purchased by AOL for $4.2 billion.

Within a few years of its formation, the Internet proved very popular, and entrepreneurs began creating companies that facilitated commerce (eBay and Amazon), web searches (Google), social networking (Facebook and Twitter), and many other activities. Those companies hired computer scientists, engineers, and mathematicians, many of whom had been trained at public universities or had even received government scholarships and research and development grants. Andreessen has noted the importance of government support early in his career. He attended the University of Illinois, a public university, and the funds for his graduate studies came from a government fellowship program. As it has been for many other scientific and business ventures, government support was vital to the early development of the Internet and electronic networking.

How Tax and Inheritance Policies
Help the Wealthy Retain Money

Government tax policy is a major factor in enabling people to create and retain wealth. How the government taxes income, determines deductions, sets tax rates, and permits financial resources to pass from generation to generation has a tremendous impact on the extent to which people accumulate resources.

For much of the country's history, there were no significant income or estate taxes, and the government relied primarily on tariffs for income. The federal government enacted its first, temporary, income tax in 1861, to finance its expenditures on the Civil War. It set the tax rate at 3 percent of income greater than $800, and that provision continued in force until the early 1870s, when it lapsed. In 1894, as part of a tariff reduction, Congress passed legislation that applied a 2 percent surcharge on personal income greater than $4,000. That tax was designed to generate revenue for the growing federal government and reduce the tariff duties on goods coming into the United States from abroad. Financial experts believed that the tariffs, which they considered too high, forced up prices, thereby affecting poor people disproportionately. Legislators argued successfully that the government needed an alternative revenue source.

However, just as some individuals do today, wealthy interests protested the income tax, claiming that it was "the entering wedge of socialism." One of the lions of Wall Street, William Gutherie, "raised money for [a] lawsuit among his clients, found a willing litigant named Pollock, and launched an attack that he carried all the way to the highest court."[10] Following hearings in 1895 on *Pollock v. Farmers' Loan & Trust Co.*, the Supreme Court struck down the tax on grounds that the Constitution required direct taxes on interest or personal property to be apportioned by population across the states.[11] In its landmark ruling, the court argued that the income surcharge was such a tax and therefore subject to the Constitution's population apportionment provision.

It was almost two decades later, in 1913, that the Sixteenth Amendment, which gave Congress the "power to lay and collect taxes on incomes, from whatever source derived, without apportionment among the several States, and without regard to any census or enumeration," was added to the Constitution. Congress set the top rate at 7 percent on annual income over $500,000.[12] The top rate affected very few people because not many individuals earned more than half a million dollars a year during that period.

Since then, there have been dramatic fluctuations in the tax rate, taxable income categories, and deductions. The top marginal rate rose to 77 percent during World War I, dropped to 24 percent in 1928, rose to 94 percent in 1944 during World War II, dropped to 50 percent in 1981 and to 28 percent in 1988, rose to 39.6 percent in 1994, dropped to 35 percent in 2004, and rose back to 39.6 percent at the end of 2013.[13] Some of the greatest public controversies now concern deductions and income carve-outs not subject to federal taxes. It is no accident that fights over tax policy are at center stage in Washington and at the heart of partisan disputes over the budget, the debt ceiling, and the role that government plays in society. Twice in the past two decades, the U.S. federal government has shut down because of divisive partisan fights over taxes and spending.

For many years, Congress has allowed individuals tax exemptions under specified circumstances for a range of expenditures. In addition, money earned from capital investments has been treated differently from income and taxed at a lower rate. That provision allows those with capital gains to reduce their tax obligations to a considerable degree. An analysis of the finances of the top 400 American taxpayers reveals that they earned an average of $202 million a year and paid an effective income tax rate of less than 20 percent—that is, a lower rate than the maximum rate paid by individuals earning as little as $35,500.[14]

Those who earn income through private equity investments or hedge funds benefit from other tax rules that are considerably more generous than those governing ordinary income. So-called "carried interest" regulations allow hedge fund managers to declare profits greater than the amount that they contributed to the hedge fund as long-term capital gains, taxed at around 20 percent—not as ordinary income, subject to a marginal 39.6 percent tax rate. That allows them to avoid a large share of the taxes that they would have paid if their gains were treated as ordinary income.[15]

An example of the impact of tax rules can be seen in the case of Henry Kravis and George Roberts, who earned a total of $327 million in 2013 from their private equity firm, KKR. Nearly all their compensation came in the form of dividends and carried interest, not salary income. Kravis garnered dividends of $117.2 million and $43.3 million in carried interest, while Roberts received $121 million in dividends and $43.3 million in carried interest. The remaining $2.2 million of their compensation came in the form of more conventional salary and benefits.[16] Having their money paid in dividends and carried interest almost certainly saved them millions in income taxes.

One of the biggest fiscal fights concerns the estate tax, a levy on money that passes to heirs following the death of an individual. According to current tax law, the first $5.25 million of an estate is exempt from taxes, but amounts above that level are subject to a 40 percent federal tax (plus any state estate taxes). This law is much more generous than the previous policy, changed during the tax-cutting years of the George W. Bush administration. In 2001, for example, only $675,000 was exempt from the estate tax, and amounts above that were taxed at 55 percent.[17]

Other provisions, called "dynasty trusts," help the wealthy pass more resources on to their heirs. Some of these trusts are officially based in South Dakota because the state lacks a state income tax on investments and has a trust law that shields people from estate taxes. South Dakota thus makes it possible for wealthy individuals, including nonresidents, to avoid estate taxes because, unlike most other places, it does not limit the length of a trust to the lifetime of the heir (plus 21 years). That provision helps the super rich "shield a big fortune from estate taxes for centuries as it hands out cash to great-great-great grandchildren and beyond."[18]

For example, casino industry billionaire Sheldon Adelson has avoided $2.8 billion in gift taxes since 2010 "by shuffling his company stock in and out of more than 30 trusts."[19] Doing so allowed him to transfer $7.9 billion to his family members. He is not alone in this practice. According to the U.S. Securities and Exchange Commission, hundreds of wealthy individuals have employed a legal tax shelter—the Walton grantor retained annuity trust (GRAT), after Audrey Walton, an heir to the Wal-Mart fortune—to save billions in taxes over the past decade.

The impact of these tax policies on wealth accumulation is considerable. If one looks at historical variations in income and estate taxes, it becomes clear that current policy is much more generous with respect to wealth accumulation and generational transfer than the policies of one, two, or three decades ago. The United States has gone from an era of high marginal individual income tax rates and high estate taxes to much lower levels today. It also is kinder than many other developed nations to rich people.

Advocates claim that lower taxes encourage the wealthy to invest their incomes in productive enterprises, thus boosting the entire economy. The evidence is mixed, however. Analysis by Brookings Institution scholars William Gale and Samara Potter of the 2001 Bush tax cuts, which favored the wealthy, found that they reduced investment, depressed economic activity, and raised interest rates.[20]

Industry-Specific Legislation

Wealth creation also is affected by government actions intended to benefit specific industries. These actions may come in the form of special laws, tax breaks, regulatory rulings, or public procurement decisions. The U.S. tax code is thousands of pages long and filled with complex rules affecting every company in the country, large or small, successful or otherwise. The adoption or repeal of specific tax provisions or regulatory interpretations can mean thousands or millions of dollars to the businesses affected. Government policies helped entrepreneurs amass the real estate, finance, technology, and retailing fortunes described in previous chapters. Along with other individuals, billionaires got help through favorable tax breaks, government subsidies, or regulatory decisions. They engage in "rent-seeking" behavior that uses the government to boost their economic fortunes.[21]

In a recent CBS News *60 Minutes* interview, Elon Musk described 2008 as "the worst year of my life." He had made $180 million selling his PayPal company to eBay. But after investing most of his money in a space transport firm called SpaceX and an electric car company known as Tesla, he was nearly bankrupt. He had borrowed a lot of money, and it was not clear that his new businesses would survive. He told the interviewer that "I never thought I was someone who could ever be capable of a nervous breakdown. I felt this is the closest I've ever come, because it seemed . . . pretty dark."[22] Yet after three failed space launches, the fourth worked. His company turned around and soon was awarded a $1.6 billion National Air and Space Administration contract. That financial support boosted his company and helped him to get other launch orders.

In addition, up to fifty billionaires in the United States receive farm subsidies for agricultural operations that they control, even if they might have trouble distinguishing a soy bean from an alfalfa seed. Individuals such as Charles Schwab, George Kaiser, Truett Cathy, and Paul Allen obtained those taxpayer-funded subsidies through congressional legislation originally designed to assist working farmers. Some of them also have benefited from federally subsidized crop insurance because the insurance program is not subject to income tests. These programs have made it possible for the super rich to receive public subsidies despite having billions in wealth.[23]

Agriculture and space exploration are just the tip of the iceberg. The government makes major policy decisions affecting offshore drilling, mining on public lands, manufacturing, finance, and exports, among many other areas. For example, the energy sector demonstrates clearly how government actions affect businesses. In the field of alternative energy, for example, Congress has adopted investment tax credits for solar energy products. Homeowners can receive a tax credit of 30 percent of the purchase price of qualifying solar energy devices—a credit that has helped the solar energy industry to flourish and offer products that are becoming competitive with those fueled by other energy sources. Over the past several decades, however, tax policies on solar products have been inconsistent. The tax break has been extended seven times, but it has been allowed to lapse three times.[24] The first investment tax credit for renewable energy was adopted in 1978 following dramatic increases in oil prices by nations aligned with the Organization of Petroleum Exporting Countries. To try to offset the effects of the increases, Congress passed legislation providing generous tax credits for individuals and businesses that purchased solar-powered products.

The credit lapsed in 1986 during the Ronald Reagan administration. Reagan wanted to reduce the role of the government in the U.S. economy and saw decreasing federal support for renewable energy as one way to do that. The policy change created considerable uncertainty for the industry and generally had a detrimental impact on solar companies. In following years, the credit dropped to as low as 10 percent of the purchase price of solar products, while at other times it rose to 30 percent. Industry leaders complain that policy volatility in this area has undermined budding companies and made it difficult for entrepreneurs to succeed in the face of low-cost foreign competition. Business leaders argue that they need predictability in government policy to be successful.

Federal regulatory policy can encourage whole new sectors to flourish. One example is high-frequency stock trading, also known as "flash" trading. Before 2000, people could buy or sell stocks in amounts of one-quarter, one-eighth, or one-sixteenth of a dollar. However, reformers argued that more precise decimal pricing would improve market efficiency and expedite trading.[25] They took their case to the Securities and Exchange Commission (SEC), claiming that it was unfair to price stock transactions in fractions when the financial sector as a whole operated on penny pricing. The agency's commissioners agreed, and in 2000 the SEC passed a rule requiring all U.S. stock exchanges to switch stock valuations from fractions to decimals. The policy change to decimal stock pricing, along with the use of powerful computers, allowed the emerging practice of high-frequency stock trading to flourish. Firms could look for small discrepancies in pricing between individual stocks and market indices and profit by rapidly buying or selling large numbers of shares.

The volume of high-frequency trading increased dramatically in the wake of the shift in SEC regulations. Within a decade, this kind of trading was responsible for more than 60 percent of all the stocks traded in the United States. In 2009, for example, high-speed trading accounted for 3.25 billion of the 6 billion shares transacted each day. It has been estimated that in that year alone the high-frequency trading industry made about $5 billion buying and selling stocks.[26] Today, high-speed trades account for about half of Wall Street's stock market volume.[27] Critics complain that high-frequency trading forces executives to focus on short-term results linked to daily and hourly stock prices to the exclusion of longer-term considerations. In their opinion, such trading has been detrimental because it distracts executives from focusing on a longer time horizon that would be better both for individual companies and for the country as a whole.[28]

Traders also benefited because they were able to purchase early access to *Business Wire* and *Marketwired* news releases that announced corporate earnings, Federal Reserve monthly manufacturing surveys, and ADP monthly employment numbers. Because they gained access "fractions of a second ahead of less fleet-footed investors," they were able to make high-speed trades on that material before others could. An example of this took place on December 5, 2013. Ulta Salon, Cosmetics & Fragrance announced that it had missed analysts' expectations for its quarterly earnings. Before that information was released to the general public, $800,000 of the company's stock was sold, allowing those selling the stock to avoid the losses that accrued to those who traded seconds later.[29]

Writer Michael Lewis critiqued high-speed trading in his recent book *Flash Boys: A Wall Street Revolt.*[30] He claims that the U.S. stock market is rigged for insiders because these investors trade ahead of ordinary investors in their stock transactions. Rather than treating everyone the same, he says, these firms abuse their position and therefore gain an unfair advantage. Yet despite these concerns, the industry has flourished, and the result has been highly lucrative fees for those who run the trading firms. Founders of companies such as Knight Capital, Getco, Citadel, and Renaissance Technologies have made enormous amounts of money, and the amount of financial assets under their control has grown tremendously. In some cases, businesses have sought to combine the advantages of decimal trading with favorable tax policies. For example, the Internal Revenue Service has accused some of these firms of dodging taxes by reclassifying their short-term profits as long-term capital gains. According to the IRS, that practice helped companies generate profits of 80 percent.[31]

Many other companies have benefited from tax breaks given to them specifically, often to encourage them to make investments to bring jobs to particular states and communities. For example, when Dell, Inc. decided to build its company headquarters in a suburb of Austin, Texas, the company received a state government–provided package of "sales-tax rebates, property-tax cuts, and $50 million in tax-free financing." That encouraged the company to remain in Texas and increase the number of jobs there. Later, in 1999, Dell received $200 million in city and state incentives to construct a Nashville manufacturing facility, which led the company to shift jobs from Texas and locate more of its manufacturing in Tennessee.[32]

However, those incentives did not stop Dell from shifting jobs from Nashville when it received even more generous financial enticements from another city. In 2002, it switched half of the Nashville factory's workforce to another facility in a nearby city after officials there offered the company $6 million in tax concessions. By 2004, in return for tax breaks abroad that were even more generous than those available from domestic governments, the company had outsourced many of its jobs overseas and employed more people abroad than in the United States. That outmigration improved the finances of the corporation, helping it to generate even larger revenues and generous compensation packages for its executives.[33]

Living in Washington, D.C., I see firsthand how federal government regulatory policies can help or harm specific sectors or individual companies. Many people view government politics as fights over ideology, but in reality, much of the lobbying concerns the distribution or protection of material benefits. It is no accident that K Street lobby firms are among the fastest growing in the country. Companies employ skilled lobbyists to seek small regulatory changes that can make them millions of dollars; in other cases, they lobby for administrative actions that can hurt their competitors. Firms in the information technology area, for example, are greatly affected by federal privacy, procurement, and antitrust policies. Companies can deliver services to consumers much more easily and profitably if regulations require consumers explicitly to opt out of delivery than if consumers must give approval upfront by opting in.

The Value of Social Networking

Wealth creation is helped enormously by social networking—the old-fashioned, face-to-face kind, not just social media interactions over the Internet. Social, economic, and political contacts help entrepreneurs gain access to financial capital, political intelligence, and government connections. The right ties help business people make deals, gain valuable information, or get government contracts. Sometimes they may get insight into potential growth areas; at other times, a relationship pays off in a crucial business transaction.

According to David Rothkopf in his book *Superclass*, 6,000 "global elites" hold high positions in government, business, and the media, and therefore exercise powerful influence over national and international policy.[34] A number of organizations serve to bring these leaders together. For example, in the United States the Council on Foreign Relations encourages the study and analysis of specific global policy problems and convenes task forces on which experts and business people debate particular challenges and write papers on how to deal with them. The World Economic Forum is a global organization that works on a wide range of international issues, not just the economy. Every January, its gathering in Davos, Switzerland, is attended by top business, political, and civic leaders from around the world, providing a valuable opportunity for social networking and intelligence sharing. The Aspen Institute, which brings together leaders from a number of sectors for educational programs on important issues, holds another gathering that is attended by the wealthy. Its Ideas Festival, held each summer in Colorado, offers a smorgasbord of ideas to be shared among the economic, political, and media elite and is a popular venue for the affluent to connect with one another.

At one roundtable in Aspen organized jointly by the Aspen Institute and the Brookings Institution, I met financier George Soros. Despite his role in founding left-of-center activist organizations such as MoveOn, he is a man who gives little hint of the strong agenda that he pushes to fight social and economic injustice. We spoke about his efforts to encourage international development, especially in Eastern Europe, where he was born. He makes major decisions in a remarkably intuitive manner. He has earned an enormous amount of money on currency transactions by questioning the conventional wisdom. In 1992, for example, he earned an extraordinary amount by betting against the British pound. From my brief meeting with him, it was apparent that he trusted his own instincts, even if others did not share his viewpoint.

The 83-year-old Soros attracted considerable press attention in 2013 when he married a 42-year-old education consultant named Tamiko Bolton. Their wedding reception at the Caramoor Center for Music and the Arts in Westchester County, New York, was attended by more than 500 people. The guests constituted a Who's Who of the politically and economically powerful: World Bank president Jim Yong Kim, rock star Bono, Christine Lagarde of the International Monetary Fund, fellow billionaires Julian Robertson and Paul Tudor Jones, and Nancy Pelosi, the Democratic leader of the U.S. House of Representatives.[35] High-level gatherings provide valuable opportunities for leaders to meet one another, swap gossip, and share insights.

Unethical or Illegal Networking

Some social networking goes beyond information sharing to insider trading.[36] One case that attracted considerable legal attention involved billionaire Raj Rajaratnam and his Galleon Group hedge fund. Working secretly with Rajat Gupta of McKinsey & Company and Goldman Sachs, Rajaratnam used inside tips to make millions of dollars on stock trading. When Gupta received information regarding company earnings, stock market developments, mergers and acquisitions, or major stock investments, he would pass it along to Rajaratnam, who would execute trades and thereby profit from that knowledge before it became publicly available. Both men were convicted of securities fraud and sentenced to prison. As of early 2014, Rajaratnam was incarcerated at a federal medical facility in Massachusetts, while Gupta remained free pending an appeal of his 2012 conviction.

A book entitled *The Billionaire's Apprentice*, by Anita Raghavan, explores the tangled web created by these individuals and shows how both profited enormously from their insider trading.[37]

For example, when Rajaratnam found out from Gupta that Warren Buffett was going to invest $5 billion in Goldman Sachs during the height of the 2008 financial meltdown, Rajaratnam traded on that knowledge and made a large amount of money.

Another example involves Steven A. Cohen and his company, SAC Capital Advisors. Cohen made his fortune through hedge fund investments and lucrative fund management fees. Hedge fund management is one of the most profitable businesses in the U.S. economy. However, after years of investigation, the government found evidence that some of the success of Cohen's firm was built illegally, by trading on inside information. In mid-2013, the company paid $616 million in fines to the Securities and Exchange Commission to settle allegations of insider trading. According to the suit, traders at the firm profited illegally in trading on two pharmaceutical companies (Elan and Wyeth) after receiving secret information from a medical doctor about difficulties that arose in clinical trials of an anti–Alzheimer's disease medication.

Other traders at the same firm have pleaded guilty to insider trading in technology companies, such as Dell.[38] Overall, nine traders at the company were indicted for insider trading, two (including Mathew Martoma) have been found guilty, and six pled guilty.[39] The charges illustrate the temptations that arise in making these kinds of financial transactions. Some dealers seek to gain a competitive advantage by trading on secret information, knowing that when the information becomes public, it is going to move market share prices up or down in a significant way.

Suspicious trading led the Securities and Exchange Commission to file an administrative proceeding alleging that Cohen and his colleagues ignored "red flags" about possible insider trading among company employees. Although the company had compliance policies, the agency published e-mails showing that its executives were aware that its traders had obtained confidential information about upcoming earnings reports and were trading on that material. Prosecutors called the company "a veritable magnet of market cheaters" and said that it had systematic schemes for making money from inside information. The SEC claimed that the firm's actions were "substantial, pervasive and on a scale without known precedent in the history of hedge funds."[40] Those charges led to an additional $1.2 billion fine from the Securities and Exchange Commission and the company's agreement to end its management of outside money. The plea bargain required the company to plead guilty to insider trading and limit its operations to managing Cohen's personal investments.[41]

How Society Aids Wealth Creation

Wealth creation is not a one-person act, despite the myth that some billionaires peddle. The notion of a genius who comes up with a novel invention does indeed have a basis in fact, although it's rarely a case of one or two people working by themselves at the kitchen table or in a garage. Many of the billionaires that I have met developed great ideas that made them rich. But most often, these visionary entrepreneurs worked with teams of people to put their ideas into action, and they were able to commercialize their products and make money with the assistance of societal and government forces.

Directly or indirectly, the public sector educates the workforce, builds the infrastructure, invests in research and development, provides tax breaks, awards contracts, and makes regulatory decisions that are essential to the success of many businesses. These public and social investments lay the groundwork for smart, talented business leaders to innovate, create new products, and develop their enterprises. Some sectors are especially dependent on government. For example, oil, gas, and mining depend considerably on public permits, tax laws, regulation, and in many cases low-cost access to public lands. The information technology industry relies on highly educated workers and the Internet infrastructure, which was built in the early years through government research and development dollars. Banks and other financial service companies need securities and tax laws that encourage investment and trading. Casinos require government licenses to operate—and government social programs to help deal with the consequences of gambling in local communities. Defense companies rely entirely on the government to buy their expensive weapons systems and services. Although business leaders believe that their firms would generate more money without as much government regulation, it would be hard for them to make money without the infrastructure and services provided by the public sector.

With the assistance of government contracts, favorable legislation, or helpful regulatory actions, business leaders in every sector of the economy create jobs and expand their firms. For this reason, executives in general and billionaires in particular have responsibilities to society as a whole. Rather than take the perspective that they owe nothing to the general public and have little obligation to assist others, it is in their self-interest to support the government programs that helped their own businesses succeed and to provide opportunities for other people. As noted decades ago by auto manufacturer Henry Ford, many of these individuals are customers or could be customers if afforded reasonable chances for personal economic advancement.

PART III

WHAT CAN BE DONE?

9 Better Transparency, Governance, and Opportunity

THE POLITICAL SYSTEM in the United States and those in many other countries are beset by weak accountability, lack of transparency, excessive partisanship, and other aspects of unsatisfactory performance. These challenges have many roots, but the wealthification of politics is an important contributor. As outlined in earlier chapters, the super rich control a substantial proportion of the country's total wealth, have policy viewpoints that differ from those of the general population, and have numerous ways to influence political processes, often out of public view.

In addition to influencing public policy, the very rich often gain direct or indirect assistance from government even while many of them fight for a limited role for the public sector—or, at least, they favor limited public benefits for other people. They promote their views by combining electioneering activities with lobbying, issue advocacy, and new models of politically oriented philanthropy. In an era of secretive campaign finance, limited transparency, and increasingly weak news coverage, billionaires have many opportunities to turn their financial resources into political might.

Spending large amounts of money does not, of course, guarantee political, policy, or electoral success. As witnessed by the resounding defeat of the billionaires who spent hundreds of millions of dollars to defeat President Obama, political outcomes depend on many factors, such as how one-sided the dialogue is, the quality of the news coverage, the rules of the game, public opinion, and campaign strategies, among others. Billionaires and their allies can't buy elections or dictate policy outcomes in all circumstances, but their money puts them in a position where they often can determine the agenda and shape the ultimate decisions.

The increasing weakness of countervailing institutions, such as the news media and political parties, makes it difficult for the rest of society to restrain the power of the rich and other special interests. Around the world, billionaires have purchased major news outlets and provided considerable funding for party organizations and special interest groups. In a number of countries, they even have run for public office themselves. On tax issues, liberal and conservative billionaires are nearly united in opposing any higher taxes that they would have to pay. For years, their resistance to increases has made it difficult for the public sector to find the money to invest in opportunities for other people.

In this chapter, I argue that people need to address wealthification at several different levels: political, social, and economic. The country requires policies that expand transparency, strengthen governance, improve news coverage, promote tax fairness, and create more equitable educational possibilities. In essence, countries around the world should further social and economic opportunity so that more people have a better shot at personal economic advancement.

Greater Transparency

Anyone paying the slightest amount of attention recognizes that the U.S. political system is performing poorly—unless, of course, one believes that it would be better if the political system did not work at all. Washington is gripped by extreme partisanship, which prevents Congress from conducting even routine business, and cooperation between the executive and legislative branches is near historic lows. But the problem with the nation's politics is even deeper than the daily headlines suggest. There is limited transparency surrounding money and politics, and many institutions that in the past could counterbalance the power of the wealthy and other special interests have grown weak. It is difficult for financially strapped news organizations to provide quality coverage of government, and political parties have become heavily dependent on a relatively small number of wealthy and well-connected people for campaign contributions.

Supreme Court rulings in the United States have created a situation in which large amounts of secret money are flowing into elective politics and influencing public policy at all levels of government. With the *Citizens United* v. *Federal Election Commission* and *McCutcheon* v. *Federal Election Commission* decisions, it is easier than it has been in many years for wealthy individuals to spend enormous amounts of money to influence elections. The 501(c)(4) "social welfare" groups recognized by the Internal Revenue Service and the super PACs allowed by the Federal Elections Commission have blurred the boundaries between different sectors. These rulings allow the wealthy to spend millions of dollars in secret to influence elections and public policy, thereby undermining democratic accountability and representation. An analysis by the nonprofit Center for Responsive Politics shows that spending by these tax-exempt nonprofit groups grew from $5.8 million in the 2004 elections to $310.8 million in 2012. About 40 percent of donors either are not disclosed or are only partially disclosed.[1]

In the past, social welfare organizations focused on nonpartisan "do-gooding." They raised money that helped people deal with concrete problems. Grant recipients weren't especially political or partisan in how they pursued their missions. In recent years, however, new types of groups have emerged to take advantage of U.S. tax laws. With the aid of favorable legal decisions, 501(c)(4) organizations have engaged in explicitly political activity: supporting or opposing candidates, lobbying for laws and policies that they favor, and influencing public opinion. That would not be problematic if they were not acting through a "not-for-profit" organizational structure—a fact that under the tax code means that their work is, in effect, subsidized by all taxpayers. Any individual or organization can engage in electoral advocacy. Indeed, the ability to speak and organize is the essence of democracy. But political activism has broad risks for society as a whole when it takes place through tax-exempt entities that supposedly are social welfare organizations, which are not required to disclose their donors.[2]

The outpouring of activism by tax-exempt organizations has led to calls for clearer rules regarding political activity. New proposals from the Internal Revenue Service have suggested that groups must focus "exclusively" on social welfare as opposed to electioneering. Those organizations classified as 501(c)(4) would be prohibited from supporting "advertisements that mention a candidate within sixty days of an election," engaging in voter registration or get-out-the-vote efforts, or sponsoring within sixty days of a general election events at which candidates appear, even bipartisan debates.[3]

This proposal, released in November 2013, generated criticism from the left and the right. Around 150,000 comments were received from various organizations about the proposed rules.[4] Many groups complained that the proposal was overly broad, and they defended their right not to disclose their donors on the grounds that disclosure would subject them to possible political retaliation. From their standpoint, greater transparency would be problematic. The reality is that cracking down on social welfare groups may merely push electoral advocacy to other parts of the system. If people cannot influence politics through putative social welfare organizations, they may form super PACs or use other types of nonprofit organizations to circumvent IRS rules. Squeezing one part of the money balloon will push the money to other parts of the balloon.

But that fact notwithstanding, policymakers need to clarify the regulations that govern each type of advocacy. Currently, different rules govern tax exemption, deductibility of gifts, and disclosure, depending on the category of organization. That creates uncertainty for groups, donors, and regulators. Activists are not sure what restrictions they face in various areas, and regulators cannot be sure what legal authority they have to oversee political activity. The result is a Wild West of political activism. With limited disclosure and poor accountability, it is the worst of all possible worlds. The public has little access to information about what is being spent to influence elections (other than information that rich people voluntarily disclose) and how the super wealthy are using their financial resources to shape public policy. That allows the rich to influence local, national, and global debates in secret, raising serious risks for the political system as a whole.[5]

It often is difficult to trace cash flows because so-called "dark money" is just that, deliberately hidden from public view, sometimes in violation of laws or regulations. An investigation in California, for example, found that several political groups spent money on referendum campaigns without making the public disclosures required by state law. The state's Fair Political Practices Commission fined the organizations the sum of $16 million, based on the illegal contributions that they received. These groups had put considerable effort into fighting proposed tax hikes and supporting limits on union political activities. The measures were financially backed by Sheldon Adelson, Charles and David Koch, Eli Broad, Charles Schwab, and Wayne Hughes, among others.[6]

In its investigation, the commission found that "the groups are part of an intricate, interlocking network of political nonprofits that have taken on a prominent role in state and national politics in recent years, bolstered by legal and regulatory shifts, including the Supreme Court's *Citizens United* decision in 2010."[7] If voters do not know who is behind certain campaign activities, it is difficult for them to judge the donors' motives or actions.

Improved Governance, Starting with the Senate

In the opening chapter, I described the "get a senator" strategy favored by certain wealthy individuals. This is an example of how billionaires and special interests with political connections in the U.S. Senate are able to block nominations and legislation that they oppose and promote legislation that they support. Preventing congressional action is especially easy if someone gets a compliant senator to impose secret "holds," or object to "unanimous consent" motions, or engage in filibusters that prevent legislation from reaching a vote, even when it has majority support. The virtue of this approach is that it only takes a single senator to execute the strategy.

In a decentralized political system, it is possible to achieve tremendous influence by working well-known veto points in the legislative process. The most obvious and frequently used veto point is the Senate, where entrenched interests can prevent action simply by applying various Senate rules. For example, any senator can place a secret hold on a presidential appointment to an executive branch post or federal judgeship, effectively derailing the Senate from moving forward with consideration of the appointment. This sometimes even prevents committee hearings from taking place or, more frequently, blocks nominations from reaching a vote by the full Senate.

Similarly, a single senator can slow down the legislative process by objecting to the unanimous consent needed for most votes. In the arcane world of Senate rules, there are many places where complete unanimity is required just to bring legislation to the floor for debate. If any one senator objects, the Senate cannot debate or vote until leaders of both parties agree on a plan to move ahead. It is easy for special interests to block action by having a senator object.

Finally, senators can delay or even block floor votes by filibustering a bill. By talking the bill to death, they can prevent legislative consideration and keep the leadership from scheduling a formal vote. In what some now see as the good old days, senators actually had to take to the floor and talk for hours to stop legislation. Today, they can prevent action just by threatening to filibuster. Senate experts have found a dramatic increase in the use of the filibuster in recent years. Previously filibusters were limited to matters of conscience or grave issues facing the country, but today senators filibuster major bills, minor bills, and administration nominations—anything they want to stop the majority from approving. The chamber as a whole can stop filibusters through cloture votes that end discussion. But it takes a supermajority of sixty senators to do so on major nominations or policy legislation.[8] In a polarized political system, such as the one that has prevailed in recent years, it is difficult to muster sixty votes for anything.

Several reforms would make it more difficult for small sets of influential people to stop congressional legislation or presidential appointments. Rather than allowing holds to be placed in secret, senators would make their holds public, and there would be time limits on their use. Walter Oleszek of the Congressional Research Service, who has studied this issue, notes reforms that would impose a three-day, three-week, or forty-five- or sixty-day limit on holds.[9] Such time limits would improve the transparency and accountability of Senate deliberations and prevent unreasonable delays.

In addition, the Senate should consider reforming its rules to make it more difficult for senators to stop floor action by objecting to unanimous consent requests and by mounting frequent filibusters of legislation. Majority Democrats in 2013 forced through small steps that severely limit filibusters of certain executive branch and judicial nominations. Rather than needing sixty votes to end such a filibuster, the Senate now can do so through a majority vote. Senators also should consider legislation that would alter the number of votes required to end any filibuster as debate time passed. For example, Senator Tom Harkin (D-Iowa) has proposed that the vote required for cloture should start out at sixty but drop by "a decreasing majority of senators over a period of eight days."[10]

Strengthening News Coverage

The news media play a crucial role in democratic systems. Voters count on reporters to act as an early warning system with respect to influence peddling and other political abuses. With the concentration of income among the the super rich and their political activism, it is especially important for the media to inform the public about the role that moneyed and other special interests play in government and society.[11] However, there are reasons why news organizations' reporting and ability to hold political leaders accountable have become weakened. For starters, newspapers and other print news media—historically the major sources of serious coverage of government news—have lost subscribers and advertisers to the Internet and have cut back their news reporting in response.

Another factor is that billionaires have co-opted major parts of the news industry by buying top newspapers, magazines, television networks, and Internet portals. In the United States, individuals such as Michael Bloomberg, Rupert Murdoch, John Henry, and Jeff Bezos control major news outlets. Murdoch, who owns Fox News, has attracted the greatest controversy; critics decry what they say is a conservative bias at the television network due to his ownership. This kind of criticism comes up in numerous countries around the world where the rich own major communications outlets. Outside observers always worry that personal ownership by the rich makes it difficult for reporters to act as a check on the wealthy.

In addition, too much of contemporary reporting relies on the "Noah's ark" approach of pairing opposites to comment on the news. This approach reinforces political polarization and makes it difficult for people to grasp the essence of policy debates. Discussions of billionaires, for example, often condemn them either as the greedy "1 percent" or praise them as noble entrepreneurs, with no nuance in between. That does little to inform civil dialogue about money and politics.

The Internet offers some potential help. Through its interactive features and use of data visualization and information mapping, it has the potential to improve diversity in news coverage and provide greater depth in reporting. Journalists have limited space in their print-based articles, but online they can link to in-depth reports and provide people with ways to get much-needed additional information.

Tech investor Marc Andreessen says that there are several media practices that hold the industry back. For example, in a widely publicized series of tweets, he says that traditional news organizations have a bloated cost structure, are too married to objectivity as an industry norm, and suffer from too much market competition. He suggests that media companies need to realign costs with revenues, become less hierarchical, avoid false equivalences in coverage, and identify niches where they can build audiences and make money.[12]

Search engines represent a way to improve the quality and depth of news coverage. Right now, wealthy people and corporations drive much of the news coverage through their ownership of prominent platforms and expertise in political messaging. Major search algorithms elevate articles covered by those outlets on the grounds that they generate a lot of page views and therefore are more helpful than others that do not. This technique, however, biases the presentation of information, giving priority to popularity as opposed to thoughtfulness, reasonableness, or diversity of perspectives. Digital firms should add criteria to their search engines that highlight information quality as opposed to mere popularity. So-called "editor's picks" could direct news consumers toward high-quality information sources that present diverse viewpoints and in-depth reporting and analysis.

Better Opportunity

Auto magnate Henry Ford was a far-sighted capitalist who understood the importance of customers to his business. When asked why he paid his factory workers double the rate ($5 a day) extended by other manufacturers, he explained that he saw them as purchasers of his products. Paying good wages was vital to his company because it would enable his employees to buy cars.[13] That was not an altruistic sentiment. He understood that it made long-term corporate sense to have prosperous workers. Decently paid employees would build a viable middle class and that would be good for business, he reasoned. Some executives today appear to have lost that perspective. In a drive to keep corporate costs low (and profits high), they pay workers as little as possible, cut or even try to eliminate pensions, and offer the minimum in terms of health care benefits.[14] They support organizations that advocate against social welfare benefits for workers and policies that provide access to educational opportunities. In certain cases, they seem to reject Ford's insight from many decades ago that capitalism requires robust consumers and basic fairness within the system as a whole.

There is little question that income inequality has been a persistent problem throughout human civilization and remains a pressing challenge in the contemporary period. Yet the research presented in this volume shows that the United States and the world as a whole have alternated between periods of greater and lesser inequality. There has been no constancy in the level of income concentration over various points in time. The particular level at any given point depends on public policies, tax levels, inheritance policies, and social welfare provisions as well as overall economic conditions. Despite arguments about its immutability, high income inequality is not a fixed fact of human existence. Levels of inequality actually have varied substantially over time and across societies.

Eras in which economic inequality was pronounced often have been problematic for the middle class and have featured economic crises that undermined general prosperity and stability. That certainly was the case in the 1920s and the 2000s, the two periods exhibiting the greatest inequality in the United States in the modern era. The first period ended with a Great Depression, while the

FIGURE 9-1. Preferences about Wealth Distribution
Percent

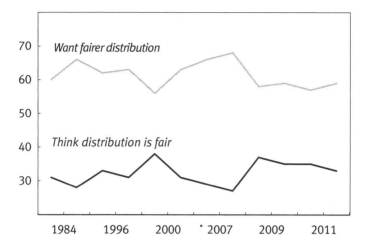

Source: Frank Newport, "Majority in U.S. Want Wealth More Evenly Distributed," Gallup
Organization, April 17, 2013.

second has seen the turmoil of the Great Recession and its resulting
financial collapse and lingering high unemployment.

There have been shifts over time in how Americans feel about the
distribution of wealth. Over the past 30 years, the Gallup Organization has asked people the following question: "Do you feel that the
distribution of money and wealth in this country today is fair, or do
you feel that the money and wealth in this country should be more
evenly distributed among a larger percentage of the people?" Figure
9-1 shows the results for 1984 through 2013. A clear majority of
people over this time period supported a more even distribution.
An average of 61 percent of Americans say that they want a more
even wealth distribution, while around 32 percent say that they
believe the current pattern is fair.[15] The high point in perceptions
of American inequality occurred in 2008, when 68 percent felt that
the current distribution should be more even. That was right after

FIGURE 9-2. Preferences about Taxing Wealth

Percent

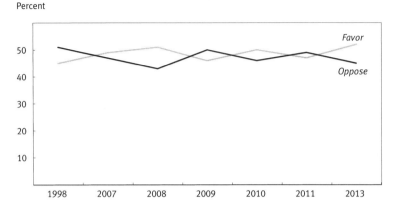

Source: Frank Newport, "Majority in U.S. Want Wealth More Evenly Distributed," Gallup Organization, April 17, 2013.

the collapse of the stock market and the subsequent financial crisis. People were concerned about economic sustainability and feared that high inequality was part of the cause of the country's poor economic performance.[16]

As a result of their preference for greater equity, a majority of Americans now favor increasing taxes on the rich as one way to produce a fairer distribution of financial resources. For the past couple of decades, Gallup has asked, "Do you think our government should or should not redistribute wealth by heavy taxes on the rich?"[17]

Over time, pro-tax sentiments have edged up. In 1998, 45 percent of Americans favored "heavy taxes on the rich" as a way to redistribute wealth, while 51 percent opposed them (see figure 9-2). By 2013, however, those numbers had reversed. At that time, 52 percent supported heavy taxes on the rich and 45 percent opposed them.

In addition, the Pew Research Center undertook a national survey in 2014 on public feelings about income inequality. It found that during the last 10 years, 65 percent of Americans felt that the "gap between rich and everyone else" had increased, 8 percent believed that it had decreased, and 25 percent thought that it had stayed the same. Sixty-nine percent said that the government should do "a lot" or "something" to reduce the gap, while 26 percent believed that the government should do nothing or not much. Fifty-four percent said that the best way to reduce poverty was to raise taxes on the wealthy and corporations to expand programs for the poor. When asked why some people are poor while others are rich, 51 percent said someone becomes rich "because he or she had more advantages than others," while 38 percent said it was "because he or she worked harder than others."[18]

Fairer Tax Policies

The U.S. tax code is neither fair nor efficient. Although tax law is supposedly "progressive" in that the stated rates are greater on higher incomes and the really poor are exempt from income taxes, in actual practice it reinforces inequality and undermines mobility through a number of provisions. It has many exclusions that allow wealthy people to shield much—and in some cases even all—of their income from taxation and pass resources to their heirs at low rates of taxation. For example, a study by the Congressional Budget Office found that the top 1 percent of earners reaped 17 percent of the tax benefits from credits and deductions and that the top 20 percent got 50 percent of the benefits overall.[19]

Overall, the top tax deductions (many of which benefit middle-class earners as well as the wealthy) cost the federal government around $925 billion in revenue each year. That is almost as much as is collected through income taxes in general. In recent years, for example, a total of $1.1 trillion was collected through individual income taxes.[20] If there were no deductions, the government could cut income taxes in half and maintain about the same level of budgetary expenditures. Some of these deductions benefit a broad swath of people, while others help the wealthy disproportionately.

Among the largest exclusions are the following: employer-provided health insurance (around $260 billion in tax savings), favorable treatment of dividends and capital gains ($160 billion), retirement savings ($140 billion), state and local taxes ($80 billion), mortgage interest ($70 billion), child tax credit ($60 billion), earned income tax credit ($60 billion), capital gains benefits from assets received following someone's death ($50 billion), charitable contributions ($40 billion), Social Security benefits ($35 billion), and "carried interest" ($17.4 billion).[21]

Three of those deductions are especially advantageous to the super wealthy: those for capital gains, for carried interest for hedge fund and private equity investors, and for estate taxes.[22] Capital gains rules help the wealthy in particular by treating income earned through investment appreciation at lower rates than "earned income," such as salaries. Asset gains are subject to a 20 percent tax rate for assets held longer than six months. If the money is treated as ordinary income, the top marginal rate is 39.6 percent on incomes of $400,000 or more for individuals or $450,000 for couples. The Congressional Budget Office estimates that 70 percent of the financial gains derived from favorable treatment of dividends and capital gains goes to the top 1 percent of wage earners and 90 percent accrues to the top 20 percent. As a result of favorable treatment of dividends and capital gains, the after-tax income of the top 1 percent has been estimated to increase by 5 percent and that of the highest 20 percent by 2 percent.[23] Most homeowners, of whatever income bracket, also benefit from the exclusion of some of the proceeds of a home sale from capital gains taxes.

There are similar carve-outs for carried interest, earnings from the fees that hedge fund and private equity fund managers charge investors for supervising portfolios.[24] Under current law, these earnings are taxed at the same 20 percent rate as long-term capital gains. Fund managers claim that the favorable treatment is justified because they need to be compensated for risking their capital. Critics, however, point out that managers benefit in some cases despite having little personal money involved.[25] The previously obscure issue of carried interest came to the fore during the 2012 presidential campaign because Republican candidate Mitt Romney had benefited from the tax break during the years he ran a major private equity firm, Bain Capital. If the earnings were taxed as ordinary income, a number of high-earning individuals likely would pay a much higher rate, since the maximum marginal rate in 2014 is 39.6 percent.[26] The Congressional Budget Office estimated last year that taxing carried interest as ordinary income would generate $17.4 billion in additional tax revenue for the government over the 2014–23 decade.[27]

Policies on estate taxes help the super wealthy pass money across generations in several different ways. The federal tax code allows anyone to leave up to $5 million to heirs tax free.[28] This figure is adjusted for inflation, so it rose to $5.25 million in 2013. Since only 4,000 households in the United States have assets higher than $10.5 million (the combined total of the estate tax exemption for a married couple), the United States has virtually eliminated the estate tax for most people. Showing how dramatically the estate tax has been scaled back over recent years, as recently as 2001 individual estates were subject to a 55 percent tax on amounts over $675,000. Congress sharply cut back the estate tax during the George W. Bush administration in response to a campaign by wealthy landowners and others who called it the "death tax."

In another generous provision benefiting primarily the wealthy, current rules tax gains on assets from the day that they are inherited, not on gains from the day that the assets were originally acquired. This provision saves the wealthy $258 billion over a five-year period.[29] Eliminating the exclusion of capital gains at death through this rule, called "step-up in basis," would add considerable progressivity to the tax code. Right now, according to the Congressional Budget Office, 65 percent of this tax benefit goes to the top 20 percent of wage earners.[30]

Some ultra-wealthy individuals also have employed "dynasty trusts" based in South Dakota to avoid the federal estate tax. It has been estimated that $121 billion has been shielded from federal taxes by people taking advantage of the South Dakota law, which allows trusts to last beyond the conventional period of an individual's lifetime plus 21 years.[31] Since South Dakota is the only place in the United States that has such generous tax provisions, political leaders should close that loophole in the name of tax fairness vis-à-vis the other forty-nine states.

To combat the cumulative impact of pro-wealthy deductions, some leaders have proposed the "Buffet Rule" (named after its principal advocate, the Omaha investor Warren Buffet), which would levy a 30 percent minimum tax on those earning over $1 million annually. Buffet's rationale for this tax is that it is unfair if the wealthy pay a lower tax rate than their employees—in Buffet's case, his executive assistant. If enacted, this tax—which would apply to around 200,000 U.S. taxpayers (or 0.06 percent of the total)—would raise around $367 billion over the next decade.[32]

Many wealthy people feel that U.S. income taxes are too high. Yet according to the Organization for Economic Cooperation and Development (OECD), the total income tax rate in the United States is well below that of other Western nations. While the combined rate for U.S. individual income and payroll taxes totals 31.3 percent, the rate is 55.8 in Belgium, 49.3 percent in Germany, 49.1 percent in Austria, 49 percent in Hungary, and 48.9 percent in France. The average for the OECD as a whole is 36 percent; with a rank of twenty-sixth among thirty-five nations, the United States is well below that number.[33]

Corporate Jet Deductions

Another point of contention in tax policy concerns the deductibility of expenses for private and corporate jets, which are very expensive to purchase, operate, and maintain. Light jets seating five to eight individuals cost from $3 to $8 million each, while large executive jets that can transport up to twelve passengers run between $17 and $45 million. Once the plane is purchased, annual operating costs for pilots, fuel, and insurance can total more than $200,000.[34] Yet despite the high cost, having a private aircraft is a perk strongly desired by business executives. Many of them travel as often as several times a month, so having a company plane, which helps executives move around the world in a convenient and efficient manner, is a huge time-saver; in addition, it offers a dramatic boost in terms of ease, personal comfort, and productivity.

Tax provisions in this area were sweetened after the 9/11 terrorist attacks and then maintained in the aftermath of the global financial crisis. Sales of jets dropped after both events, and jet manufacturers, who say that their industry employs 1.2 million people in the United States,[35] complained that they needed special help to regain their financial footing. Even in 2014, private jet sales were half of what they had been the decade before.[36]

Current tax law specifies that companies can write off the costs of corporate jets used for business purposes over a five-year period. This is more generous than the provisions for charter or commercial planes, which must be depreciated over seven years. It has been estimated that ending this provision would save the U.S. Treasury around $3 billion over 10 years.[37]

Executives can write off certain business expenses related to jets as long as they meet Internal Revenue Service rules. The write-offs include costs such as pilot salaries, maintenance, fuel, insurance, and take-off and landing fees. But there are detailed regulations concerning deductibility. For example, deductions must be for "ordinary and necessary" business expenses and costs must be related to the "active conduct of the taxpayer's trade or business." Executives must keep logs that distinguish between personal and business uses of the aircraft and cannot deduct any expenses for "entertainment, amusement, or recreation activities."[38]

In general, U.S. tax provisions on corporate jets are much more generous than those of other nations. Few of the European billionaires that I know fly on corporate jets. They fly first class, but they do so on commercial airlines, and they go to airports and wade through security lines just as most other travelers do. They are not insulated from commercial air travel, as are American billionaires who have their own planes and fly out of separate hangars. The United Kingdom, for example, raised its value-added taxes on private jets in 2011 in response to European Union Commission proceedings that concluded that British tax laws were overly generous compared with those of other European nations. The commission ordered the United Kingdom to raise its aircraft sales tax from zero to 20 percent.[39]

It is much harder to finance aircraft purchases in Europe. Ever since the 2010 Basel III accords, European banks have imposed very strict rules on risk assessment and lending practices. Buyers are required to keep sufficient reserves, and they must justify the creditworthiness and collateral requirements for aircraft loans. One corporate client complained that in "purchasing an airplane from a European bank, [he] recently faced the kind of scrutiny normally reserved for convicted felons."[40] His company, a large firm, had to provide data on costs, depreciation schedules, business benefits, and travel frequency before the loan was approved.

According to the General Aviation Manufacturers Association, 11,261 private jets currently are registered in the United States while only 7,997 are registered abroad. In terms of the future market for private jets, it is estimated that 49.7 percent of expected orders will be placed in the United States, 20.8 percent in Europe, 11.8 percent in Asia, 11.6 percent in Central and South America, and 6.1 percent in the Middle East.[41]

It is easy to understand the convenience associated with private jets. In a commencement speech at Duke University, billionaire Oprah Winfrey said of her plane: "That is what makes me feel successful. Of all the wonderful things that have happened, including getting a doctorate, an honorary doctorate from Duke, what really makes me feel successful is being able to use my life in service to someone else's

. . . and it is really fantastic to have your own jet, and anybody who says it isn't is lying to you. That jet thing is really good."[42] I experienced this convenience firsthand a couple of years ago. Following a board meeting, a trustee offered me and some colleagues a ride on his corporate jet. The sleek plane provided large windows, wi-fi Internet service, quality cuisine, and fast speed (four hours coast to coast). It definitely beat the red-eye coach flight on which my co-workers and I had been booked previously. But that fact notwithstanding, U.S. tax law is much more generous than European law in subsidizing corporate jets, and its current provisions are much more generous that provisions from a decade ago. We need to weigh the costs and benefits of these tax subsidies and compare them with those of policies that would create opportunities for a broader set of Americans.

More Reasonable Executive Compensation

The skyrocketing compensation of business executives around the world has contributed to the income gap between executives and company employees. A few decades ago, chief executives made five or ten times the salary of the average employee in their company, but now they earn 50 to 100 times more than the typical worker. From 1978 to 2011, the average compensation of CEOs—including salary, benefits, and stock options—rose 725 percent while it rose only 5.7 percent for the average worker.[43] The rationale for increasing executive compensation emphasizes the need to maintain competitiveness with other businesses. Corporate boards and executives insist that they need to compete in the marketplace when recruiting and retaining talented leaders. They have boosted executive pay and provided very generous stock options to attract leaders who deliver effective results. Companies justify high compensation based on its alleged link to better business performance. Yet research has shown little connection between executive pay and company performance. The research company Obermatt "compared the compensation of C.E.O.s at publicly traded firms and their performance and found no correlation between the two."[44] This research suggests that high pay does not guarantee quality performance.

In 2010, Congress passed the Dodd-Frank Act to improve transparency and oversight in the financial industry. Among other provisions was a requirement that corporate shareholders vote on executive compensation at least once every three years. This so-called "say on pay" provision was designed to give those who own company equity a chance to express their views on executive performance and high-level compensation. While the provision has drawn attention to this topic, in practice it has had little impact. Bowing to business pressure, the law specified that such votes would be only advisory in nature. Even if executive compensation fails to get majority support from shareholders, that lack of support has no legal bearing on the leader's actual pay package. And in any event, shareholders have approved 97 percent of the executive packages put before them.[45]

Furthering Mobility

Better equity can be obtained not just through adopting a progressive tax code but through improving education, health care, and other social benefits. People should have reasonable opportunities for individual advancement. The country needs more options than are currently available for creative people to emerge and have a chance to build the kinds of innovations that have been seen in the past. As pointed out by George Mason University economist Tyler Cowan, the United States needs to keep investing in long-term solutions in order to escape the grip of what he calls the "great stagnation."[46]

Research by the Boston Consulting Group for the Sutton Trust in Great Britain found that there, "closing the educational attainment gap could add 4% to Gross Domestic Product."[47] Investing in human capital can have surprisingly large social and economic benefits, especially for those of humble origins. Unless students who are educated in a system characterized by what writer Jonathan Kozol calls "savage inequalities" are given opportunities to create better prospects for themselves, they are cheated out of their future.[48] A surprisingly large number of billionaires come from working-class backgrounds. Their origins may be humble, but through talent, vision, and high motivation, they develop ideas and put themselves in a position to make major contributions. In addition, many of them receive significant help from public institutions along the way: they attend taxpayer-supported colleges and universities; some receive government scholarships or fellowships, especially in the areas of science and technology; and others built companies that benefit directly from federal investments in research and development.

Public boosts, which have helped many individuals become wealthy and increase their fortune, also can be productive investments for low- or middle-income recipients. The government can promote social and economic opportunity through various kinds of assistance programs. The most direct form of government aid to the poor, including the working poor, is what economists call "cash transfers," or money given directly to the poor, often with certain conditions attached. The United States uses only a few kinds of cash transfer—for example, disability and unemployment benefits and welfare assistance for needy families. But several federal and state government programs have a similar impact—for example, food stamps, housing subsidies, free or low-cost health insurance, and income tax credits. A 2012 study by the Organization for Economic Cooperation and Development found that cash transfers had the greatest impact on reducing overall income inequality among the thirty-four member nations. In these developed countries, 75 percent of reductions in inequality took place through cash transfers linked to education, family support, and housing benefits, while 25 percent occurred through progressive tax policies.[49] Most of OECD countries used a range of tax policies, educational assistance, housing aid, and family benefits to promote fairness in their systems.

Indeed, a new OCED report found that the Great Recession had hit the bottom tier the hardest and had been especially damaging to young people looking for employment.[50] In general, the OECD found that income concentration at the top is lower when taxes and social benefit policies are fairer. Nations that adopt progressive tax and spending policies are more likely to have lower income and asset inequality. Wealth distribution is subject to the effects of public policy, and countries that pay attention to the ramifications of their policies often end up with fairer income patterns.

The OECD study described three models for improving fairness. The Nordic model, followed in Scandinavia, is "characterized by large and mostly universal cash transfers, a high level of spending on in-kind services, and a tax mix which promotes redistribution." The Continental Europe approach, taken in Germany and France, uses "large cash transfers with the lion's share for old-age pensions—i.e., redistribution income mostly over the lifecycle instead of across individuals—and a tax mix which does not promote redistribution across individuals." The Anglo-Saxon model, employed by the United States, the United Kingdom, and Japan, is "characterized by small cash transfers, and a tax mix which promotes income redistribution."[51]

Any one of these models can be effective in promoting mobility as long as tax revenues are sufficient to fund needed government investments. The key point is that nations need to promote some modicum of economic fairness through their tax policies and social welfare provisions. They need to engage in what Brown University political scientist Mark Blyth calls "capitalism with airbags."[52]

Ending the Race to the Bottom

One of the challenges to improving economic fairness is the mobility of financial capital. Billionaires are not restricted to single states or countries. They can move themselves, their money, and even their companies around the world to those venues that are most favorable to them in terms of taxes, regulations, and business law. This practice has become increasingly common as countries and jurisdictions within countries compete for the money of the well-to-do. Kemal Derviş, Global Development vice president at the Brookings Institution, has argued that "capital is seeking to avoid the burden-sharing which makes modern society possible. If every country tries to race towards the lowest rate, then in the end nobody gains." According to Derviş, the big losers "are those who do not have the option of exiting the nation-state: the middle-class citizen and the medium-size business."[53] They lack the geographic mobility of wealthy individuals.

Only some billionaires actually move their places of residence to reduce their tax bills, but a large number use off-shore havens to shield their financial assets from taxation. The Cayman Islands, the Channel Islands, and Switzerland are among the best-known havens for billionaires and others to park their cash, free from the prying eyes of tax collectors. When Russian billionaire Dmitry Rybolovlev filed for divorce, his wife Elena sued him in six jurisdictions: the United Kingdom, the United States, Singapore, Switzerland, the British Virgin Islands, and Cyprus. She alleged that her husband employed a "multitude of third parties" to hide his financial assets. Even though he lives in Monaco, his potash fertilizer companies were based in Cyprus and his artwork, jewelry, and apartments were scattered in various places around the globe. Overall it is estimated that 30 percent of the 200 wealthiest individuals in the world use offshore holding companies to house their financial assets.[54]

Among the wealthy for whom hiding assets away in tax havens is not enough, a number of tax havens offer beautiful settings, arts, and culture as well as low taxes. Among the popular places for the rich to move to are the Cayman Islands, Hong Kong, Luxembourg, Singapore, and Switzerland. Research shows that only one-third of the billionaires who live in those areas actually grew up there.[55] Virgin Airlines founder Richard Branson, for example, attracted negative press attention after he moved his official residence to uninhabited Necker Island in the Caribbean in 2007. The move meant that he, as a nonresident of Britain, was "not liable for tax on personal income generated outside Britain." Branson claimed that the relocation was not for tax reasons, explaining that "I have not left Britain for tax reasons but for my love of the beautiful British Virgin Islands. . . . There is no better place to stay active, and I can kitesurf, surf, play tennis, swim, do Pilates, and just play."[56] He noted that his companies continue to pay hundreds of millions in corporate taxes. In 2012, Liliane Bettencourt was accused of buying a home in Switzerland to avoid paying the high French wealth tax and exit fee. Her new abode, which cost 62 million francs, gave her an official residence in Zurich. This followed several years of bad press related to her funding of conservative politicians in France.

Income tax rates on top earners range widely around the world. After France, where the top rate is 75 percent, the country with the highest upper rate is Denmark, at 60.2 percent, followed by the United Kingdom and Austria, at 50 percent. In the United States, the highest income tax rate is 39.6 percent.[57] Sudden increases in taxes can be a motivating factor when wealthy people decide to leave their home countries. For example, in 2013 Bernard Arnault, the luxury goods magnate, relocated after French president François Hollande announced plans to raise the country's top income tax rate to 75 percent. Arnault officially moved to Belgium and shifted his money for "family inheritance reasons." He applied for a Belgian passport and, according to a news report, "transferred his 31 per cent stake in Groupe Arnault, the family holding that controls LVMH, to Pilinvest, a Belgian firm that he specifically set up for the purpose." The transaction was valued at around $8.2 billion. Unlike France, Belgium has no wealth tax and its inheritance levy is 3 percent; the rate in France, in contrast, is 11 percent.[58] Shortly thereafter, however, he decided to remain a French citizen and reversed his move. He explained that is was important for him to stay in France during a time of social and economic challenges and that he did not want his personal migration to be seen as tax avoidance.[59] Even though he returned to France, much of his money appears to remain safely in other countries outside the reach of French authorities.

Billionaire François-Henri Pinault and his wife, actress Salma Hayek, moved from Paris to London in 2014. When asked about the relocation, Hayek said, "it's not for tax purposes. We are still paying taxes here in France. We think that London has a lot more to offer than just a better tax situation."[60]

As France discovered in the cases of Arnault and wealthy actor Gerard Depardieu, raising income taxes to 75 percent can lead to emigration to another country (first Belgium, then Russia, in Depardieu's case). The same thing occurred with Facebook co-founder Eduardo Saverin, who moved to Asia to avoid U.S. tax increases. But empirical evidence has found that high taxes on the wealthy do not necessarily lead to millionaire migration. When economists Charles Varner and Cristobal Young analyzed California data on the in- and out-migration of millionaires, they discovered that "migration accounts for 1.2 percent of the annual changes in the millionaire population."[61] Looking at before- and after-migration data following imposition of the 2005 Mental Health Services Tax, which added a 1 percent surcharge on taxable income greater than $1 million, they found that "the highest-income Californians were less likely to leave the state after the millionaire tax was passed." Indeed, getting divorced was a better predictor of migration than tax law changes.

In another study, which focused on New Jersey's adoption of a tax on millionaires, Young and Varner found that rising housing prices were a much stronger factor than the tax law shift in explaining millionaire migration. Some millionaires left the state, but so did other high earners who were not subject to the new tax. According to the authors, housing booms enable migration because it allows people to sell their homes quickly and in a lucrative manner.[62]

A few nations are encouraging relocation by offering passports with little residency requirement. Malta, for example, allows foreigners to purchase passports for 650,000 euros (around $893,000) with no residency requirement.[63] Portugal and Spain already allow residency in exchange for short visits to their countries. Estonia and Latvia are considering similar moves.

Other countries, such as the United States and France, have enacted an "exit tax" to deal with the migration of wealthy people. This tax—an extra fee imposed on citizens with assets of more than $2 million who give up their passports—enables governments to address the mobility of the super rich and impose restrictions on moving money around. Even so, for the truly super rich, even high fees might seem worth the investment if emigrants save millions more in taxes. In 2013, about 3,000 Americans renounced their citizenship or gave up their green cards, more than three times the number (932) who did so in 2012.[64] Not all of them did it to preserve their wealth, but having exit rules in place helps national authorities manage issues related to capital migration.

Legislation intended to help the U.S. government keep track of financial assets held abroad was recently passed. The Foreign Account Tax Compliance Act of 2010 "requires foreign financial institutions to report all assets owned by Americans."[65] This law is designed to improve accountability and keep people from shifting money into secret accounts abroad to avoid U.S. taxes.

Another important tax issue for the super wealthy is the estate tax. A number of nations have undermined progressivity by dismantling the estate tax completely. For example, Canada, Austria, and Sweden have eliminated the estate tax and the United States has gotten rid of it for most people by raising the amount of property exempt from taxation to $5.25 million per person. The campaign to label this a "death tax" instead of a wealth surcharge has effectively undermined public support for the charge and led to its elimination or reduction in a number of countries. This is a sharp change from the situation following World War II, when many countries had estate taxes as high as 77 percent.[66]

Finally, one of the most far-reaching proposals is Thomas Piketty's idea of a "wealth tax" on financial and nonfinancial assets.

In his book *Capital in the Twenty-First Century*, Piketty argues that wealth is increasing among a small group of individuals and that capital appreciation is rising at a more rapid rate than wages. To deal with increasing disparities, he proposes a 1 percent tax on net assets over 1 million euros and a 2 percent tax on those over 5 million euros.[67] He admits that such an idea is utopian and not likely to be adopted anytime soon. But he argues that a wealth tax would have the most impact of the various measures to address asset disparities and thereby reduce the dangers of oligarchical politics. He claims that the risks of the latter are so severe as to warrant new taxes on great wealth.

10 *Hope for the Future*

AMID WIDESPREAD CONCERNS about stagnating opportunity in the United States and many other developed countries, past history offers evidence that investing in people pays ample dividends for society as a whole. My personal experience, for example, demonstrates the value of public-supported education and health care. During my rural youth, my family had little money for health care. One spring day in 1966, when I was 11 years old, I developed a sore throat. Thinking that it was not very serious, my parents did not take me to the doctor. Physicians cost money, and they didn't have health insurance.

A few days later, on a Sunday morning, I awoke and could barely move. My joints were inflamed, and it was clear that something was seriously wrong. My parents rushed me to the doctor. (In those days, in an emergency you could see your family doctor on the weekend.) He took one look at my symptoms (a terrible sore throat, high fever, and inflamed joints) and told my parents to take me straight to the hospital. I had developed rheumatic fever, a bacterial disease that attacks the joints and the valves of the heart.

At the beginning of the twentieth century, this illness was the leading cause of death among school-age children. As late as 1940, according to medical historian Peter English, 2 percent of school children were infected with rheumatic fever.[1] A significant percentage of those afflicted with the acute disease died. But by the end of the century, improved treatment through antibiotics had reduced the incidence to 0.05 individuals per 1,000 population. The death rate dropped nearly to zero by 1960. After 1970, with the exception of a few isolated flare-ups, almost nobody in developed nations got the disease. In the last part of the twentieth century, it became a disease of what was then known as the Third World. My hometown of Fairhaven, Ohio, wasn't exactly the Third World, but I had the illness. Fortunately, I got quick medical care in a publicly funded hospital that saved my life. Twice a day in the hospital, I received injections of penicillin. Within two weeks, the fever was under control and my joint pain gone.

The health care that I received turned out to be a productive social and economic investment. After a full medical recovery, I continued my education in public schools and universities. I earned a Ph.D. in political science, taught in the Ivy League, and became a vice president at the country's leading think tank. It is clear that modest investments in education and health care were quite beneficial in lifting me out of poverty.[2] And mine is not an isolated example. Analysis by Brookings senior fellows Henry Aaron and Gary Burtless finds that investing in health care improves income distribution. Using data from U.S. entitlement programs, they find that the Affordable Care Act, for example, already has raised income for those in the bottom fifth of the nation's income distribution by 5.3 percent (including the cash value of the health insurance).[3] That demonstrates the value of public investment in health care for a broad range of people.

The Importance of Mobility

An economy's ability to grow and develop depends on consumers having sufficient money to buy basic goods and services—without it, they have no purchasing power and cannot invest in education and other sources of human capital.[4] According to Princeton University economist Alan Krueger, however, wages for lower- and middle-class families have stagnated in recent decades.[5] Meanwhile, Wealth-X CEO Mykolas Rambus predicts that "there will be 1,700 to 1,800 new billionaires created globally over the next eight to ten years."[6]

Weak and in many cases nonexistent growth in income below the top level makes it difficult for the country to maintain a viable middle class and provide opportunities for upward social mobility. As Henry Ford knew but many of today's business leaders seem to have forgotten, to keep the economy growing, workers need sufficient money to purchase products. In the United States, consumer spending—on discretionary as well as essential items—constitutes two-thirds of the overall economy and drives economic growth. When people purchase goods and services, they create markets, generate jobs, and stimulate even more wage growth, enabling the cycle to continue.

Research by Raj Chetty, Nathaniel Hendren, Patrick Kline, and Emmanuel Saez has shown that places in the United States where the middle class is bigger experience greater social and economic mobility across generations than areas where the middle class is smaller. Children born in these areas have higher odds of receiving an adequate education and earning good salaries than do children born in areas with less of a strong middle class.[7] Even during periods of slow income growth, such as the current period, investment in education pays off for American workers. Those with college or post-graduate degrees earn significantly more than those without college degrees. According to Jennifer Day and Eric Newburger, people who have college degrees earn an average of $2.1 million over the course of their working careers while high school graduates earn only $1.2 million.[8]

Yet, as noted by Suzanne Mettler in her book *Degrees of Inequality*, the cost of higher education has pushed college beyond the means of many U.S. students.[9] With annual expenses running over $55,000 at leading private universities and tuitions on the rise at public institutions, it is difficult for families experiencing low wage growth to send their children to college. In recent years, college completion rates have suffered and dropout rates have risen. The result has been what Princeton economist Alan Krueger calls a "Great Gatsby Curve." In comparing inequality in advanced economies with intergenerational mobility, he finds that "higher income inequality [is] associated with lower intergenerational mobility."[10] In other words, when income inequality is high, there are fewer opportunities for people to do better than their parents. Lack of financial resources keeps people from making investments that promote their own advancement as well as that of their children. Without educational advancement and intergenerational mobility, it is hard for workers to get the knowledge, jobs, and incomes needed for social and economic advancement.

Health, Well-Being, and Happiness

Income concentration is not just an economic challenge. Some researchers have posited a deleterious relationship between inequality and overall health and well-being.[11] Ohio State University economist Richard Steckel, for example, demonstrates a significant connection between nutritional status and income inequality. As one might expect, countries with higher inequality tend to have more people suffering from poor nutrition. People who cannot afford to purchase adequate amounts of nutritious food are less healthy and die earlier than those with higher incomes.[12] According to economists Melissa Kearney and Phillip Levine, being poor also is associated with feelings of despair and a greater likelihood of teenage pregnancy.[13]

In looking at inequality's impact on a variety of health outcomes, Bruce Kennedy, Ichiro Kawachi, and Deborah Prothrow-Stith find unfavorable links to heart disease, infant mortality, and low birth weights, among other things.[14] Poor people typically lack access to quality health care, and that translates into higher rates of disease and death, especially for infants and children. People in countries with higher incomes live longer.[15]

British public health researcher Richard Wilkinson has done extensive research that makes the same point. In examining the cross-national links between inequality and life expectancy, he notes that nations—such as the United States—with greater inequality have higher levels of personal stress, infectious diseases, and chronic illnesses than do countries—such as several in Scandinavia—with lower levels of income inequality. As a result of those maladies, the average lifespan tends to be shorter in countries with high rates of inequality.[16] Wilkinson's research shows that the links between income level and measures such as life expectancy exist even in developed countries, not just in the poorer countries of Africa, Asia, and Latin America. For example, in the United States a Social Security Administration research project discovered that "the life expectancy of male workers retiring at 65 had risen six years in the top half of the income distribution but only 1.3 years in the bottom half over the previous three decades."[17] Those with money tend to receive better health care and lead healthier lifestyles, and that translates into longer lives.

In contrast, those who experience discrimination or who do not have adequate financial resources suffer from a variety of conditions that limit their overall life expectancy. An analysis in 2013 by the National Center for Health Statistics found that blacks have an average life expectancy of 75 years, 4 years below that of whites (79 years). According to the study, blacks have higher levels of "heart disease, cancer, homicide, diabetes, and infant mortality."[18]

Some researchers have linked inequality to personal unhappiness. Shigehiro Oishi, Selin Kesebir, and Ed Diener, who used General Social Survey data from 1972 to 2008 to study over 53,000 individuals, discovered that "Americans were on average happier in the years with less national income inequality than in the years with more national income inequality."[19] The mechanism the researchers identify to explain this relationship is the level of perceived fairness. Years with greater inequality, they note, also saw an increase in the perception that other people were unfair and therefore a drop in social trust. Believing that other people are unfair and untrustworthy limits people's levels of happiness across the board. If individuals see blatant unfairness, it negatively affects their entire perspective about their society.

For these reasons, writer Kentaro Toyama calls for "happiness-based economies." He says that "a more even distribution of income would correlate with greater total happiness."[20] If nations put more financial resources into education or raised marginal tax rates on their wealthiest citizens, he claims, it would boost the well-being of the entire society. Political scientist Benjamin Radcliff, at the University of Notre Dame, goes even further. In his book *The Political Economy of Human Happiness*, he argues that personal well-being is served by fair-minded policies. Drawing on cross-national surveys, he finds that people "live more positive and rewarding lives in countries (and states) that have bigger governments, large welfare states, stronger labor movements, and more economic regulation (controlling for other factors)."[21] In his book *Bottlenecks: A New Theory of Equal Opportunity*, Joseph Fishkin, an assistant professor at the University of Texas School of Law, calls for "opportunity pluralism."[22] Fishkin says that financial well-being should not be a zero-sum game in which a few win at the expense of the many. Instead, societies should aim to broaden social and economic opportunities and promote greater fairness.

The Personal Complications of Wealth

Beyond the systemic impact of inequality, great wealth can be problematic because it often complicates the personal relationships of those who have it. In looking at the family connections of the well-to-do, complications abound, especially for children of the rich. Wealthy patriarchs and matriarchs have to guard against the rivalries, resentments, and jealousy that may arise when families have extraordinary amounts of money. The level of intrafamily conflict can rise dramatically when millions of dollars are involved. Big money can turn marriage, divorce, social relationships, and individual conflicts into high-stakes matters.

In China, a nine-year-old boy provided a vivid demonstration of this problem when he sued his billionaire father for child support. In 2010, Zhao Bingxian, who made his money through lucrative business investments, filed for divorce from his wife Lu Juan. During the contentious divorce proceedings, Zhao cut off all financial support for his son, who filed suit to have the money restored.[23] Another Chinese billionaire, Cecil Chao Sze-tsung, demonstrated the complications of wealth within his own family when he offered 1 billion Hong Kong dollars (around US$129 million) to any man who married his lesbian daughter, Gigi Chao, who has had a female partner for nine years. The father explained, "I don't want to interfere with my daughter's private life. I only hope for her to have a good marriage and children as well as inherit my business." Speaking to the press after this offer was made, his daughter commented, "I don't think my dad's offering of any amount of money would be able to attract a man I would find attractive."[24]

In Australia, the children of the country's richest woman, Gina Rinehart, sued her for misconduct. As the trustee of the family trust, she delayed the date when her four kids could receive their money. Children John and Bianca Rinehart challenged that decision in court, insisting their mother should be forbidden to make that move.[25]

Children of the super wealthy suffer from personal pressures that are very different from those confronting people of lesser means. When they are growing up, other individuals treat them differently because of their family's wealth. That may lead them to wonder whether people are genuinely relating to them as individuals.

The Kennedy family presents an example of this syndrome among the super wealthy. It once was estimated that one-quarter of the members of the Kennedy "third generation" suffered from alcohol or drug problems. Some of them have died from drug overdoses, and many have checked into treatment houses or rehabilitation clinics.[26]

An American psychologist testifying on behalf of Texas teenager Ethan Couch came up with the term "affluenza" to describe the condition of bad behavior that "stemmed from having wealthy, privileged parents who never set limits." The term arose in the case of Couch, who, when charged in a drunk driving case in which four people died, used his upbringing as his legal defense. His attorney's argument was that children who have no limits experience impulse control challenges that can lead to a range of problems. Based on her research, Arizona State University psychology professor Suniya Luthar claims that "we've found the level of serious adjustment problems ranging from depression, anxiety, delinquency, substance abuse [is] higher among kids of upper-middle-class families."[27]

The Need for Better Understanding

Given the systemic and personal ramifications of having great personal wealth, I often have talked with the super rich about the importance of maintaining social and economic opportunities for society as a whole. Many of them understand its importance and direct much of their philanthropy toward education and health care. They see the virtue of social investments and want to make sure that the less fortunate receive a fair shake.

But others remain unconvinced. Venture capital firm founder Tom Perkins, for example, attracted great attention with his January 2014 letter to the editor at the *Wall Street Journal* when he compared criticisms of the top 1 percent with Nazi attacks on Jews in 1938 during Kristallnacht. Demonizing the wealthy, he said, reflects a "rising tide of hatred of the successful one percent."[28] Following those comments, Perkins proposed that only taxpayers be allowed to vote in U.S. elections and that the wealthy should have extra voting privileges. "You pay a million in taxes, you get a million votes," he advised.[29] Perkins later apologized for the comparison to Kristallnacht but stood by the essence of his criticism of those who worry about the rich. "The message is, any time the majority starts to demonize a minority, no matter what it is, it's wrong and dangerous," he told *Bloomberg*. "And no good ever comes from it."[30] Norwegian billionaire Olav Thon openly worries about complacency among young people in his native country. He said that he worried that they have been spoiled by the Scandinavian nation's generous welfare system. "You can't feed a cat with cream and food in the kitchen and expect him to go catch mice," he explained.[31]

The sharp responses by some of the wealthy hit home one day during a conversation I had with a successful investor. We were discussing pension fund investments in alternative instruments. This individual did not understand why ordinary people had difficulty comprehending the value of investing public pensions in hedge funds and private equities. I was taken aback by this person's inability to understand the public controversy over hedge funds. Because he was a high-level investor himself, he could not understand the perspective of those struggling to make ends meet who were concerned about high investment fees and complex investment instruments developed by Wall Street firms that many people did not trust. Because he had a deep understanding of those instruments, which might seem exotic to others, hedge fund investing was a given. It was hard for him to comprehend that most Americans have little understanding of complicated investment vehicles developed by supposed experts on Wall Street—the same kinds of experts who were responsible for the 2008 financial crisis.

Rarified Lifestyles

In 1925, F. Scott Fitzgerald wrote a short story entitled "The Rich Boy," which opened with these widely quoted lines: "Let me tell you about the very rich. They are different from you and me. They possess and enjoy early, and it does something to them, makes them soft where we are hard, and cynical where we are trustful, in a way that, unless you were born rich, it is very difficult to understand. They think, deep in their hearts, that they are better than we are because we had to discover the compensations and refuges of life for ourselves. Even when they enter deep into our world or sink below us, they still think that they are better than we are."[32]

With their abundant financial resources, the super rich lead lives that differ considerably from those of people of ordinary means.[33] They are insulated from many routine annoyances of day-to-day life. They have private transportation, which shields them from the inconvenience of dealing with traffic, parking, and airport security.[34] They send their children to exclusive private schools that provide an opportunity to receive the best educations. Inequity even extends to the skies. One commentator wryly noted that "the 1 percent fly first class; the .1 percent fly Netjets; the .01 fly their own planes."[35] Others have referred to billionaires as the .000001.[36]

A few of the wealthy express very high opinions of their own contributions to society. Ken Langone, the billionaire cofounder of the Home Depot chain, joins Tom Perkins in being upset with those who demonize the wealthy. Complaining about the political rhetoric surrounding inequality, he bluntly declared that "if it wasn't for us fat cats and the endowments that we fund, every university in the country would be fucked."[37]

Life for the super rich can be insular, especially for those who spend much of their time in the company of others who are famous or wealthy. They attend conferences, retreats, and gatherings that cater to the well-to-do—limiting their contact with those who are less well-to-do. And for those seeking to practice the mating principles outlined earlier, there even are dating websites that cater to the super wealthy. The site BillionaireFish.com, for example, advertises itself as "the largest and most trusted billionaire dating site where you can date wealthy men."[38] Members are hand-picked by company staff and asked to verify their incomes and professions. If someone's taste tilts more toward mere millionaires, MillionaireMatch.com provides connections in that not-quite-so-exclusive league.

People like to read or watch stories about rich individuals, but the idiosyncrasies of the most fortunate sometimes attract public ridicule. During a September 2012 nationally televised football game against the New York Giants, Dallas Cowboys owner Jerry Jones had his son-in-law Shy Anderson clean his eye glasses for him.[39] The video was replayed over and over to make the point that "out-of-touch" wealthy people were not willing to do mundane tasks for themselves. When Jones later criticized a New York Giants player for allegedly faking an injury to slow down the clock at the end of a close game, Giants defensive tackle Cullen Jenkins questioned Jones's eyesight, saying that "maybe he should get his son-in-law to clean his glasses a little better."[40]

The impudent exercise of wealth sometimes even annoys other rich people. One Palm Beach billionaire that I know complains about a wealthy neighbor who flies a helicopter a couple of miles up the Florida coast to a golf course instead of taking a car. Flying the noisy helicopter low overhead on weekend mornings, he disturbs the peace and quiet of the coastal community, eliciting eye rolling and head shaking from his neighbors below.

Facebook CEO Mark Zuckerberg, one of the world's youngest billionaires, has come up with a novel way to stay grounded amid all the attention that accompanies great wealth. During his September 18, 2013, visit to Washington, D.C., I heard him outline a philosophy that was unusual for a super-wealthy person. He said that his goal was to connect with other people and "not do a lot of things you could only do if you have a lot of money." He has set himself the goal of having, every day, a "meaningful conversation with someone I don't know who doesn't work at Facebook." His wife, Priscilla Chan, helps him maintain his balance. Recently, he started to learn Mandarin. In speaking with his wife, he complained that he could have short conversations with Chinese speakers but had difficulty listening in Mandarin. Without missing a beat, she joked, "Mark, you have difficulty listening in English!"

Rising Awareness

Despite the insularity of some of the wealthy, there are encouraging signs that public awareness of inequality, opportunity, and fairness is rising. Opinion surveys confirm that voters want more fairness in tax and budgetary policies. In certain cases in recent years, they have acted on those beliefs by electing candidates who campaign on a fairness platform. A number of news organizations and opinion leaders, such as the *New York Times*, *Forbes*, and *Bloomberg Businessweek,* are devoting considerable resources to reporting on problems associated with rising inequality. The *Times*, for example, has a regular feature in this area entitled "The Great Divide," in addition to columnists who frequently write about inequality.[41] Think tanks, universities, and nonprofits have launched initiatives on this subject as well.

Some wealthy people also have spoken out about aspects of these issues. For example, billionaire investor David Rubenstein said that "we have growing economic inequality. It's getting much worse as a result of the recession, and we have to do something about that."[42] Warren Buffet has said that it is unfair that he has a lower effective tax rate than his secretary and has suggested a minimum tax on the wealthy (a proposal known as the Buffet Rule). Media mogul Leo Hindery Jr. formed a group called "Patriotic Millionaires" that called for the end of Bush tax cuts for those earning over $1 million a year.[43] Even Peter Thiel, a libertarian, has publicly backed a California ballot measure proposed by conservative Republican Ron Unz that would increase the state's minimum wage to $12 an hour. Thiel said that he supported a higher minimum wage as an alternative to people "going on welfare."[44]

Some national and international leaders are focusing on inequality and unfairness. In a profile of Senator Elizabeth Warren (D-Massachusetts), Noam Scheiber of the *New Republic* notes the schism between those who "are angrier, more disaffected, and altogether more populist than they've been in years" and others who "still fundamentally believe the economy functions best with a large, powerful, highly complex financial sector."[45] In a speech to the National Consumer Law Center, Senator Warren, a liberal critic of Wall Street, clearly put herself into the first category. She complained that "the system is rigged for powerful interests and against working families. We could talk about a lot of ways the system is rigged—lobbyists, campaign finance, the court system. But I want to raise a very specific issue that we need to spotlight: how much powerful interests benefit from a system that is complicated and opaque."[46]

Even Pope Francis has weighed in on this topic. In his first papal statement, the pope wrote that "some people continue to defend trickle-down theories which assume that economic growth, encouraged by a free market, will inevitably succeed in bringing about greater justice and inclusiveness in the world. [But] this opinion, which has never been confirmed by the facts, expresses a crude and naïve trust in the goodness of those wielding economic power and in the sacralized workings of the prevailing economic system."[47]

Others do not agree with the emphasis on economic populism. Andrew Stern, the former president of the Service Employees International Union, cautions that "it's really not helpful for the Democrats to turn this into an attack on the one percent. I don't think it's in the American spirit." Brookings senior fellow William Galston predicts that a strategy of "pure undistilled populism" will not work.[48] Former secretary of the treasury Larry Summers remarked that "the politics of envy are the wrong politics in America. The better politics are the politics of inclusion, where everyone shares in economic growth."[49] Billionaire Ken Langone of Home Depot put it even more bluntly in response to Pope Francis's call for greater fairness and justice. Langone warned that "wealthy people such as himself are feeling ostracized by the Pope's messages in support of the poor, and might stop giving to charity if the Pope continues to make statements criticizing capitalism and income inequality."[50]

Encouraging Billionaires to Sign the Giving Pledge

Charitable giving to nonprofit organizations is a way in which many members of the super wealthy have directly benefited society. Billionaires have provided generous gifts to universities, hospitals, museums and the arts, social services, and think tanks. These gifts allow the organizations to do good things with the money, and the wealthy get a tax break. One recent stimulus for big-money support of charity is the voluntary Giving Pledge, whereby wealthy individuals pledge to give away half of their assets during their lifetime instead of transferring them to the next generation. To date, the pledge, launched in 2010 by Bill and Melinda Gates, has been signed by fewer than 10 percent of the world's billionaires.[51] Most of the signers live in the United States, although a few have come from other places around the world. Warren Buffet, an early signer of the pledge, encourages his fellow billionaires to be generous. It would be good for the world, he says, and it would not cause undue damage to the lifestyles of the very wealthy. "If you have trouble living on $500 million, I'm gonna put out a book, *How to Live on $500 Million*," he said. "Think about whether the other $500 million might do more for humanity than it will for you and your family."[52]

On the pledge organization's website, pledge signatories publish letters outlining their motivation and goals for charitable giving. One example comes from Sara Blakely, the chief executive officer of Spanx, a women's undergarment company. One of the world's youngest self-made female billionaires, Blakely wrote the following description of her philanthropic interests:

I have so much gratitude for being a woman in America. I never lose sight that I was born in the right country, at the right time. And, I never lose sight of the fact that there are millions of women around the world who are not dealt the same deck of cards upon their birth. Simply because of their gender, they are not given the same chance I had to create my

208 HOPE FOR THE FUTURE

own success and follow my dreams. It is for those women that I make this pledge."[53]

From Malaysia, Vincent Tan Chee Yioun of the Berjaya Group explained the importance of giving back to his community:

Coming from a relatively poor family and without the benefit of a formal tertiary education, I have been blessed with material success beyond my wildest imagination. Yes, I have worked hard and smart, but there are many who undoubtedly have worked harder and who are far smarter than I and yet have not achieved the same level of material success. My success could not have been possible without divine blessings. I am also keenly aware that there is only so much money that a person needs for himself and his family and this brings home the sense that when one is blessed with great wealth beyond what is needed, there is a corresponding moral and social responsibility to put the money to good use. For this reason, I have for many years done my part to help the less fortunate and underprivileged through monetary donations and other means of material support. I have also established a foundation known as Better Malaysia Foundation to organize and focus these efforts with the aim of giving back to the community and generally making Malaysia a better place."[54]

The Case of the National Football League

The National Football League (NFL) is a powerful example of an industry, run by a central authority, that promotes a level playing field for all participants and employs policies explicitly based on fairness. Professional football represents one of the most successful sectors in the U.S. economy. Since 1985, the Harris Poll has asked adult fans to name their favorite sport. In 2011, "35 percent of fans call[ed] the NFL their favorite sport, followed by Major League Baseball (14 percent), college football (11 percent), auto racing (7 percent), the NBA (6 percent), the NHL (5 percent) and college basketball (3 percent)." Nielson ratings confirm the NFL's popularity. The Super Bowl routinely attracts more than 100 million viewers, which makes it the most widely watched TV show in the United States.[55] Professional football is very popular with a broad segment of the public (including many politically conservative, working-class individuals) despite pro-fairness policies that undoubtedly would be extremely controversial if advocated by the government. These include salary caps for each team, a draft of college players in which poorly performing teams are given priority over better teams, and equal sharing of television revenues by all the teams. In the NFL, rich teams are not allowed to outspend poor teams. In 2013, for example, each team was limited to an overall player payroll of $123 million.[56] General managers can allocate salaries however they want among individual players, but to ensure that competition is fair across geographic markets and owner wealth, their total expenditures can be no higher than the salary cap. With the sport's upsurge, the NFL has contracts for around $42 billion in television revenue over the next decade. This money is split evenly among the thirty-two franchises, with each team getting $170 million annually.[57]

Its business model clearly is very different from that of professional baseball. In baseball, there are huge disparities between wealthy and poorer teams, and the rich teams spend much higher amounts on player slaries. For example, with $90 million in revenue just from its YES local television network, the New York Yankees had a 2012 payroll of $197 million, while the San Diego Padres and the Oakland Athletics had total payrolls of $55 million.[58] That financial disparity allows "big-market" teams to compete more aggressively than "small-market" locales for marquee players.

The NFL uses centralized regulations and collective bargaining with a players' union to negotiate contracts that control players' personal behavior. The contract limits what players can and cannot do and even has provisions regulating their on-field wardrobe (including shoe color). Violators can be fined, suspended, or barred from league play. The NFL commissioner can impose major penalties on players or owners for conduct detrimental to league standards. Despite having strict governance and formal principles based on fairness in competition, professional football is wildly popular among the general public in all regions of the country. Its business model is embraced by people of very different socioeconomic backgrounds and political perspectives because it produces healthy competition among the teams, exciting games, and lots of media coverage.

Conclusion

There are many obstacles to making progress in improving opportunity and fairness. Entrenched interests fight change and come up with self-interested justifications for maintaining the status quo. Many others understand that the country has serious problems with inequality and lack of fairness, but they direct most of their ire at the government rather than the special interests that often benefit from government policies and programs. In recent years, for example, the most vigorous populist movement has been the Tea Party, whose members are angry at the government over high debt levels and a health care reform that they oppose. But that trend notwithstanding, it is important to understand the political role of the super rich and how income concentration has contributed to the evident dysfunction of the U.S. political system, particularly at the national level. Activist billionaires have become adept at taking advantage of veto points in the legislative process, promoting their causes through elections and referendums and using the machinery of government to protect their business interests. This is true in many countries besides the United States.

It is the combination of high income concentration, distinctive political viewpoints among the super wealthy, lack of transparency in money and politics, and weak countervailing institutions such as news media and political parties that threatens basic governance and representative democracy. These problems are most apparent in the developing world, where a number of nations lack effective rule of law, do not have merit-based institutions, and do little to promote social and economic opportunity for their people. Yet as demonstrated in this volume, the United States and other Western democracies are not immune to these maladies. When there is secrecy in campaign funding, poor news coverage, or one-sided political dialogue, American institutions also are vulnerable to the power of big money in the political process.

In a provocative essay, political scientist Norm Ornstein recently asked, "Could America become a banana republic?"[59] He raised this question following an anticorruption conference that the Brookings Institution held in Prague in 2014. At that event, people from China, the Czech Republic, Egypt, India, Italy, Kenya, South Africa, Turkey, Ukraine, the United Kingdom, and the United States traded stories about crony capitalism, oligarchs, princelings, tycoons, and billionaires who used wealth to advance their own personal or business interests.

In such a setting, it is easy for Americans to be complacent, claiming that problems with oligarchy would never occur in an advanced democracy with a free press and strong rule of law. But in the context of income inequality, wrong-headed Supreme Court decisions, poor media coverage, and weak transparency, Ornstein fears that corruption will become more common and that lawmaking will return "to the kind of favor-trading bazaar that was common in the Gilded Age." With highly polarized elections and narrow margins between winning and losing, America has more to fear than most people realize. At a time of dysfunctional governance and fragmented institutions, society needs shock absorbers that shield it from major political and economic breakdowns. Billionaires can assist by using their own resources and influence to encourage better governance and wider opportunities for the personal and economic advancement of others. This includes supporting—rather than spending millions of dollars in political campaigns to oppose—government and nongovernment programs that help people gain the benefits of education, health care, and workforce development. Billionaires, perhaps more than anyone else, should be able to understand that people need opportunities if they are to achieve economic success and personal fulfillment. Many billionaires rose from humble origins and made vast fortunes. Along the way, they received important boosts. Paying that help forward would provide others with the kind of beneficial assistance that they received and allow for the creation of the healthy, educated workforce that is necessary to the social and economic advancement of all nations in the world today.

Acknowledgments

BOOKS PERCOLATE FOR considerable time before they end up in their final form. I started to think about this project during the 2012 presidential election, when a number of very wealthy individuals poured large amounts of money into the candidates' coffers. Since then, it has become apparent that such support is not an aberration but evidence of a substantial wave of campaign financing of sometimes unknown origin that is inundating the American political system and that of many other countries around the globe. I wrote this volume to draw attention to this topic and suggest ways to improve the situation.

Along the way, I was blessed with terrific research, editorial, and writing assistance. Tyler Cowan and John Felton reviewed the manuscript and offered invaluable comments and suggestions; the analysis and writing is much better for their help and wise counsel. In addition, I am indebted to E. J. Dionne, Tom Mann, Elaine Kamarck, Jim Morone, Peter Andreas, David Nassar, Christine Jacobs, Courtney Dunakin, Ashley Bennett, and Karin Rosnizeck for conversations about the book. Hillary Schaub, Elizabeth Valentini, Ashley Gabrielle, Joshua Bleiberg, Sonia Vora, and Joseph Goodman provided valuable research assistance. A number of individuals at the Brookings Institution Press deserve a special thank you. Valentina Kalk, who directs the press, was a tremendous source of good advice about the book. Janet Walker was very helpful in supervising the book production process, and Susan Woollen deserves credit for managing the cover design process. Eileen Hughes did an outstanding job copy editing the manuscript. None of these individuals is responsible for the interpretations presented in this volume.

Appendix

TABLE A-1. Number of Billionaires in Various Countries

United States	492	Indonesia	19
China	152	Sweden	19
Russia	111	Israel	18
Germany	85	Mexico	16
Brazil	65	Singapore	16
India	56	Malaysia	13
United Kingdom	47	Chile	12
Hong Kong	45	Thailand	11
France	43	Philippines	10
Italy	35	Austria	10
Canada	32	Norway	9
Australia	29	Ukraine	9
Taiwan	28	Peru	8
Japan	27	Egypt	8
South Korea	27	South Africa	8
Spain	26	Netherlands	7
Turkey	24	Saudi Arabia	7
Switzerland	21	Czech Republic	6

Denmark	6	Belgium	3
Lebanon	6	Oman	2
Ireland	5	Macau	2
Kuwait	5	New Zealand	2
Argentina	5	Algeria	1
Kazakhstan	5	Georgia	1
Poland	5	Lithuania	1
Columbia	4	Romania	1
Finland	4	St. Kitts	1
United Arab Emirates	4	Angola	1
Morocco	4	Guernsey	1
Cyprus	4	Nepal	1
Nigeria	4	Swaziland	1
Greece	3	Tanzania	1
Monaco	3	Uganda	1
Portugal	3	Vietnam	1
Venezuela	3		

Source: *Forbes, "The World's Billionaires."*

TABLE A-2. Number of Billionaires in Various American States

California	111	Minnesota	5
New York	88	Missouri	5
Texas	50	Kansas	5
Florida	34	Arkansas	4
Illinois	19	Indiana	4
Connecticut	13	Montana	4
Maryland	13	Ohio	4
Washington	12	North Carolina	3
Michigan	11	Nebraska	3
Wisconsin	9	Oregon	2
Massachusetts	9	Virginia	2
Pennsylvania	9	Hawaii	1
Arizona	9	Iowa	1
Colorado	8	Kentucky	1
Nevada	8	Louisiana	1
Georgia	7	New Hampshire	1
New Jersey	6	Rhode Island	1
Tennessee	6	South Carolina	1
Wyoming	6	Utah	1
Oklahoma	5	West Virginia	1

Source: Forbes, "The World's Billionaires."

Notes

Chapter One

1. Luisa Kroll, "Inside the 2013 Forbes 400," *Forbes*, September 16, 2013. Also see Arthur Kennickell, "Ponds and Streams: Wealth and Income in the U.S., 1989 to 2007," Federal Reserve Board Working Paper, January 7, 2009.

2. Marco Cagetti and Mariacristina de Nardi, "Wealth Inequality," *Macroeconomic Dynamics*, vol. 12 (2008), p. 285.

3. Thomas Piketty and Emmanuel Saez, "Income Inequality in the United States, 1913–1998," *Quarterly Journal of Economics*, vol. 118 (2003), pp. 1–39. For 1999 to 2012 numbers, see the web page of Emmanuel Saez (http://emlab.berkeley.edu/users/saez). Also see Richard Burkhauser and others, "Recent Trends in Top Income Shares in the USA: Reconciling Estimates from March CPS and IRS Tax Return Data," Working Paper (Cambridge, Mass.: National Bureau of Economic Research, September 2009). Also see Thomas Piketty, *Capital in the Twenty-first Century* (Harvard University Press, 2014).

4. The 2012 income numbers come from Emmanuel Saez, "Striking It Richer: The Evolution of Top Incomes in the United States," unpublished paper, September 3, 2013.

5. Ed Harris and Frank Sammartino, "Trends in the Distribution of Household Income, 1979–2009" (Congressional Budget Office, August 6, 2012).

6. Piketty, *Capital in the Twenty-First Century*.

7. "Selected Measures of Household Income Dispersion: 1967 to 2010," *Current Population Reports* (U.S. Census Bureau, 2011), table A-3.

8. Alex Cobham and Andy Sumner, "Is It All About the Tails? The Palma Measure of Income Inequality" (Washington: Center for Global Development, September, 2013).

9. Tami Luhby, "Wealth Inequality between Blacks and Whites Worsens," *CNN Money*, February 27, 2013 (http://money.cnn.com/2013/02/27/news/economy/wealth-whites-blacks/).

10. Jennifer Hochschild, Vesla Weaver, and Traci Burch, *Creating a New Racial Order: How Immigration, Multiracialism, Genomics, and the Young Can Remake Race in America* (Princeton University Press, 2012).

11. Thomas Piketty and Gabriel Zucman, "Capital Is Back: Wealth-Income Ratios in Rich Countries, 1700–2012," unpublished paper, July 26, 2013.

12. Edward Wong, "Survey in China Shows a Wide Gap in Income," *New York Times*, July 20, 2013, p. A9, and Tom Orlik and Sophia Cheng, "New Survey Finds China Unequal, Unemployed, and Untrusting," *Wall Street Journal*, July 26, 2013. Also see Song Xiaowu, Wang Feng, and Wang Tianfu, *China Faces Inequality: Studies in Income Distribution* (Beijing: Social Sciences Academic Press, 2013).

13. "China's Richest Man Says Wealth Gap Not a Priority," Agence France-Presse, July 17, 2013.

14. Adam Pasick, "Chinese Billionaire Unconcerned about Rich-Poor Gap Is Attacked by Knife-Wielding Jobseeker," *Quartz*, September 18, 2013.

15. James Davies and others, "The World Distribution of Household Wealth," Discussion Paper 2008/03 (United Nations World Institute for Development Economics Research, February 2008), p. 7.

16. Branko Milanovic, "Global Inequality and the Global Inequality Extraction Ratio: The Story of the Past Two Centuries" (World Bank, September 2009) (http://elibrary.worldbank.org/doi/book/10.1596/1813-9450-5044). Also see Branko Milanovic, *The Haves and Have-Nots: A Brief and Idiosyncratic History of Global Inequality* (New York: Basic Books, 2012) and Sudhir Arnand and Paul Segal, "What Do We Know about Global Income Inequality?," *Journal of Economic Literature*, vol. 46 (March 2008), p. 57.

17. Benjamin Page, Larry Bartels, and Jason Seawright, "Democracy and the Policy Preferences of Wealthy Americans," *Perspectives on Politics*, vol. 11 (March 2013).

18. Ibid., p. 55.

19. Kay Lehman Schlozman, Sidney Verba, and Henry Brady, *The Unheavenly Chorus: Unequal Political Voice and the Broken Promise of American Democracy* (Princeton University Press, 2012).

20. Lee Drutman, "The 1,000 Donors Most Likely to Benefit from McCutcheon—and What They Are Most Likely to Do" (Sunlight Foundation, October 2, 2013).

21. Page, Bartels, and Seawright, "Democracy and the Policy Preferences of Wealthy Americans," pp. 53–54.

22. "American National Election Study 2012 Preliminary Release Codebook," University of Michigan, June 13, 2013, p. 1039.

23. Page, Bartels, and Seawright, "Democracy and the Policy Preferences of Wealthy Americans."

24. Ibid.

25. Credit Suisse Research Institute, *Global Wealth Databook: 2012* (October 2012), p. 127.

26. Page, Bartels, and Seawright, "Democracy and the Policy Preferences of Wealthy Americans."

27. Rachael Bade, "Rand Paul in Cross Hairs of Tax Evasion War," *Politico*, March 2, 2014.

28. Michael Schmidt, Eric Lipton, and Alexandra Stevenson, "After Big Bet, Hedge Fund Pulls the Levers of Power," *New York Times*, March 9, 2014.

29. Martin Gilens, *Affluence and Influence: Economic Inequality and Political Power in America* (Princeton University Press, 2012).

30. Martin Gilens and Benjamin Page, "Testing Theories of American Politics: Elites, Interest Groups, and Average Citizens," *Perspectives on Politics* (Fall 2014, forthcoming), p. 2.

31. Matea Gold, "Newt Gingrich Says Wealthy Donors Like Sheldon Adelson Have Too Much Influence," *Washington Post*, March 28, 2014.

32. Nicholas Confessore, "Big-Money Donors Demand Larger Say in Party Strategy," *New York Times*, March 2, 2014, p. 1.

33. Joseph Stiglitz, *The Price of Inequality* (New York: W.W. Norton, 2012).

34. Jacob Hacker and Paul Pierson, *Winner-Take-All Politics: How Washington Made the Rich Richer—and Turned Its Back on the Middle Class* (New York: Simon and Schuster, 2011).

35. Larry Bartels, *Unequal Democracy: The Political Economy of the New Gilded Age* (Princeton University Press, 2010).

36. For additional details on the media decline, see Darrell West and Beth Stone, "Nudging News Producers and Consumers toward More Thoughtful, Less Polarized Discourse," Strengthening American Democracy Series 20 (Brookings, February 2014).

37. "The State of the News Media 2013," March 18, 2013. (Washington: Pew Research Center, Project for Excellence in Journalism).

38. Jennifer Dorroh, "Statehouse Exodus," *American Journalism Review* (April-May 2009).

39. Robert Reich, *Beyond Outrage* (New York: Vintage, 2012).

40. Confessore, "Big-Money Donors Demand Larger Say in Party Strategy."

41. "Author Dean Starkman on the Watchdog That Didn't Bark," *GoLocalProv*, February 7, 2014. Also see Dean Starkman, *The Watchdog That Didn't Bark* (Columbia University Press, 2014).

42. Chrystia Freeland, *Plutocrats: The Rise of the New Global Super Rich and the Fall of Everyone Else* (New York: Penguin Books, 2012).

43. Arthur Brooks, "The Downside of Inciting Envy," *New York Times*, March 2, 2014, p. 12.

44. Adam Bonica and others, "Why Hasn't Democracy Slowed Rising Inequality?," *Journal of Economic Perspectives*, vol. 27, no. 3 (Summer 2013), p. 108.

45. Lee Drutman, "Are the 1% of the 1% Pulling Politics in a Conservative Direction?" (Sunlight Foundation, June 26, 2013).

46. Gregory Mankiw, "Defending the One Percent," *Journal of Economic Perspectives*, vol. 27, no. 3 (June 8, 2013), p. 2. Also see his column at Gregory Mankiw, "Yes, the Wealthy Can Be Deserving," *New York Times*, February 15, 2014.

47. David Corn, "Romney Tells Millionaire Donors What He Really Thinks of Obama Voters," *Mother Jones*, September 17, 2012.

48. Richard Reeves, "1% v. 99%? No, It's Affluent, Squeezed, and Entrenched Poverty" (Brookings Institution, February 19, 2014).

49. Richard Reeves, "What the Inequality Debate Leaves Out," CNN, January 7, 2014. Also see Raj Chetty and others, "Where Is the Land of Opportunity? The Geography of Intergenerational Mobility in the U.S." (Cambridge, Mass.: National Bureau of Economic Research, January 2014).

50. Jason DeBacker and others, "Rising Inequality: Transitory or Permanent? New Evidence from a Panel of U.S. Tax Returns," paper presented at the Brookings Panel on Economic Activity Conference, Washington, March 21, 2013.

51. Reich, *Beyond Outrage*.

52. Paul Krugman, "Favoring Wealth over Work," *New York Times*, March 22, 2014.

53. "Earnings and Unemployment Rates by Educational Attainment" (U.S. Bureau of Labor Statistics, December 19, 2013). Also see Greg Duncan and Richard Murnane, *Restoring Opportunity: The Crisis of Inequality and the Challenge for American Education* (Harvard Education Press and the Russell Sage Foundation, 2013).

54. Ron Haskins, "Poverty and Opportunity," testimony before the U.S. House of Representatives, Committee on the Budget, January 28, 2014.

55. Jeremy Greenwood and others, "Marry Your Like: Assortative Mating and Income Inequality," Working Paper 19829 (Cambridge, Mass.: National Bureau of Economic Research, January 2014).

56. Julia Isaacs, "Economic Mobility of Families across Generations," in *Getting Ahead or Losing Ground: Economic Mobility in America*, by Julia Isaacs, Isabel Sawhill, and Ron Haskins (Brookings Institution and Pew Charitable Trust, February 2008), p. 19.

57. Thomas Harjes, "Globalization and Income Inequality," Working Paper (International Monetary Fund, July 2007), p. 3.

58. The Electoral Integrity Project, "Risks of Flawed or Failing Elections" (University of Sydney, Australia, February 24, 2014).

59. Robert Jones and others, "Do Americans Believe Capitalism and Government Are Working?," Public Religion Research Institute and Brookings Institution Governance Studies Program, July 18, 2013, p. 7 (http://publicreligion.org/research/2013/07/economic-values-survey-07-2013/).

Chapter Two

1. Kenneth Vogel, "Koch World Reboots," *Politico*, February 20, 2013.

2. Ibid. Also see Kenneth Vogel, "Koch World 2014," *Politico*, January 24, 2014.

3. Charles Riley, "Can 46 Rich Dudes Buy an Election?," *CNN Money*, March 26, 2012.

4. Julie Patel, "Pro-Obama Nonprofits Boosted by Undisclosed Donors" (Center for Public Integrity, November 21, 2013).

5. Portions of this chapter are drawn from Darrell West, *Checkbook Democracy: How Money Corrupts Political Campaigns* (Northeastern University Press, 2000).

6. Darrell West, *Air Wars: Television Advertising and Social Media in Election Campaigns* (Washington: Congressional Quarterly Press, 2013).

7. *Buckley v. Valeo*, 424 U.S. 1 (1976).

8. West, *Air Wars*.

9. Alan Morrison, "Focusing on the Wrong IRS 501(c)(4) Scandal," *Huffington Post*, May 29, 2013.

10. Nicholas Confessore, "Power Surge for Donors as Terrain Is Reshaped on Campaign Money," *New York Times*, April 2, 2014.

11. *McCutcheon v. Federal Election Commission*, Justice Breyer, dissenting opinion, April 2, 2014, p. 2.

12. Eliza Newlin Carney, "Air Strikes," *National Journal*, June 15, 1996, pp. 1313–17; and Peter Stone, "Business Strikes Back," *National Journal*, October 25, 1997, pp. 2130–33.

13. Alfred Stepan and Juan Linz, "Comparative Perspectives on Inequality and the Quality of Democracy in the United States," *Perspectives on Politics*, December, 2011, p. 841.

14. Lawrence Lessig, *Republic, Lost: How Money Corrupts Congress— And A Plan to Stop It* (New York: Grand Central Publishing, 2011).

15. Vogel, "Koch World Reboots."

16. See the Center for Responsive Politics, "2012 Top Donors to Outside Spending Groups" (www.OpenSecrets.org).

17. Peter Baker, "Obama Campaign Seeks to Recast Romney as a Raiser of Taxes on the Middle Class," *New York Times*, August 3, 2012, p. A14.

18. Leslie McCall, *The Undeserving Rich: American Beliefs about Inequality, Opportunity, and Redistribution* (Cambridge University Press, 2013).

19. Mark Halperin and John Heilemann, *Double Down: Game Change 2012* (New York: Penguin Press, 2013), p. 248.

20. "Results of The New York Times/CBS Poll," *New York Times*, July 18, 2012. (www.nytimes.com/interactive/2012/07/19/us/nytcbspoll-results. html?ref=us). This was a national survey of 942 registered voters conducted July 11–16, 2012.

21. Jack Gillum, "Why George Soros Waited So Long to Donate $1 Million to Help Obama," *Christian Science Monitor*, September 28, 2012.

22. Halperin and Heilemann, *Double Down*, p. 31. Also reported in James Hohmann, "The 5 Biggest Losers in 'Double Down,'" *Politico*, November 1, 2013.

23. Chris Cillizza, "What George Soros' Donations Tell Us about 2012," *Washington Post*, May 8, 2012.

24. Caitlin McDevitt, "Oprah's New 'Favorite Thing': Politics," *Politico*, August 10, 2013.

25. Gregory Giroux, "Oprah Joins Donors of $82 Million for Obama Victory Fund," October 19, 2012 (http://go.bloomberg.com/political-capital/tag/obama-victory-fund/).

26. Thomas Kaplan, "Catsimatidis Campaigns with Heart, Tongue, and Checkbook Unfettered," *New York Times*, September 2, 2013.

27. "Mayor Bloomberg Delivers Remarks at 2007 Conservative Party Conference," *New York Times*, July 2, 2007.

28. Ben Smith, "Mike Bloomberg Won't Be There to Buy Everyone Off in De Blasio's New York," *BuzzFeed*, November 11, 2013 (www.buzzfeed.com/bensmith/mike-bloomberg-wont-be-there-to-buy-everyone-off-in-de-blasi).

29. Michael Barbaro and Kitty Bennett, "Cost of Being Mayor? $650 Million, if He's Rich," *New York Times*, December 29, 2013.

30. Ibid.

31. Michael Grynbaum, "De Blasio Focuses on Inequality as He Courts Business Elite," *New York Times*, October 4, 2013.

32. Michael Grynbaum and Susanne Craig, "Wooing 'Hometown Industry,' de Blasio Meets Wary Wall St.," *New York Times*, October 11, 2013.

33. Chris Smith, "In Conversation: Michael Bloomberg," *New York*, September 7, 2013.

34. Philip Caulfield, "Meg Whitman Loses California Governor Race Despite $160 Million Tab," *New York Daily News*, November 3, 2010.

35. Ray Gustini, "What Loss of Competent, Uber-Rich Meg Whitman Says about American Politics," *The Atlantic*, November 3, 2010.

36. Robert Reich, "Why Billionaire Political Investors Will Keep Pouring Money Into Politics—Until They're Stopped," December 11, 2012 (http://robertreich.org).

37. Mike Allen and Jim Vandehei, "The Koch Brothers' Secret Bank," *Politico*, September 11, 2013.

38. Matea Gold and Philip Rucker, "Billionaire Mogul Sheldon Adelson Looks for Mainstream Republican Who Can Win in 2016," *Washington Post*, March 25, 2014.

39. Ibid.

40. Carl Hulse and Ashley Parker, "Koch Group, Spending Freely, Hones Attack on Government," *New York Times*, March 20, 2014.

41. Ibid.

42. Burgess Everett, "Harry Reid Continues Showdown with Kochs," *Politico*, March 4, 2014.

43. Ibid.

44. Amanda Terkel, "Mark Begich Goes After Koch Brothers in First Campaign TV Ad," *Huffington Post*, March 10, 2014.

45. Charles Koch, "I'm Fighting to Restore a Free Society," *Wall Street Journal*, April 2, 2014.

46. Evan Halper, "McConnell Says Liberal California Billionaire Just Like the Kochs," *Los Angeles Times*, March 4, 2014.

47. Holly Yeager, "Soros Group Triples Its Lobbying Spending," *Washington Post*, February 23, 2014.

48. Matea Gold, "Billionaire Soros Backs Pro-Hillary Clinton Super PAC," *Washington Post*, October 25, 2013, p. A3.

49. "Hillary's Billionaires," *Washington Free Beacon*, February 3, 2014.

50. Peter Nicholas, "Hillary Clinton's Phantom Presence in 2016 Campaign Freezes Other Democrats," *Wall Street Journal*, April 6, 2014.

Chapter Three

1. Kenneth Vogel, *2.5 Billion Dollars, One Suspicious Vehicle, and a Pimp—on the Trail of the Ultra-Rich Hijacking American Politics* (New York: Public Affairs, 2014).

2. Clare O'Connor, "High Roller: How Billionaire Peter Lewis Is Bankrolling Marijuana Legalization," *Forbes*, April 20, 2012.

3. Clare O'Connor, "Billionaire Peter Lewis: My War On Drug Laws," *Forbes*, September 21, 2011.

4. Alexander Burns and Kenneth Vogel, "Mega-Donors Plan GOP War Council," *Politico*, February 18, 2014.

5. Sean Sullivan, "Meet the Billionaire Hedge Fund Manager Quietly Shaping the GOP Gay Marriage Debate," *Washington Post*, May 3, 2013.

6. Anna Palmer and Jake Sherman, "Billionaires Push Republicans on Gay Rights Bill," *Politico*, April 9, 2014.

7. Michael Shear, "Amazon's Founder Pledges $2.5 Million in Support of Same-Sex Marriage," *New York Times*, July 27, 2012.

8. "FWD.us Immigration Ad Targets Rush Limbaugh, Sean Hannity Fans," *Huffington Post*, May 30, 2013.

9. Seung Min Kim, "Facebook-Linked Group Pushes GOP on Immigration," *Politico*, March 3, 2014.

10. Maggie Haberman, Anna Palmer, and John Bresnahan, "Bloomberg Storms D.C. on Guns, Immigration," *Politico*, January 30, 2013, p. 1.

11. Jeremy Peters, "Bloomberg Plans a $50 Million Challenge to the N.R.A.," *New York Times*, April 15, 2014.

12. Tarini Parti, "Bloomberg Super PAC Spent over $9M Last Fall," *Politico*, February 1, 2013, p. 10.

13. Steven Yaccino, "Candidate Who Backs Gun Control Wins Race," *New York Times*, February 26, 2013.

14. Jack Healy, "National Gun Debate Hits Close to Home in Colorado Recall Vote," *New York Times*, September 2, 2013.

15. Keith Coffman, "Colorado Voters Oust Democratic State Senators over Gun Control," *Reuters*, September 11, 2013.

16. Michael Barbaro, "Anxious Allies Aiding Booker in Senate Bid," *New York Times*, October 6, 2013.

17. Maggie Haberman and James Hohmann, "Bloomberg Ad Hits Cuccinelli on Guns," *Politico*, October 23, 2013, p. 6.

18. James Hohmann and Maggie Haberman, "Michael Bloomberg to Buy Big for Terry McAuliffe," *Politico*, October 21, 2013.

19. Michael Scherer, "Michael Bloomberg Wants to Be Mayor of the World," *Time*, October 21, 2013.

20. Jane Mayer, "State for Sale," *New Yorker*, October 10, 2011.

21. Ian Millhiser, "How One Multi-Millionaire Is Turning North Carolina into A Tea Party Utopia," Center for American Progress, April 8, 2013. Also see Trip Gabriel, "Protests Aim at One Man Who Moved State to Right," *New York Times*, December 14, 2013; and Bill McDiarmid, "Is the 'Common School' Ideal Doomed in North Carolina?," *Real Clear Education*, March 17, 2014.

22. Collin Eaton, "Houston Billionaire Philanthropist Taking Act to California," *Houston Business Journal*, June 26, 2013.

23. Randal Edgar and Katherine Gregg, "Taveras Campaign Critical of Billionaire's Role," *Providence Journal*, March 1, 2014.

24. John Arnold, "Attacks and Vitriol Will Not Deter Me from Supporting Fixes to Public Policy," *Chronicle of Philanthropy*, March 31, 2014.

25. David Sirota, "The Plot against Pensions," Institute for America's Future, 2013, p. 1.

26. Carl Hulse, "Ads Attacking Health Law Stagger Outspent Democrats," *New York Times*, January 15, 2014.

27. Sheryl Stolberg and Mike McIntire, "A Crisis Months in the Planning," *New York Times*, October 6, 2013.

28. Jeremy Peters, "Conservatives' Aggressive Ad Campaign Seeks to Cast Doubt on Health Law," *New York Times*, July 7, 2013, p. 12; and Glenn Kessler, "'Billions' Spent on Attacking Obamacare?," *Washington Post*, April 4, 2014.

29. Jeremy Peters, "Koch Brothers' Group Uses Health Care Law to Attack Democrats," *New York Times*, November 19, 2013. Also see Hulse, "Ads Attacking on Health Law Stagger Outspent Democrats"; and Carl Hulse and Ashley Parker, "Koch Group, Spending Freely, Hones Attack on Government," *New York Times*, March 20, 2014.

30. Stephanie Simon, "Koch Group, Unions Battle over Colorado Schools Race," *Politico*, November 2, 2013.

31. Rachael Bade, "Norquist, Koch Group Take on Tennessee Republicans for Tax Sin," *Politico*, March 23, 2014.

32. John Eligon, "Koch Group Has Ambitions in Small Races," *New York Times*, November 3, 2013.

33. Robert Kuttner, "Billionaires against Social Security," *Huffington Post*, October 20, 2013.

34. Michael Hiltzik, "Unmasking the Most Influential Billionaire in U.S. Politics," *Los Angeles Times*, October 2, 2012.

35. Peter Wallsten and Tom Hamburger, "Adelson Launches Campaign to Ban Internet Gambling," *Washington Post*, November 17, 2013.

36. Ibid.

37. William D. Cohan, "How the Billionaires' Shadow Government Works," Bloomberg, October 20, 2013.

38. Darren Goode, "Climate Billionaire Aims to Set Stage for 2016," *Politico*, February 18, 2014.

39. Alexander Burns and Andrew Restuccia, "Inside a Green Billionaire's Virginia Crusade," *Politico*, November 11, 2013.

40. Ibid.

41. Alexander Burns, "Billionaire Environmentalist Goes Big in Virginia Governor's Race," *Politico*, August 4, 2013.

42. Joshua Green, "The Wrath of a Green Billionaire," *Bloomberg Businessweek*, April 29–May 5, 2013, p. 24.

43. David Sears and Jack Citrin, *Tax Revolt: Something for Nothing in California* (Harvard University Press, 1985).

44. Harry Esteve, "Oregon Voters Pass Tax Increasing Measures by Big Margin," *The Oregonian*, January 26, 2010.

45. Brent Walth, "The Closing Tally on the Measures 66 and 67 Campaigns: $12.5 Million," *The Oregonian*, March 3, 2010.

46. Esteve, "Oregon Voters Pass Tax Increasing Measures by Big Margin."

47. Ibid.

48. Harry Esteve, "Oregon Legislature Approves Nike Tax Deal in One-Day Special Session," *The Oregonian*, December 14, 2012.

49. James Walker, "Stephen Ross: Committed to Miami," ESPN, September 9, 2013.

50. Marc Caputo, "Blocked from Taxpayer Cash for Miami Stadium, Steve Ross Gives $200 M. to UM. As in Michigan," *Miami Herald*, September 4, 2013.

51. Kevin Delaney and Rick Eckstein, *Public Dollars, Private Stadiums: The Battle over Building Sports Stadiums* (Rutgers University Press, 2003); and Neil deMause and Joanna Cagan, *Field of Schemes: How the Great Stadium Swindle Turns Public Money into Private Profit* (University of Nebraska Press/Bison Books, 2008).

52. Michele Dargan, "Dolphins Owner Ross Donates $200 Million to Alma Mater," *Palm Beach Daily News*, October 27, 2013.

53. Walker, "Stephen Ross: Committed to Miami."

54. Alexander Burns and Maggie Haberman, "2013: Year of the Liberal Billionaire," *Politico*, November 1, 2013.

Chapter Four

1. Mike Allen, "Capitol Playbook," *Politico*, November 21, 2013.

2. Michael Scherer, "Michael Bloomberg Wants to Be Mayor of the World," *Time*, October 21, 2013.

3. Allen, "Capitol Playbook."

4. Michael Barbaro, "Bloomberg Focuses on Rest (as in Rest of World)," *New York Times*, December 15, 2013, p. 1.

5. See Brown University, Taubman Center for Public Policy and American Institutions, at www.brown.edu/academics/Taubman_Center/.

6. Zoltan Acs, *Why Philanthropy Matters: How the Wealthy Give, and What It Means for Our Economic Well-Being* (Princeton University Press, 2013).

7. "Charitable Giving Statistics," in *Giving USA* (National Philanthropic Trust, 2012) (www.nptrust.org/philanthropic-resources/charitable-giving-statistics/).

8. Maria DiMento, "America's Wealthiest Donors Slow Their Giving," *Chronicle of Philanthropy*, January 1, 2013.

9. William Broad, "Billionaires with Big Ideas Are Privatizing American Science," *New York Times*, March 16, 2014, p. A1.

10. Nick Anderson, "Bloomberg Pledges $350 Million to Johns Hopkins University," *Washington Post*, January 26, 2013.

11. Personal e-mail communication from David Rubenstin to the author, September 12, 2013.

12. Neely Tucker, "$21.3 Million Bid Will Keep Copy of Magna Carta in U.S.," *Washington Post*, December 20, 2007.

13. Thomas Heath, "Billionaire David Rubenstein Buys Colonial-Era Bay Psalm Book for $14.2 Million," *Washington Post*, November 28, 2013.

14. Leslie Milk and Mary Yarrison, "Washingtonians of the Year 2012: David Rubenstein: Philanthropy That Unites Washington," *Washingtonian*, January 14, 2013, p. 56.

15. Amy Schiller, "Can Billionaire Philanthropists Replace the Federal Government?," *The Nation*, October 11, 2013.

16. National Center for Charitable Statistics, "Quick Facts About Nonprofits" (Urban Institute, 2011) (http://nccs.urban.org/statistics/quickfacts.cfm).

17. Matthew Bishop and Michael Green, *Philanthrocapitalism: How Giving Can Save the World* (New York: Bloomsbury Press, 2009).

18. Laura Arrillaga-Andreessen, *Giving 2.0: Transform Your Giving and Our World* (San Francisco: Jossey-Bass, 2011).

19. Paul Brest and Hal Harvey, *Money Well Spent: A Strategic Plan for Smart Philanthropies* (New York: Bloomberg Press, 2008).

20. Elizabeth Blair, "Charity Watchdog Shakes Up Ratings to Focus On Results," *National Public Radio*, October 22, 2013.

21. Doug Donovan, "Hewlett Ends Effort to Get Donors to Make Dispassionate Choices on Giving," *Chronicle of Philanthropy*, April 3, 2014.

22. "Foundation Fact Sheet" (Bill and Melinda Gates Foundation, July 3, 2013).

23. Carol Loomis, "Warren Buffet Gives Away His Fortune," *CNN Money*, June 25, 2006.

24. Randall Lane, "The 50 Philanthropists Who Have Given Away the Most Money," *Forbes*, December 2, 2013.

25. "The Opportunity to Make a Difference," *Harvard Magazine*, September, 2013.

26. Brad Stone, "Bill Gates: Philanthropist," *Bloomberg Businessweek*, August 12–25, 2013, p. 54.

27. Ron Dicker, "Bill Gates: 'Philanthropy Should Be Taking Bigger Risks Than Business,'" *Huffington Post*, September 25, 2013.

28. Schiller, "Can Billionaire Philanthropists Replace the Federal Government?"

29. Deyan Sudjie, "Is This the End of the Guggenheim Dream?," *The Guardian*, January 22, 2005.

30. Mike McKenna, "CWRU Philanthropist Peter B. Lewis Dies at the Age of 80," *The Observer*, March 18, 2014.

31. Bob Colacello, "How Do You Solve a Problem Like MOCA?," *Vanity Fair*, March, 2013; and Kelly Crow, "L.A. Museum Chief Set to Step Down after Rocky Tenure," *Wall Street Journal*, July 23, 2013.

32. "TransCanada Snubs Invite from Billionaire Keystone XL Foe, Calling It 'Political Grandstanding,'" *Canadian Press*, November 28, 2013.

33. Evan Halper, "Tom Steyer May Be Liberals' Answer to the Koch Brothers," *Los Angeles Times*, December 21, 2013.

34. "TransCanada Snubs Invite from Billionaire Keystone XL Foe, Calling It 'Political Grandstanding,'" *Financial Post*, November 28, 2013 (http://business.financialpost.com/2013/11/28/transcanada-snubs-invite-from-billionaire-keystone-xl-foe-calling-it-political-grandstanding/?__lsa=b708-c0e3).

35. Ibid.

36. Darrell West, Tom Anton, and Jack Combs, "Public Opinion in Rhode Island" (Brown University Center for Public Policy, 1994).

37. Tara Loader Wilkinson, "Why Only 5% of Billionaires Have Signed the Giving Pledge," *Wealth-X*, November 15, 2013.

38. "World Giving Index" (Charities Aid Foundation, December 2012).

39. Alexander Karp, Gary Tobin, and Aryeh Weinberg, "An Exceptional Nation: American Philanthropy Is Different Because America Is Different," *Philanthropy Roundtable*, December 1, 2004.

40. John Micklethwait and Adrian Wooldridge, *The Right Nation: Conservative Power in America* (New York: Penguin Press, 2004).

41. See the description of the foundation at www.carlosslim.com.

42. Dolia Estevez, "Mexican Billionaire Carlos Slim's Philanthropic 'Generosity' Gets the Nod from a Kennedy Scion," *Forbes*, October 16, 2013.

43. "Aliko Dangote Announces N200bn Endowment for Dangote Foundation," *The Will*, March 5, 2014; and "Africa's Richest Man Aliko Dangote Gives N20bn to Charity in 2 Years," *Wazobia Journal*, January 21, 2013.

44. Sammy Said, "Richest Self-Made Women Billionaires," *The Richest*, March 2012.

45. Tom Metcalf and Manuel Baigorri, "Spain's Richest Woman Emerges with $5 Billion Zara Stake," Bloomberg, November 1, 2013.

46. Timothy Heritage, "Putin Critics Worry as Russia Clampdown Spreads," *Chicago Tribune*, May 30, 2013.

47. "Prize Offered to Africa's Leaders," BBC News, October 26, 2006.

48. "Mozambique Ex-Leader wins Prize," BBC News, October 22, 2008.

49. "Festus Mogae Wins Ibrahim Prize," BBC News, October 20, 2008.

50. "Cape Verde Ex-Leader Pedro Pires Wins Mo Ibrahim Prize," BBC News, October 10, 2011.

Chapter Five

1. "Profile of Bidzina Ivanishvili," *Forbes*, March 2011. See this profile, which is updated regularly, at www.forbes.com/profile/bidzina-ivanishvili/.

2. Wendell Steavenson, "The Good Oligarch," *Prospect Magazine*, July 21, 2010.

3. Henry Meyer, "A Billionaire Spreads Riches by the Black Sea," *Bloomberg Businessweek*, August 29, 2013, pp. 18–20.

4. "Billionaire Prime Minister's Pick for President Easily Wins in Georgia," *Washington Post*, October 27, 2013.

5. "Ivanishvili Launches a New NGO," *Georgia Today*, January 23, 2014.

6. Shaun Walker, "Georgia's Billionaire PM Wants to Give Up Office, but Will He Relinguish Power?," *The Guardian*, October 19, 2013.

7. David Herszenhorn, "Georgia Elects New President, but Real Power Will Rest with Next Premier," *New York Times*, Octobver 27, 2013.

8. David Herszenhorn, "Exiting President Reflects on Georgia," *New York Times*, November 18, 2013, p. A9.

9. Jim Yardley and Gaia Pianigiani, "Dealing a Blow to Berlusconi, an Italian Senate Panel Recommends His Expulsion," *New York Times*, October 5, 2013; Jim Yardley, "Berlusconi Expelled from Senate in Italy after 2 Decades in Government," *New York Times*, November 27, 2013; "Berlusconi Given Community Service for Tax Fraud," Associated Press, April 15, 2014.

10. Guy Dinmore, "Berlusconi Planning to Stand for European Elections," *Irish Times*, February 7, 2014.

11. Gavin Jones, "Italy's Highest Court Confirms Berlusconi Ban from Public Office," Reuters, March 18, 2014 (http://news.yahoo.com/italy-court-confirms-berlusconi-ban-public-office-214443257--sector.html).

12. Angelique Chrisafis, "French Billionaire Serge Dassault Fights Corruption Scandal," *The Guardian*, September 20, 2013.

13. "French Billionaire Dassault Faces Custody in Corruption Case," Yahoo News, February 12, 2014; "French Billionaire Senator Dassault Loses Immunity over Graft Claims," France 24, February 13, 2014; and "French Police Question Billionaire Serge Dassault over Alleged Vote-Buying," *The Guardian*, February 19, 2014.

14. Andrew Darby, "Clive Palmer Denies PUP Broke Law with Tasmania Election Ads," *Sydney Morning Herald*, March 11, 2014.

15. Rachel Morton, "Colorful Billionaire Wins Queensland Seat," 3 News, November 3, 2013.

16. Daryl Passmore, Liam Walsh, and Jason Tin, "It's Business as Usual for Nouveau Riche Billionaire Clive Palmer, Head of a Conflicting Manner Born," *The Courier-Mail*, November 16, 2013.

17. Georgina Prodhan, "Canadian Billionaire Stronach to End Foray into Austrian Politics," Reuters, October 23, 2013.

18. "Frank Stronach Puts Himself in the Race to Become the Next Chancellor of Austria," *Jewish Business News*, September 27, 2013; "Canadian Billionaire Frank Stronach Enters Austria's Parliament," Associated Press, September 29, 2013; and "Billionaire Stronach to Quit Parliament after Setbacks," *Oman Observer*, Janaury 29, 2014.

19. Naazneen Karmali, "Is Billionaire Nandan Nilekani Preparing to Plunge into Politics?," *Forbes*, September 17, 2013.

20. "Billionaire Nandan Nilekani Tells Bangalore Voters He Can't Be Bought," *South China Morning Post*, April 16, 2014.

21. Kevin Hewison, "Thanksin Shinawatra and the Reshaping of Thai Politics," *Contemporary Politics*, vol. 16 (June 2010), pp. 119–33.

22. Chico Harlan, "Battle over Long-Deposed Leader Thaksin Shinawatra Threatens Thailand's Democracy," *Washington Post*, March 1, 2014.

23. "Thaksin Shinawatra Corruption Claims Stoke Thai Protest Outrage," NDTV, January 20, 2014.

24. "Thaksin Shinawatra and Family," *Forbes*, March 2014.

25. Poypiti Amatatham, "Court Voids Thailand's February Election, Adding to Political Turmoil," *New York Times*, March 21, 2014.

26. "Can Sarzoky Survive the Bettencourt Scandal?," *Vanity Fair*, July 6, 2010.

27. "Does Andrej Babis Have Bigger Political Ambitions?," *The Economist*, July 17, 2013.

28. Peter Laca, "Czech Billionaire Risks Helping Communist Comeback," *Bloomberg News*, October 21, 2013.

29. Peter Laca and Lenka Ponikelska, "Czech Election Winner Feuds before Talks with Billionaire," *Bloomberg*, October 28, 2013.

30. Sean Hanley, "How the Czech Social Democrats Were Derailed by a Billionaire Populist," Policy Network, November 12, 2013.

31. "Central Europe's Berlusconi?," *The Economist*, November 2, 2013.

32. "Czech Billionaire Sets aside Business for Power Politics," *Tengri News*, January 21, 2014.

33. Peter Laca, "Czech Premier Battles Tycoon Minister as Budget Talks Loom," *Bloomberg News*, April 4, 2014.

34. "Finding a Better Future," Dartmouth Tuck Communications, June 21, 2010.

35. "Influential Businessman Bakala Sent Half a Million to Schwarzenberg Candidacy," *Kurzy.cz*, November 26, 2012.

36. Ibid.

37. Andrew Kramer and David Herszenhorn, "Midas Touch in St. Petersburg: Friends of Putin Glow Brightly," *New York Times*, March 1, 2012.

38. Ilya Khrennikov, "Putini's Billionaire Ally Buys Half of Tele2 Russia Operator," *Bloomberg*, October 17, 2013.

39. Kramer and Herszenhorn, "Midas Touch in St. Petersburg."

40. David Herszenhorn, "Opposition Leader Asserts Broad Problems in Moscow Race," *New York Times*, September 13, 2013, p. A6.

41. Andrew Kramer, "Political Endurance Test for Russian Billionaire," *New York Times*, August 28, 2013.

42. "Our Crony-Capitalism Index: Planet Plutocrat," *The Economist*, March 15, 2014.

43. Manu Joseph, "Indian Billionaires Get a Pass," *New York Times*, October 23, 2013.

44. Alexis Okeowo, "Africa's Richest Man Is Just Getting Started," *Bloomberg Businessweek*, March 7, 2013, pp. 52–56.

45. Andrew Kramer, "Ukraine Turns to Its Oligarchs for Political Help," *New York Times*, March 2, 2014.

46. Andrew Kramer, "Hopes of Many Riding on Wealthy Chocolatier," *New York Times*, March 30, 2014, p. A12.

47. David Barboza and Sharon LaFraniere, "'Princelings' in China Use Family Ties to Gain Riches," *New York Times*, May 17, 2012.

48. David Barboza, "Billions in Hidden Riches for Family of Chinese Leader," *New York Times*, October 25, 2012.

49. David Barboza, "Lobbying, a Windfall, and a Leader's Family," *New York Times*, November 24, 2012.

50. Nariman Gizitdinov, "Kazakh Billionaire Says He's Got Nothing to Hide," *Bloomberg Markets*, November 13, 2013.

51. Edward Wong, "China Detains a Billionaire for Activism," *New York Times*, September 14, 2013, p. A4.

52. Chris Buckley, "China Arrests Prominent Businessman Who Backed Rights Causes," *New York Times*, October 21, 2013.

53. Andrew Browne and Paul Mozur, "Alibaba's Co-Founders Delve into Philanthropy," *Wall Street Journal*, April 25, 2014.

Chapter Six

1. World Bank, "World Development Indicators," September 23, 2013.

2. Barbara Ortutay, "Microsoft CEO Ballmer to Leave Post Next Year," *Providence Journal*, August 24, 2013, p. A9.

3. Walter Isaacson, "Bill Gates, Inside the Gates," *Harvard Magazine*, September 20, 2013.

4. Ibid.

5. William Page and John Lopatka, *The Microsoft Case: Antitrust, High Technology, and Consumer Welfare* (University of Chigago Press, 2009).

6. "Bloomberg Billionaires Index Methodology," *Bloomberg Businessweek*, January 18, 2013.

7. Ibid.

8. Ibid.

9. Using different valuation measures, the first global census by Wealth-X and UBS says that there are 2,170 billionaires around the world. See Wealth-X, "First Global Census Shows Record of 2,170 Billionaires Worldwide," November 6, 2013 (www.wealthx.com/articles/2013/first-global-census-shows-record-of-2170-billionaires-worldwide/).

10. Wealth-X and UBS, "Billionaire Census," 2013, pp. 11–15 (www.billionairecensus.com).

11. Ibid., p. 21.

12. E-mail communication from Fauzi Ahmad, Wealth-X, November 17, 2013.

13. Julie Creswell, "For Rich, '13 Was Good for Making, and Spending, Money," *New York Times*, March 5, 2014. Also see Knight Frank, "Wealth Report," 2014 (www.thewealthreport.net).

14. Lisa Kroll, "Inside the 2014 Forbes Billionaires List: Facts and Figures," *Forbes*, March 3, 2014.

15. Robert Frank, "How Many Chinese Billionaires?," CNBC, March 4, 2014. For information on the Hurun Report, see www.hurun.net/usen/.

16. Shan Li, "Saudi Prince Sues Forbes over His Rank on Billionaires List," *Los Angeles Times*, June 8, 2013.

17. Gwynn Guilford, "Forbes and Bloomberg Share a Fascination with Billionaires but Don't Agree on Much beyond That," *Yahoo News*, March 4, 2013.

18. Kerry Dolan, "Prince Alwaleed and the Curious Case of Kingdom Holding Stock," *Forbes*, March 25, 2013.

19. Dolia Estevez, "Billionaire Telecom Tycoon Carlos Slim Pushes Back against Mexican Government Crackdown on Monopolies," *Forbes*, April 3, 2014.

20. "The Reclusive Billionaire: Secret Life of Zara Boss Amancio Ortega and His 'Fast Fashion' Empire," *Reuters*, March 5, 2013.

21. Maureen Dowd, "America's Billionaire," *New York Times*, September 22, 2013, p. 11.

22. Nancy Gohring, "Larry Ellison Admits It: Quick, Cheap, and Cloud Are the Future," *Cite World*, June 27, 2013.

23. Charles Koch, *The Science of Success* (New York: John Wiley and Sons, 2007).

24. Eric Malnic and Rich Connell, "Controller Says Her Error Caused Runway Collision," *Los Angeles Times*, May 8, 1991.

25. Robert Frank, "Vegas Tycoon: 'So I Lost $25 Billion,'" *Wall Street Journal*, November 22, 2010.

26. Mousumi Saha Kumar, "Christy Walton and Family," *Success Stories*, November 11, 2011 (www.successstories.co.in/christy-walton-family/).

27. Charles Fishman, *The Wal-Mart Effect: How the World's Most Powerful Company Really Works—And How It's Transforming the American Economy* (New York: Penguin Press, 2006).

28. Clare O'Connor, "Inside the World of Walmart Billionaire Alice Walton, America's Richest Art Collector," *Forbes*, September 16, 2013.

29. "Planet Plutocrat," *The Economist*, March 15, 2014.

30. "The World's Billionaires," *Forbes*, March 3, 2014 (www.forbes.com/billionaires/).

31. The estimate for total global wealth comes from Credit Suisse, Global Wealth Database 2012 (www.credit-suisse.com/news/doc/credit_suisse_global_wealth_databook.pdf), section 2.2, p. 17.

32. "The World's Billionaires," *Forbes*.

33. Dan Alexander, "Meet The Richest Billionaire in Every State," *Forbes*, March 7, 2014.

34. Katherine Ryder, "Does Baidu's Robin Li Have the Hardest Job in the World?," *Fortune*, September 27, 2011.

35. Michelle Yun, "Li Ka-shing Pays $1.3 Billion for Dutch Waste Processor," *Bloomberg News*, June 17, 2013.

36. Robert Jarman, "Alisher Usmanov: The Biggest Oligarch of Them All and Probably the Richest Man in Britain," *Vintage Magazine*, October 6, 2012.

37. Sudhir Suryawanshi, "Mukesh Ambani," *DNA India*, June 14, 2013.

38. James Clear, "The Biggest Takeaway from Sir Richard Branson's Rags-to-Billionaire Success," *Business Insider*, November 27, 2013.

39. Joe Leahy, "Brazilian Tycoon Eike Batista's Empire Crumbles amid OGX Woes," *Financial Times*, July 3, 2013; and Dan Alexander, "Fumbled Fortunes: Meet the Ex-Billionaires Who Lost Their Riches," *Forbes*, March 4, 2014.

40. Kenneth Rapoza, "The Dramatic Fall of Brazil's Eike Batista," *Forbes*, October 1, 2013; and Alanna Petroff, "Brazil's Beleaguered OGX Files for Bankruptcy," *CNN Money*, October 31, 2013.

41. Pauline Chiou, "Richer Than Trump or Oprah: Meet China's Female Property Magnate," *CNN*, July 3, 2013. Also see CBS News, *60 Minutes*, August 11, 2013.

42. "The Myth of Fu Wah's Chen Lihua," *China Times*, December 20, 2012.

43. Lily Kuo, "Half of the World's Self-Made Women Billionaires Are from China," *Quartz*, September 17, 2013.

44. Gabriel Kahn, "Patrick Soon-Shiong, Richest Man in LA, Is on a Philanthropic Mission to Improve Health Care," *Huffington Post*, April 21, 2013.

45. Howard Fineman, "Meet Patrick Soon-Shiong, The LA Billionaire Reinventing Your Health Care," *Huffington Post*, December 1, 2013.

46. Brian Solomon, "Jennifer Pritzker Becomes First Transgender Billionaire," *Forbes*, September 16, 2013.

47. Natalie Robehmed, "Meet the World's LGBT Billionaires," *Forbes*, March 3, 2014.

48. Mykolas Rambus, "Technopreneurs: Driving Innovation, Amassing Fortunes," Wealth-X, February 18, 2014.

49. Sarah Lacy, "Is Mark Zuckerberg the New Bill Gates?," *Pando Daily*, June 20, 2013.

Chapter Seven

1. A. Alfred Taubman, *Threshold Resistance: The Extraordinary Career of a Luxury Retail Pioneer* (New York: Harper Business, 2007).

2. Malcolm Gladwell, "The Terrazzo Jungle," *New Yorker*, March 15, 2004.

3. Michael Bloomberg, *Bloomberg by Bloomberg* (New York: John Wiley and Sons, 1997); and Zachary Seward, "This is How Much a Bloomberg Terminal Costs," *Quartz*, May 15, 2013.

4. Michael Grynbaum, "Bloomberg Shares a Few Secrets to Success: Be Early, Stay Late, and Hold It In," *New York Times*, August 24, 2013, p. A15.

5. Michael Hiltzik, *Dealers of Lightning: Xerox PARC and the Dawn of the Computer Age* (New York: Harper Collins, 1999).

6. Geoff Hollister, *Out of Nowhere: The Inside Story of How Nike Marketed the Culture of Running* (Aachen, Germany: Meyer und Meyer Fachverlag und Buchhandel GmbH, 2008).

7. Jennifer Steinhauser, "A Billionaire Philanthropist in Washington Who's Big on 'Patriotic Giving,'" *New York Times*, February 20, 2014.

8. David Montgomery, "David Rubenstein, Co-Founder of Carlyle Group and Washington Philanthropist," *Washington Post*, May 14, 2012.

9. Ibid.

10. Andrew Zolli and Ann Marie Healy, *Resilience: Why Things Bounce Back* (New York: Free Press, 2012).

11. Brad Stone, *The Everything Store: Jeff Bezos and the Age of Amazon* (New York: Little, Brown, and Company, 2013).

12. "Taking the Long View," *The Economist*, March 3, 2012.

13. Jeff Bezos, "Five Time-Tested Success Tips from Amazon Founder Jeff Bezos," *Forbes*, April 30, 2013.

14. Paul Farhi, "Jeffrey Bezos, *Washington Post*'s Next Owner, Aims for a New 'Golden Era' at the Newspaper," *Washington Post*, September 3, 2013.

15. Peter Whoriskey, Jia Lynn Yang, and Cecilia Kang, "Amazon Founder Jeff Bezos Known for Patience, Focus on Detail in His Business Ventures," *Washington Post*, August 5, 2013.

16. David Streitfeld and Christine Haughney, "He's 'Going to Break Some Eggs,'" *New York Times*, August 18, 2013.

Chapter Eight

1. Roger Ebert, "Trading Places," *Chicago Sun-Times*, June 9, 1983.

2. Eric Jackson, *The PayPal Wars: Battles with eBay, the Media, the Mafia, and the Rest of Planet Earth* (Los Angeles: World Ahead Publishing, 2004).

3. George Packer, "No Death, No Taxes: The Libertarian Futurism of a Silicon Valley Billionaire," *New Yorker*, November 28, 2011.

4. Gregory Ferenstein, "Thiel Fellows Program Is 'Most Misdirected Piece of Philanthropy,' Says Larry Summers," *Tech Crunch*, October 10, 2013.

5. Peter Thiel, "The Education of a Libertarian," Cato Institute, April 13, 2009 (www.cato-unbound.org/2009/04/13/peter-thiel/education-libertarian).

6. Ibid.

7. Jacob Hacker and Paul Pierson, *Winner-Take-All Politics: How Washington Made the Rich Richer—And Turned Its Back on the Middle Class* (New York: Simon and Schuster, 2011); and Larry Bartels, *Unequal Democracy: The Political Economy of the New Gilded Age* (Princeton University Press, 2010).

8. Joseph Stiglitz and Michael Doyle, "Make Eliminating Extreme Inequality a Sustainable Development Goal," *Ethics and International Affairs*, March 20, 2014.

9. Darrell West, *Digital Government: Technology and Public Sector Performance* (Princeton University Press, 2005), pp. 2–3.

10. Lawrence Friedman, *A History of American Law*, 3rd. ed. (New York: Touchstone, 2005), p. 429.

11. Richard Joseph, *The Origins of the American Income Tax* (Syracuse University Press, 2004).

12. John Steele Gordon, *Empire of Wealth* (New York: Harper Perennial, 2005).

13. John Witte, *The Politics and Development of the Federal Income Tax* (University of Wisconsin Press, 1986).

14. James Stewart, "High Income, Low Taxes, and Never a Bad Year," *New York Times*, November 2, 2013, p. B1.

15. Peter Orszag, "Testimony on the Taxation of Carried Interest," Congressional Budget Office, July 11, 2007 (www.cbo.gov/publication/18823).

16. Ryan Dezember, "KKR Co-Founders Take Home $327 Million in 2013," *Wall Street Journal*, February 24, 2014.

17. Ian Shapiro and Michael Graetz, *Death by a Thousand Cuts: The Fight over Taxing Inherited Wealth* (Princeton University Press, 2005).

18. Zachary Mider, "Little Tax Haven on the Prairie," *Bloomberg Businessweek*, January 13–19, 2014, pp. 38–39.

19. Zachary Mider, "An Accidental Tax Break for America's Wealthiest People," *Washington Post*, December 29, 2013, p. G3.

20. William Gale and Samara Potter, "An Economic Evaluation of the Economic Growth and Tax Relief Reconciliation Act of 2001," *National Tax Journal* (March 2002), pp. 133–34.

21. Anne Krueger, "The Political Economy of the Rent-Seeking Society," *American Economic Review*, vol. 64 (1974), pp. 291–303.

22. "60 Minutes: Billionaire Elon Musk on 2008," CBS News, March 28, 2014.

23. Rob Nixon, "Billionaires Received U.S. Farm Subsidies, Report Finds," *New York Times*, November 7, 2013; and Christine Stuart, "DeLauro Questions Billionaire Farm Subsidies," *CT News*, November 13, 2013.

24. Molly Sherlock, "Impact of Tax Policies on the Commercial Application of Renewable Energy Technology," testimony before the House

Subcommittee on Energy and Environment, April 19, 2012, p. 3 (www. google.com/#q=Molly+Sherlock%2C+%E2%80%9CImpact+of+Tax+Polici es+on+the+Commercial+Application+of+Renewable+Energy+Technology% 2C%E2%80%9D+).

25. Roland Jones, "Stock Exchanges Trade Fractions for Decimals," ABC News, August 23, 2000 (http://abcnews.go.com/Business/story?id=89457).

26. Matthew Philips, "How the Robots Lost," *Bloomberg Businessweek*, June 6, 2013, pp. 62–66.

27. Scott Patterson and Jenny Strasburg, "High-Speed Trading Firms Face New U.S. Scrutiny," *Wall Street Journal*, March 18, 2014.

28. Mark Mizruchi, *The Fracturing of the American Corporate Elite* (Harvard University Press, 2013).

29. Scott Patterson, "Speed Traders Get an Edge," *Wall Street Journal*, February 6, 2014.

30. Michael Lewis, *Flash Boys: A Wall Street Revolt* (New York: W. W. Norton, 2014).

31. Hamilton Nolan, "Super-Successful Hedge Fund Reportedly a Huge Tax Dodger," *Gawker*, July 1, 2013.

32. Josh Harkinson, "How a Homegrown Geek Outsourced, Downsized, and Tax-Breaked His Way to the Top," *Mother Jones,* March-April 2011.

33. Ibid.

34. David Rothkopf, *Superclass: The Global Power Elite and the World They Are Making* (New York: Farrar, Straus and Giroux, 2009).

35. Jennifer Ablan, "Billionaire Soros Weds Consultant in Third Marriage," Reuters, September 21, 2013.

36. Mizruchi, *The Fracturing of the American Corporate Elite.*

37. Anita Raghavan, *The Billionaire's Apprentice: The Rise of the Indian-American Elite and the Fall of the Galleon Hedge Fund* (New York: Business Plus, 2013).

38. Peter Lattman, "Big Hedge Fund Pays $616 Million in Trading Cases," *New York Times*, March 16, 2013, p. 1.

39. Ben Protess and Peter Lattman, "Hedge Fund Starts to Balk over Inquiry," *New York Times*, May 18, 2013, p. 1; and Ben Protess, Matthew Goldstein, and Alexandra Stevenson, "Former SAC Trader Is Convicted of Insider Trading," *New York Times*, December 18, 2013.

40. Peter Lattman and Ben Protess, "SAC Capital Is Indicted and Called a Magnet for Cheating," *New York Times*, July 25, 2013.

41. Ben Protess and Peter Lattman, "SAC Deal Could End Its Advisory Business," *New York Times*, October 18, 2013; and Ben Protess and Peter Lattman, "After a Decade, SAC Capital Blinks," *New York Times*, November 4, 2013. Also see Christopher Matthews and John Carreyrou, "Ex-SAC Trader Found Guilty," *Wall Street Journal*, February 6, 2014.

Chapter Nine

1. Quoted in Thomas Edsall, "In Defense of Anonymous Political Giving," *New York Times*, March 18, 2014.

2. Bradley Smith, "The Latest IRS Power Grab," *Wall Street Journal*, December 8, 2013.

3. Nicholas Confessore, "New Rules Would Rein In Nonprofits' Political Role," *New York Times*, November 26, 2013.

4. Susan Page, "IRS Chief: New Rule on Way for Non-Profits," *USA Today*, April 15, 2014.

5. Lucy Bernholz and Rob Reich, "Social Economy Policy Forecast 2013" (Stanford University, Stanford Center on Philanthropy and Civil Society, September 2013), pp. 13–15.

6. Chris Megerian and Anthony York, "California Fines Groups $16 Million for Funneling Money to Campaigns," *Los Angeles Times*, October 25, 2013.

7. Nicholas Confessore, "Koch-Linked Group Admits Spending Violations," *New York Times*, October 25, 2013, p. A19.

8. Thomas Mann and Norman Ornstein, *It's Even Worse Than It Looks* (New York: Basic Books, 2012), pp. 84–89.

9. Walter Oleszek, "Proposals to Reform 'Holds' in the Senate" (Congressional Research Service, December 20, 2007).

10. Tom Harkin, "Examining the Filibuster: Legislative Proposals to Change Senate Procedures," testimony before Senate Rules Committee, September 22, 2010.

11. Portions of this section are drawn from Darrell West and Beth Stone, "Nudging News Producers and Consumers toward More Thoughtful, Less Polarized Discourse" (Brookings, February 2014).

12. Mathew Ingram, "Is Marc Andreessen Right about What Is Holding the Media Industry Back? Mostly, Yes," Gigaom, February 13, 2014.

13. Steven Watts, *The People's Tycoon: Henry Ford and the American Century* (New York: Random House, 2006).

14. Mark Mizruchi, *The Fracturing of the American Corporate Elite* (Harvard University Press, 2013).

15. Frank Newport, "Majority in U.S. Want Wealth More Evenly Distributed," Gallup Organization, April 17, 2013.

16. Leslie McCall, *The Undeserving Rich: American Beliefs about Inequality, Opportunity, and Redistribution* (Cambridge University Press, 2013).

17. Newport, "Majority in U.S. Want Wealth More Evenly Distributed."

18. Pew Research Center for the People & the Press, "Most See Inequality Growing, but Partisans Differ over Solutions," January 23, 2014.

19. Lori Montgomery, "Richest 20 Percent Get Half the Overall Savings from U.S. Tax Breaks, CBO Says," *Washington Post*, May 29, 2013.

20. Lam Thuy Vo and Jacob Goldstein, "What America Pays In Taxes," *Planet Money*, April 13, 2012.

21. Montgomery, "Richest 20 Percent Get Half the Overall Savings from U.S. Tax Breaks."

22. John Witte, *The Politics and Development of the Federal Income Tax* (University of Wisconsin Press, 1986).

23. Congressional Budget Office, "The Distribution of Major Tax Expenditures in the Individual Income Tax System," May 2013, p. 3.

24. Peter Orszag, director of the Congressional Budget Office, "The Taxation of Carried Interest," testimony before the Senate Finance Committee, July 11, 2007 (www.finance.senate.gov/imo/media/doc/071107testpo2.pdf).

25. Les Leopold, *How to Make a Million Dollars an Hour: Why Hedge Funds Get Away with Siphoning Off America's Wealth* (New York: John Wiley and Sons, 2013).

26. "Obama Sets Sights on 'Carried Interest,' Lucrative Tax Deduction Used by Romney," *Huffington Post*, February 4, 2013.

27. Congressional Budget Office, "Options for Reducing the Deficit: Revenues–Option 11, Tax Carried Interest as Ordinary Income," November 13, 2013 (www.cbo.gov/budget-options/2013/44804)

28. Sam Pizzigati, "Tax-Free Gifts Solidify Dynastic Wealth," *Providence Journal*, February 13, 2013.

29. Figure quoted in Jeanne Sahadi, "The 4 Worst Tax Breaks," *CNN Money*, June 3, 2013.

30. Congressional Budget Office, "The Distribution of Major Tax Expenditures in the Individual Income Tax System," p. 16.

31. Zachary Mider, "Moguls Rent South Dakota Addresses to Shelter Wealth Forever," *Bloomberg News*, December 27, 2013.

32. Josh Boak, "Buffett Rule's Impact?," *Politico*, January 26, 2012.

33. Floyd Norris, "Total Taxes on Wages Are Rising," *New York Times*, April 12, 2014, p. B3.

34. Lawrence Delevingne, "How to Buy Your Own Private Jet," *Business Insider*, September 15, 2009.

35. Eric Lichtblau, "Industry Set for Fight to Keep Corporate Jet Tax Breaks," *New York Times*, July 7, 2011.

36. Tara Loader Wilkinson, "Private Jet Firms Navigate a Post-Crisis World," Wealth-X, February 19, 2014.

37. Richard Rubin and Andrew Zajac, "Corporate Jet Tax Gets Six Obama Mentions, $3 Billion Estimate," *Bloomberg News*, June 30, 2011.

38. Shirley Dennis-Escoffier, "IRS Finalizes Deduction Limits for Corporate Jets" (Wiley Periodicals, 2013) (http://onlinelibrary.wiley.com/doi/10.1002/jcaf.21866/abstract).

39. KPMG, "Private Jet Ownership: Do You Understand the Tax Costs?" (2012).

40. Jeff Wieand, "The Changing Face of Aircraft Lending," *Business Jet Traveler*, February 26, 2013; and Charles Alcock, "For Aircraft Buyers in Europe, Loans Come with Strings Attached," *Aviation International News*, December 2012, pp. 18–20.

41. David Ewalt, "Thirty Amazing Facts About Private Jets," *Forbes*, February 13, 2913.

42. Ibid.

43. Mizruchi, *The Fracturing of the American Corporate Elite*.

44. Adam Davidson, "Greed is Good," *New York Times Sunday Magazine*, June 2, 2013, pp. 14–6.

45. Ibid.

46. Tyler Cowan, *The Great Stagnation: How America Ate All the Low-Hanging Fruit of Modern History, Got Sick, and Will (Eventually) Feel Better* (New York: Dutton, 2011).

47. Quoted in Richard Reeves, "The Economic Case for Social Mobility" (Brookings, August 16, 2013) (www.brookings.edu/research/opinions/2013/08/16-economic-case-social-mobility-reeves).

48. Jonathan Kozol, *Savage Inequalities: Children in America's Schools* (New York: Broadway Books, 2012).

49. Isabelle Joumard, Mauro Pisu, and Debra Bloch, "Less Income Inequality and More Growth: Are They Compatible?," OECD Working Paper 926, part 3, January 10, 2012, p. 6.

50. Organization for Economic Cooperation and Development, "Urgent Action Needed to Tackle Rising Inequality and Social Divisions" (March 18, 2014) (www.oecd.org/social/urgent-action-needed-to-tackle-rising-inequality-and-social-divisions-says-oecd.htm).

51. Joumard, Pisu, and Bloch, "Less Income Inequality and More Growth: Are They Compatible?," p. 7.

52. Mark Blyth, *Austerity: The History of a Dangerous Idea* (Oxford University Press, 2013).

53. Quoted in Chrystia Freeland, "When State and Capital Split Apart," *New York Times*, March 28, 2013.

54. David de Jong and Robert LaFranco, "Where Trillions Go to Hide," *Bloomberg Businessweek*, May 6–12, 2013, pp. 43–44.

55. Tara Loader Wilkinson, "Nationality Swapping: The Latest Craze of the World's Ultra Rich," Wealth-X, November 20, 2013.

56. Virginia Harrison, "Branson: My Island Life Isn't a Tax Dodge," *CNN Money*, October 14, 2013.

57. Jeanne Sahadi, "Top Income Tax Rate: How the U.S. Really Compares," *CNN Money*, April 1, 2013.

58. Peter Allen, "France's Richest Man Moves to Belgium and Takes Multi-Billion Pound Fortune with Him 'to Avoid New Socialist Super-Tax,'" *Daily Mail*, Janury 24, 2013.

59. "LVMH's Arnault Withdraws Belgium Citizenship Bid," *Wall Street Journal*, April 10, 2013.

60. Stephen Johns, "Hollywood Star Salma Hayek and Her Billionaire Husband Move from Paris to London," *Daily Mail*, March 1, 2014.

61. Charles Varner and Cristobal Young, "Millionaire Migration in California: The Impact of Top Tax Rates," p. 3, unpublished working paper, Stanford University, 2012.

62. Cristobal Young and Charles Varner, "Millionaire Migration and State Taxation of Top Incomes: Evidence from a Natural Experiment," *National Tax Journal*, vol. 64 (June 2011).

63. Julie Creswell, "For Rich, '13 Was Good for Making, and Spending, Money," *New York Times*, March 5, 2014.

64. Susan Johnston, "Financial Considerations for Expats," *Mainstreet*, March 19, 2014 (www.mainstreet.com/article/smart-spending/financial-considerations-expats?page=1).

65. Internal Revenue Service, "Foreign Account Tax Compliance Act," January 2014.

66. Kenneth Scheve and David Stasavage, "Is the Estate Tax Doomed?," *New York Times*, March 24, 2013.

67. Thomas Piketty, *Capital in the Twenty-First Century* (Harvard University Press, 2014), p. 517.

Chapter Ten

1. Peter English, *Rheumatic Fever in America and Great Britain: A Biological, Epidemiological, and Medical History* (Rutgers University Press, 1999).

2. Jonathan Kozol, *Savage Inequalities: Children in America's Schools* (New York: Broadway Books, 2012).

3. Henry Aaron and Gary Burtless, "Potential Effects of the Affordable Care Act on Income Inequality" (Brookings, January 24, 2014), p. 6 (www.brookings.edu/research/papers/2014/01/potential-effects-affordable-care-act-income-inequality-aaron-burtless).

4. Richard Reeves, "The Economic Case for Social Mobility" (Brookings, August 16, 2013).

5. Alan Krueger, "The Rise and Consequences of Inequality" (Council of Economic Advisers, January 12, 2012), figure 4.

6. Tara Loader Wilkinson and Will Citrin, "A Conversation with Wealth-X CEO Mykolas Rambus," Wealth-X, April 2, 2014.

7. Raj Chetty and others, "The Economic Impacts of Tax Expenditures: Evidence from Spatial Variation across the U.S." (Harvard University and the University of California–Berkeley, 2013).

8. Jennifer Day and Eric Newburger, "The Big Payoff: Educational Attainment and Synthetic Estimates of Work-Life Earnings" (U.S. Census Bureau, 2002).

9. Suzanne Mettler, *Degrees of Inequality: How the Politics of Higher Education Sabotaged the American Dream* (New York: Basic Books, 2014).

10. Krueger, "The Rise and Consequences of Inequality," figure 7.

11. Angus Deaton, "Health, Inequality, and Economic Development," *Journal of Economic Literature*, vol. 41 (March 2003), pp. 113–58. Also see Angus Deaton, *The Great Escape: Health, Wealth, and the Origins of Inequality* (Princeton University Press, 2013).

12. Richard Steckel, "Stature and Standard of Living," *Journal of Economic Literature*, vol. 33 (1995), pp. 1903–40.

13. Melissa Kearney and Phillip Levine, "Income Inequality and Early Non-Marital Childbearing: An Economic Exploration of the 'Culture of Despair'" (Cambridge, Mass.: National Bureau of Economic Research, June 2011).

14. Bruce Kennedy, Ichiro Kawachi, and Deborah Prothrow-Stith, "Income Distribution and Mortality: Cross-Sectional Ecological Study of the Robin Hood Index in the United States," *British Medical Journal*, vol. 312 (1996), pp. 917–21.

15. Steckel, "Stature and Standard of Living."

16. Richard Wilkinson, *Unhealthy Societies: The Affliction of Inequality* (London: Routledge, 1996). Also see Richard Wilkinson, "How Economic Inequality Harms Societies" (TED, October 2011) (www.ted.com/talks/richard_wilkinson/transcript).

17. Michael Fletcher, "Research Ties Economic Inequality to Gap in Life Expectancy," *Washington Post*, March 10, 2013.

18. Sabrina Tavernise, "Racial Disparities in Life Spans Narrow, but Persist," *New York Times*, July 18, 2013.

19. Shigehiro Oishi, Selin Kesebir, and Ed Diener, "Income Inequality and Happiness," *Psychological Science*, vol. 22 (2011), p. 1095.

20. Kentaro Toyama, "The Case for Happiness-Based Economies," *The Atlantic*, March 21, 2011.

21. Benjamin Radcliff, *The Political Economy of Human Happiness: How Voters' Choices Determine Quality of Life* (Cambridge University Press, 2013).

22. Joseph Fishkin, *Bottlenecks: A New Theory of Equal Opportunity* (Oxford University Press, 2014).

23. "Chinese Billionaire Sued for Child Support by His 9-Year-Old Son," *Huffington Post*, September 30, 2013.

24. Joanna Chiu, "A Billion Dollars for the Man Who Marries My Lesbian Daughter," *South China Morning Post*, January 23, 2014.

25. Quentin Fottrell, "Billionaires Won't Tell You," *Providence Journal*, November 17, 2013, p. B11.

26. Darrell West, *Patrick Kennedy: The Rise to Power* (Englewood Cliffs, N.J.: Prentice Hall, 2000), pp. 159–60.

27. Ashley Hayes, "'Affluenza': Is It Real?," CNN, December 13, 2013.

28. Tom Perkins, "Progressive Kristallnacht Coming?," *Wall Street Journal*, January 24, 2014.

29. Charles Riley, "Tom Perkins' Big Idea: The Rich Should Get More Votes," *CNN Money*, February 14, 2014.

30. Dara Kerr, "Tom Perkins Apologizes for His 'Kristallnacht' Reference," CNET.com, January 27, 2014 (www.cnet.com/news/tom-perkins-apologizes-for-his-kristallnacht-reference/).

31. Steven Erlanger, "In Left-Leaning Norway, Its Wealthy 'Fox' Gleefully Swings to the Right," *New York Times*, February 8, 2014, p. A7.

32. F. Scott Fitzgerald, "The Rich Boy," in *All The Sad Young Men* (New York: Scribners, 1926).

33. Bill Bishop, *The Big Sort: Why the Clustering of Like-Minded America Is Tearing Us Apart* (Boston: Mariner Books, 2009).

34. Stephanie Rosenbloom, "Leaving on a (Private) Jet Plane," *New York Times*, August 25, 2013, p. TR1.

35. James Atlas, "Class Struggle in the Sky," *New York Times*, July 7, 2013, p. SR1.

36. David Francis, "Why the Rise of Russia's Oligarchs Dooms the Country," *Fiscal Times*, October 13, 2013.

37. Mark Halperin and John Heilemann, *Double Down: Game Change 2012* (New York: Penguin Press, 2013), p. 194.

38. Newsday, "Billionaire Fish Announces the Launch of the Dating Site for the Rich and Admirers," December 5, 2013.

39. Will Brinson, "Jerry Jones Says Son-in-Law Offered to Clean Glasses During Game," CBS Sports, September 8, 2012.

40. Dan Graziano, "Cullen Jenkins Jabs at Jerry Jones," ESPN, September 12, 2013.

41. Gail Collins, "Billion Dollar Babies," *New York Times*, March 5, 2014; and Paul Krugman, "Favoring Wealth over Work," *New York Times*, March 22, 2014.

42. Ken Sweet, "Billionaire Rubenstein: DC Needs to Stop Bickering," *Associated Press*, October 28, 2013.

43. Hannah Dreier, "5 Tycoons Who Want To Close the Wealth Gap," *Talking Points Memo*, February 23, 2014.

44. Gina-Marie Cheeseman, "Republican Billionaire Peter Thiel Supports Raising the Minimum Wage," *Triple Pundit*, February 27, 2014.

45. Noam Scheiber, "Hillary's Nightmare? A Democratic Party That Realizes Its Soul Lies with Elizabeth Warren," *New Republic*, November 10, 2013.

46. Ben White and Maggie Haberman, "Wall Street's Nightmare: President Elizabeth Warren," *Politico*, November 11, 2013.

47. Zachary Goldfarb and Michelle Boorstein, "Pope Francis Denounces 'Trickle-Down' Economic Theories in Critique of Inequality," *Washington Post*, December 9, 2013.

48. Dan Balz and Philip Rucker, "For Democrats Looking to Post-Obama Era, How Populist a Future?," *Washington Post,* February 15, 2014.

49. Ben White and Maggie Haberman, "The Rich Strike Back," *Politico*, March 18, 2014.

50. David Phillips, "Billionaire Threatens Charity Donations If Pope Continues Support for the Poor," *Las Vegas Democrat Examiner*, January 1, 2014.

51. Eleanor Goldberg, "Billionaires Gave Less to Charity in 2012," *Huffington Post*, January 2, 2013.

52. Randall Lane, "The 50 Philanthropists Who Have Given Away the Most Money," *Forbes*, December 2, 2013.

53. See Sara Blakely's pledge at http://GivingPledge.org.

54. See Vincent Tan's pledge at http://GivingPledge.org.

55. Nielsen, "Football TV Ratings Soar," January 28, 2011.

56. Chris Wesseling, "NFL Sets 2013 Salary Cap at $123M, up from $120.6M," NFL.com, February 28, 2013.

57. Leigh Steinberg, "MLB Hit the Jackpot!" *Forbes*, October 4, 2012; and Monte Burke, "How the National Football League Can Reach $25 Billion in Annual Revenues," *Forbes*, August 17, 2013.

58. Steinberg, "MLB Hit the Jackpot!"

59. Norm Ornstein, "Could America Become a Banana Republic?," *National Journal*, April 16, 2014.

Index